Farewell to Football?

Farewell to Football?

• • •

An American Fan's Examination of Conscience.

Steven Liparulo

"One nation shall not raise the sword against another,
Nor shall they train for war again."

(ISAIAH 2:4)

"Therefore, if the world around you goes astray,
In you is the cause and in you let it be sought."

(DANTE, *PURGATORIO* XVI.83)

For Matt and Jaia, Tim and Jack: Father, Son, and Holy Spirit

Table of Contents

CHAPTER 1

• • •

Super Bowl XLVII: Farewell to Football? (2013)

"On Sunday, the eleventh of November, 196-, while
sitting at the bar of the New Parrot Restaurant in my
home town, Watertown, New York, awaiting the telecast
of the New York Giants-Dallas Cowboys football game, I
had what, at the time, I took to be a heart attack."

(FREDERICK EXLEY, *A FAN'S NOTES*, P. 1)

• • •

FEBRUARY 3, 2013. New Orleans. The Baltimore Ravens held a commanding 28-6 lead over the San Francisco 49ers with 13 minutes left in the third quarter when the world said farewell to football.

For half an hour, at least.

Most of the TV-watching world knew that Super Bowl XLVII in New Orleans was interrupted by a third-quarter power outage. The NFL title game has become such a big deal that it dominates not just the world of sports, but the world of broadcasting. And here was *news* among the sports festivities—the lights went out in the Mercedes Benz Superdome, and stayed out for a long time.

I may have been the only person in that largest of TV audiences whose first thoughts, once he realized what was happening—what *wasn't* happening in New Orleans—ran to the written word, a book, Michael MacCambridge writing about Lamar Hunt, founding father of the

American Football League and son of legendary Texas oilman H. L.
Hunt. But it's true, I am a football guy and a literary guy, too, and live
for good football books. I had recently been reading MacCambridge's
2012 biography *Lamar Hunt: A Life In Sports* and come upon this passage
about Lamar and New Orleans, whither he was considering moving his
AFL franchise, the Dallas Texans, in 1963:

> "Lamar, you're going to make the biggest mistake of your life,"
> warned [oilman Mack] Rankin. "Everything down there is a pay-
> off. You have not ever paid off one nickel in your life .... And
> you're going to end up down there, and the first thing that's
> going to happen to you is you're not going to pay off the police,
> you're going to get out there and there's not going to be any traf-
> fic control in the place. The next thing you know, the conces-
> sion people, you haven't paid off them, and you're going to get to
> the game and you're not gonna have any concessions. It's gonna
> be one thing right after another." (p. 127)

One thing after another, culminating in an embarrassing power outage
during America's Game? Why not? After all, there were all kinds of
conspiracy theories in the air in the Big Easy for the Super Bowl in 2013.
After all, NFL Commissioner Roger Goodell had essentially knocked the
New Orleans Saints out of action for the 2012 season, laying down heavy
punishment, suspensions not just of players but of the head coach and
defensive coordinator, for an alleged "bounty scheme" in which players,
who are paid (sometimes millions of dollars) to play in a manner that
frequently causes injuries, stood accused of having been paid (at most a
few thousand dollars) to cause injuries. So, *after all*, did this power outage stem from a lack of payoff to some corrupt Crescent City contractor,
or was it payback to the Commish for messing with the Saints?

And then my mind went spiraling through the time-tunnel—*one thing
after another, it's all about football, it's always been about football.* Personally,
I had been in the stands for at least one big-time football game when

Farewell to Football?

the lights went out, when Army played Houston some fifteen years ago. OK, *kind of* big-time, Division I college football, anyway, at Robertson Stadium in October 1998, and some power switch got thrown the wrong direction midway through the evening and the place went dark. That was the year when the Houston Cougars had gone back to playing all of their home games on campus at Robertson Stadium instead of splitting the slate with the Astrodome. An outdoor stadium, not a dome, so you could see all the city lights sparkling like jewels in the night all around the darkened arena. That probably wasn't in the plan, that "darkened arena" part.

That game had drawn my wrath even before the lights went out: early on, the Cougars faced third and two at around the Army 8-yard-line, threatening to score. They threw a pass to the tight end in the flat—and missed picking up the first down by a yard. *Why even run that play, why even release from the line of scrimmage if you aren't going to at least get past the first-down marker?* I fumed, as did most of the Houston fans around me, or anyone who understands anything about situational football. *They should have been trying to score, but at least get the first down.* But the lights going out, that was the final straw. Here the Army had brought their skydivers, the Black Knights (an appropriate if subtle pun, as it turned out), to parachute into the stadium at twilight just before the start of the game, and Houston's response was a blown fuse? My adopted city, dropping the ball, like some third-world shanty-town that can't even keep the lights turned on. This gets kind of personal with me—I'm an Army veteran. More than that, I'd served at West Point, as a Special Forces officer training cadets in hand-to-hand combat down in the sawdust pits in the heat of the summer, and I had seen the bumper stickers proclaiming "ARMY Football, not just a sport, a pathological obsession." This failure rankled me, too, as someone who had chosen the University of Houston for my final, doctoral degree, the pinnacle of an educated life, so as a Cougar—shoot, just as a run-of-the-mill football fan, I was out of there, fed up with *stupid* football, and I didn't go back to any University of Houston football games for years.

One thing after another, all about football.

Back in 1996, my first year at the university, I had stood in that very stadium, debating with a writer friend whether that Robertson Stadium, in fact, had once been Jeppesen Stadium, where Lamar Hunt's original Dallas Texans (later relocated, not to New Orleans, but to Kansas City as the Chiefs) had played the Houston Oilers (much later relocated to Tennessee, as the Titans) for the AFL title in 1962. In fact, it had been. Indeed, until the fall of 2012, when a new building on campus interposed itself, that very stadium, originally built in the early 1940's as a joint project of the Houston Independent School District and the New-Deal Works Progress Administration (probably the result of the close alliance between President Roosevelt and Houston businessman Jesse Jones), could be seen from my boss's office window at the University of Houston Writing Center. When the 2012 season was over, though, they just tore down the old stadium to make way for a new one, and we moved the Writing Center to the other side of campus, and that was the end of that.

One more closely related fact: Marjorie Chadwick's father had tossed the coin for the overtime of that December 1962 contest, and thus had been party to one of the greatest pro-football games ever played and one of the biggest nationally-televised mistakes in football history, recounted in the 2009 Showtime TV-documentary *Full Color Football*. Running back Abner Haynes, representing the Dallas Texans in the coin-toss to determine who would kick and who would receive the crucial overtime kickoff, got it tangled in his mind and proclaimed to referee Harold "Red" Bourne that "we will kick to the clock." That seemed like a big mistake, choosing to kick, giving away first possession of the ball in sudden-death overtime, when the first team to score would win the game. Dallas coach Hank Stram had a plan to force Houston's offense, led by the already-ageless George Blanda, to fight against the rising wind. Just by pronouncing those words, "we will kick," though, Haynes initiated a whole new plan. Those words, that kick, that clock, *in that stadium*, Jeppesen Stadium later rechristened Robertson Stadium, on the campus of the University of Houston. Red Bourne was my boss's father. Fifty years ago, he tossed the coin, which Marjorie brought to work to show me, in that stadium, which was just recently torn down.

One thing after another, all about football.

I had plenty of time for spiraling revelries in 2013, because the electrical problem at the Superdome went on for 30 agonizing minutes, which in Super-Bowl broadcast terms equates to millions and millions of dollars. As most of the wise-cracking blogosphere soon noted, crowing insufferably over the failings of the giant TV network, CBS Sports had about 10,000 former-player *analysts* in New Orleans to talk about the Super Bowl and not a reporter among them capable of covering the simplest of stories, a power failure at a big event. Not a problem for me, though. In the absence of old-school 5-W news, I listened to voices in my head, which I have done for most of my life, generally to profound effect. After all, Michael MacCambridge was neither the beginning nor the end of my reading. His voice rattled around in my head with stellar company like Shakespeare and Milton, Saint Augustine and Michel Foucault and Walker Percy.

I realized how steeped I was in football, though, the game and its lore, going back to the earliest days of childhood. One of the first books I remember *owning* was something like *Throw the Long Bomb, Terry,* about a rookie quarterback playing for the New York Giants. While they didn't stack up with Victorian novels or Civil War histories, football books were still all over my library (essentially, the whole little house I had bought in 2008 just before Hurricane Ike tried to blow it down), and MacCambridge's *America's Game* had represented a watershed for me in 2005, revelation of the next level of writing about football, what could truly be called *sports scholarship.* David Maraniss, most recently celebrated for his "multi-generational biography" of President Barack Obama, has written two other authoritative biographies, one of President Bill Clinton, and the other of coach Vince Lombardi. I've read one of those books (not surprising: Lombardi was a daily communicant; more surprising: Lombardi was openly accepting of his gay brother). More than reading about the sport, I had attended or shared football games on TV with some of the most important people in my life, at some of the most formative moments. Often when I was young, it was just my mother and me watching, she putting up with it because it was something I really liked. Locally, I'd taken in games at all four of the major football venues in Houston (two of which had hosted Super Bowls), with my colleagues and fellow writers (since two of those venues are on university campuses), with my best friends, with my nephew Matt Benson and his son Jaia flown in especially for a football double-header weekend. I'd watched football on TV in many distant corners of the American Empire all over the world, in all states of elevation and disrepair. For over five decades, it has been all about football.

And the thing is, the thing that nagged at me as the lame farce of CBS's TV coverage of a news event in the middle of a football game dragged on without visible leadership, I was starting to wonder how much longer this football life would go on. Is this stuff worth it anymore? Do I still keep the faith, do I still believe in whatever we venerate on Super Bowl Sunday, the nation's all-but-declared national sports High Holy Day?

The Catholic Church really does call its Easter service "the Mother of All Vigils," the greatest of all the sacred ceremonies, and I had passed through its candlelit procession, all those readings and all that music, those clouds of incense and waves of baptism, to come into full communion with the Church, a new beginning to my spiritual life in 2011. For the NFL that peak experience is the Super Bowl, maybe better allegorized as The Big Daddy—always epic, epoch-defining, always the great dividing point between Alpha and Omega, Before and After. It became Super thanks to the aforementioned Lamar Hunt, who applied the modifier from his children's Super Ball in talking about the first of these games, when in January of 1967 his Chiefs played Lombardi's Packers, fully expecting some smart wordsmith to come up with a better term eventually. You could make that watershed case for Super Bowl XLVII at the end of the 2012 season by concentrating on Joe Flacco and

Farewell to Football?

Ray Lewis, two players for the Ravens, a team making its second appearance in the title game in the current millennium (the Roman numerals, the talk of millennia, that's all part of the epic stature of the NFL, whose symbol is a shield, which Roger Goodell is constantly harping on protecting).

Quarterback Joe Flacco, along with his head coach John Harbaugh, had made the playoffs in each of his first five years (a hard mountain to climb in the parity-adjusted, salary-cap restricted NFL), but this season the Delaware product led the Ravens all the way to the summit, the Super Bowl. His generation's Joe Cool, Flacco is even-tempered and dispassionate, a level-headed star who can maintain composure in pressure situations (a previous generation's Cool, a Joe named Montana, started a game-winning Super Bowl drive by casually noticing comic actor John Candy in the stands).

At the other end of the emotional spectrum is the veteran linebacker Ray Lewis, retiring after this game and already memorialized by the NFL Films documentary series *A Football Life,* as if he'd been eulogized while still living. Depending on your perspective, Lewis is either a raving narcissist whose passions are so easily disordered that he may have taken part in a brutal stabbing murder over a decade ago (after a Super Bowl party, of course), or he is a redeemed warrior inspiring not just his team but the city of Baltimore. Either way there's nothing cool about the guy—he's like an evangelical Rorschach test. Lewis is loud about his feelings and talks a lot about God, and he was one of the few Ravens left who had played in the franchise's first Super Bowl, when Trent Dilfer was the quarterback and Brian Billick the head coach.

From Sugar Ray to Joe Cool, the torch was being passed from one generation to the next (in football, generations tend to pass pretty quickly). But the Ravens had to win the Super Bowl or the story would be a bust, since the story is whatever happens. And of course, on the San Francisco sideline there were plenty of stories, too: head coach Jim Harbaugh was going up against his brother, and quarterback Colin Kaepernick appears to sport as many tattoos as Ray Lewis but also seems to live by a very different code, and coach and quarterback would have loved to be this year's heroes with the 49ers.

For the Ravens to win, though, the game had to come back from purgatory. Just three plays from scrimmage into the third quarter, after a gargantuan song-and-dance half-time show that I found too vulgar to endure (which means in Super Bowl terms it was probably just right), and after a spectacular 108 yard kickoff return for the Ravens by Jacoby Jones, whom my hometown Houston Texans had chosen not to re-sign at the end of last season after he muffed a punt in a playoff game against the Ravens, over half of the lights in the Mercedes Benz Superdome went out (bet the carmaker loved seeing their brand stamped all over these scenes of what is known in the current vernacular as *Epic Fail*). It wasn't just the broadcast network that couldn't figure out what to do. This wasn't in the game-plan for the teams, either.

NFL players and coaches live and die by a regimen of detailed planning handed down to them in routines that still largely reflect the experience of veterans of World War II military service. Certainly in Texas, and likely across the country, football fans remember and revere Tom Landry, who translated his service as a strategic bomber pilot to meticulous training and game-day routines as a player and then as a coach, first with the New York Giants and then as head-man with the Cowboys (who eventually won the early 1960's competition against Lamar Hunt for football supremacy in Dallas). Perfectionist coaches like Landry and Paul Brown, who spent World War II coaching football in the Navy, organizational men who brought with them the practices of military and industrial management, they drove the NFL's expansion into America's favorite sport. Landry earned a master's degree in industrial engineering from the University of Houston while he was playing and coaching for the New York Giants, where Vince Lombardi joined him in 1954, having learned a little something about organization from Coach Red Blaik at the United States Military Academy at West Point.

Farewell to Football?

This new breed of leaders professionalized the sport of football in the 1950's and 1960's and the result was flawless and detailed planning, timetables perfected down to the minute. In his celebrated 1963 book *Run to Daylight* (ghost-written by W. C. Heinz), Lombardi reckoned that each hour of game-time required 14 hours of preparation. Lombardi's book takes the reader through the grinding NFL game-week, as coaches break down film of their upcoming opponents, decide on plays, install the plays on the practice field with the team, and work through game-planning routines. Their work habits remind me a lot of the mission-planning we used to do in the Army, leading patrols in Ranger school, and later on for me in Korea's Demilitarized Zone (and for a lot of guys who came after me much more recently in Iraq and Afghanistan), and long before that what Landry used to do in the Army Air Forces planning and conducting the bombing raids of the strategic air war against Germany. That process is still with me, the logic of the five-paragraph operations order: Situation, Mission, Execution, Support, and Communications. In *America's Game,* Michael MacCambridge aptly compares NFL planning and execution to Flight Control at NASA "coaching" the Apollo missions to the moon, right down to the communications headsets both coaches and flight controllers wear (p. 273).

Having been raised in this regimented and systematic approach to the game of football, which starts now around the same age as Little League baseball for a lot of American kids (not without controversy over when is the right time for kids to start sustaining head trauma through tackle football), these NFL players in New Orleans were clearly thrown off by the disruption to their routine. Of course, the Super Bowl itself is a break from the regular-season routines, with a 5:30 CST start time unique to the NFL schedule (games typically start at either noon or 3:15 CST), and an unusually long break for half-time, this year's extravaganza starring Beyonce Knowles (30 minutes, instead of the regular-season 12-minute intermission). Then in 2013 the routine broke down altogether, the lights went out, and in the eerie semi-darkness of the Superdome, some players stretched, some joked around, and some seemed to be looking for guidance from coaches, who weren't ready for this kind of improvisation. The NASA flight-controllers run through simulations for all kind of contingencies (like the oxygen-tank explosion reported from Apollo 13 on its way to the moon with the famous phrase, "Houston, we've had a problem"), while NFL coaches are much more narrow in their planning—they would have been challenged but could have handled it if San Francisco had shifted from its read-option game to a standard drop-back passing scheme. They just hadn't scouted the lights going out.

But in early 2013 there was something a bit more ominous in the air above the Super Bowl, a sense that maybe this really is a huge Before and After moment beyond the Ray Lewis hype, that we may look back not so far into the future and see this as one of the last of the games before … The Big Change. The NFL is facing up to a big problem, the realities of brain-injuries and their long-term consequences for current and former players—you know it's real because the lawyers are involved, advancing cases against the NFL (with its annual revenues of over $9 billion) representing more than 4,200 plaintiffs.

The casualties are real, too. In May of 2012, Junior Seau, an apparently ebullient soul who played in a pair of Super Bowls during his standout career as an NFL linebacker, shot himself in the chest after the fashion of safety Dave Duerson, who played in a Super Bowl with the Chicago Bears in the 1980's and another with the New York Giants at the start of the 1990's and killed himself in 2011. They are said to have chosen this method for suicide to preserve their brains, because they suspected that they would present evidence of Chronic Traumatic Encephalopathy (CTE), the result of multiple concussions during their careers in the violent NFL game. They were both proven correct—posthumously.

You know it's real because the politicians and the Hall-of-Famers are talking about it. In an interview with *The New Republic* just before the 2013 Super Bowl, President Barack Obama alluded to the likelihood of

Farewell to Football?

changes coming to the NFL, and also personalized as a parent the impact of brain injuries.

> "I'm a big football fan, but I have to tell you, if I had a son, I'd have to think long and hard before I let him play football," Obama said.
>
> "I think that those of us who love the sport are going to have to wrestle with the fact that it will probably change gradually to try to reduce some of the violence," he added. "In some cases, that may make it a little bit less exciting, but it will be a whole lot better for the players, and those of us who are fans maybe won't have to examine our consciences quite as much."

The President has some unexpected company in this line of thinking. In a January 2011 interview with Bryant Gumbel for HBO Sports, retired quarterback Troy Aikman said essentially the same thing as the President: that if he had a 10-year-old son (and like Obama, he has only daughters), he doesn't know if he would let him play football. Unlike the President, the former Cowboy has some very vivid personal experiences of what it means to take a blow to the head in the violent world of pro football, having suffered a few of the NFL's most visible and game-changing concussions on the way to winning three Super Bowls in the 1990's.

But for both the President and the Hall-of-Fame quarterback, that question has a hypothetical quality, since neither has sons. I don't have to look very far in my own life, though, to see that question working itself out in very real terms for very real fathers and sons. My nephew's son, Jaia Benson, a wise old man of 12 years, decided that even though he could dominate football the same way he dominates basketball and baseball (the Bronco League team he led as catcher made it all the way to the biggest show, the PONY World Series in Monterrey, California in 2012, where they played against teams from all over the country and around the world), he didn't need to risk his world-class brain on the football field. He'd said his farewell to football, and everyone in my family who had rejoiced when Jaia chose to live with his father instead of his mother after stormy and protracted divorce and custody proceedings had to confess relief about this choice, too. Before and After, some things had changed in the succession of generations in my family. Like me, my nephew Matt had to deal with divorced parents, but unlike me he had forged a strong bond with his father, and sports had played a big part in it. Matt had also beaten the odds and become a great father, the kind of father a wise young son would choose as his full-time parent.

On the other hand, Tim Loonam, my old Army buddy from our 1980's-era service in Korea, had a son playing Division I football as a University of Georgia Bulldog. Major Loonam, DVM, had faced fierce tribulations as a kind of "Army of One" in Iraq, the only airborne and Ranger qualified Army veterinarian supporting Air Force military working dogs attached to Marine combat units there in 2004 and 2005 (he is the vet depicted treating the title canine hero in Mike Dowling's 2011 book *Sergeant Rex*). All the while back at home Georgia head coach Mark Richt had helped the Loonam family deal with Tim's absence by including them in the Bulldog football family even though Jack was just a fifth-grader at the time, no doubt the widest-eyed fifth-grader in Georgia sitting in the stands in Athens with Coach Richt watching special teams practice as a special guest. Before and After, Tim has returned from war and started up a veterinary practice in South Carolina (a Georgia alum through and through, his email address is DawgDoc), and starting with the 2011 season, Jack was on the roster as a walk-on tight end for Coach Richt's Bulldogs, taking his lumps on the practice squad—and sporting a helmet embedded with sensors to study head impacts as part of Georgia's research into concussions. As if to double down the examination of conscience, too, Jack Loonam decided to follow in both his father's and my own footsteps and seek an Army commission through ROTC.

Farewell to Football?

As an outsider to marriage and fatherhood, I wonder how they put the pieces together, not just about football but about life, how they dealt with the inevitable challenges to enduring marriage, how they got through all the obstacles to fatherhood. We live our lives surrounded by an expansive swamp of rotten human business, whether it's war or divorce or simple stupidity, and I wonder how these men got through some of the stretches that thwarted me. I wonder how the rest of the story is going to play out for them.

I guess I could ask. It's one thing after another, but it's also one thing over and over again, this quest to understand, and maybe, as once I had been taught as an infantryman, to improve the position.

And then I began to see something, just as if it were written on the TV screen, and it might as well have been, in place of all the nothingness that was being broadcast as the power outage continued at the Super Bowl in New Orleans: these were all stories about fatherhood in the context of football, and in a lot of ways I could tell my life story—encapsulate what I understand and have misunderstood—in those two terms. Well, maybe one more. *Fatherhood, football, and love.* I hadn't been immersed in all of them throughout my life, not in equal measure, had struggled more with understanding my father and plumbing the mysteries of love than comprehending football, which is, after all, a simple game of blocking and tackling, but I had reached a certain point where if I didn't know, I could seek to understand, ask around, and tell the story for those who do, learn the story *from* and tell the story *with* those who do. And I'm pretty sure that Matt and Tim do know. The proof of the father is in the character of the son.

I can't say for certain whether President Obama understood the particularly Catholic resonance of his phrase "examine our conscience," but I did, as a fairly recent initiate into the faith (though I can see that I had been on a journey aimed at getting there for a long time). An *Examination of Conscience* is what we conduct before "going to Confession," a list of questions we review to sift the good and the bad, to locate our sins before we enter that sweaty little house where God has put a priest for our benefit and indeed to aid in our salvation, and I was starting to imagine a plan to conduct a year-long examination of conscience, from this Super Bowl to the next, with everything in between fair game for a lifelong fan of both football and critical thinking willing to plumb the depths of a question. *Why has football been such a big deal in my life, and in the lives of so many? Will I have to confess to the sin of football idolatry?* Is the dark side of football, its god-awful triumvirate of consumerism, militarism, and disordered passions, the way the game and its media coverage seems to enable some of the worst characteristics of its fans, coaches, and players, is all of that bad enough to overshadow the game itself, its intensity and quest for excellence and the frequent elegance and artistry of its competition on the field, what it gives back to the coaches and players who dedicate themselves to it, the way the game embodies positive elements of American life like teamwork, dedication, sacrifice, and commitment?

The best way to get this project started would probably be to just grind it out, as the coaches say, sift through the good and the bad. Turning up the bad right away, I had directly in front of me the TV commercials during the Super Bowl, with all their desperate urgency to be cool, to be *Mad Men*. Some people didn't grow up devout football fans like myself, some people just watch the Super Bowl for the commercials, and the commercials play to that audience with notable lack of shame. In fact, speaking as I did at one stage in my higher education and delving into the "semiotic codes" of the commercials, the fairy tale of TV ads would be quite clear, virtually unchanging beneath the surface diversity of market plentitude, and since Super Bowl Sunday is America's High Holy Day, this would count as American Theology: *Nothing*, not manners, not family loyalty, not even the law, should stand in the way of fulfilling the consumer desires aflame within us. Al Davis translation: just *consume*, baby! Lie to your children to steal their fried chicken, push old ladies out of your way to gobble down candy bars, whatever. Your only hope for any pleasure and satisfaction in this life lies in the smartest new smart phone, or possibly *also* in a car that will solve every problem in your life (those problems that your smart phone didn't already out-smart). No, *definitely* also, Also and Also and Also. Just don't stop, the ads keep telling us. What you need is what we are selling, and you need more and more of it.

This is the truth of our fallen world, the big lie at the heart of the American dream, and what's most striking about the whole business is how tremendously *ironic* the ads all are on Super Bowl Sunday, stead-fastly refusing to believe in anything, completely hollowed out of any transcendent value. Think about what's so *funny* about some of those TV commercials we laugh at.

Come to think of it, though, there is another fairy tale behind some of the commercials, so blatantly ideological and nationalistic that it tends to physically seize me with what, in Russian novels, they always call *paroxysms*. I was thoroughly exasperated by one spot for the U. S. Navy that had been running on the NFL Network for weeks, but it didn't make it onto the roster for Super Bowl Sunday. This ad got right to the heart of the matter for me, the fairy tale for the warfare state. "A global force for good," the TV spot proclaimed, as if the Navy had teamed up with the Salvation Army for some sort of bipartisan crusade for all that's good and holy—why did it have to lie and claim it was "for good"? The military *is* force—*government* is force, for that matter, no one can deny that, whether you think that's a good thing or a bad thing (*government is just a word for things we do together*, is how the happy progressives like to sing it, *together* with the power to tax and imprison and apply man-aged violence), and the military is its most explicit expression of force, and so the Navy is at its best a global force for the government, and the government has been far from good lately. (Has the government *ever* really been good? This is likely a question for a *libertarian* examination of conscience.)

Long ago, in the overheated year of the American Bicentennial, 1976, James Michener of all people had warned in *Sports In America* that athletics "are being used to buttress military goals" and that they are "being grossly misused to create a fuzzy, shallow patriotism" (p. 377).

I'm sure he could hardly imagine how completely the military saturates our sports in America today, especially since 9/11 (the Great Before and After of the American Empire), with constant uniformed presence on the sidelines and on-camera, the pre-game festivities dominated by fuzzy, shallow patriotism on steroids, massive flags and multiple anthems by soldiers and sailors and cops and firefighters, and like those desperate wannabe *Mad-Men* ads, the urgent message is that war is like sports, an American tradition, a great tradition (it certainly is great if you are a military contractor hoarding all those tax dollars being shoveled your way—if you are a wounded veteran waiting the year or so it usually takes for the Veterans Administration to process your claim, maybe not so much). As a veteran myself, I've spent years trying to untangle these knots, and I can't say I've been very successful, but I know there's something about the whole business I'm not buying anymore, if I ever did. While I honor my brothers and sisters who have served, are serving now, and will serve in the future, and I know that we must somehow provide for the common defense, I know too that when Laura Nyro invoked Isaiah 2 in "Save the Country" during bloody times back in 1968, she sang it for me and for many: "In my mind I can't study war no more."

But football is all-in on war.

Sifting the Good and the Bad: Next up would have to be the disordered passions of some of the worst player behavior, epitomized by this running back I'd recently read about who played for the Panthers and the Raiders and had been sued by three different women for child support for six illegitimate children he had fathered. Apparently this is a common thing in the NFL, all this renegade fertility, like a parody of the very concept of fatherhood—there's a player on the Jets who has "fathered" twelve children by eight different women. What kind of "fatherhood" is that? Jason Whitlock, an ESPN columnist who for years has been writing against the grain and questioning trends like mass incarceration and the "war on drugs," described this phenomenon in sports as "Hurricane Illegitimacy," arguing that "as long as 68 percent of black women who have children are unwed, there are no cures for the social maladies preventing black progress." Even worse, during the 2012 season, a player for the Kansas City Chiefs had shot and killed his girlfriend, mother of his illegitimate daughter, and then drove to the practice facility, where he killed himself in view of the head coach. You can sift out a lot of disorder in football players without even rooting around in that whole tangle of brain-injury problems.

You can't have a Bad Football without bad fans, though, fans with seriously disordered passions. Way back in 1973 Howard Cosell was writing about the "myth of the fan," a mistaken notion of entitlement held by "somebody who pays his money to get into the ball park and says that gives him the right to heap insulting verbal abuse that amounts to public slander upon a man" (p. 358). How far have we come? Well, the technology is a whole lot better now, cameras everywhere, everyone wired, everything potentially networked, enabling a strain of fan narcissism that reflects the on-field spectacle of touchdown or sack celebrations by the more narcissistic of players (Ray Lewis consistently made a spectacle of himself in pre-game introductions that may never be topped for intensity and sustained commitment to self-aggrandizing). The cultural logic is simple enough, our American catechism—"it's all about me," and for the player that means celebrating the personal triumph of a touchdown even if his team is down by thirty points. For the fan, it's all about turning the game into an opportunity to make an on-screen appearance of his own, usually by very visibly and frantically overreacting to what is, after all, a kid's game. The word "fan" is a diminutive of "fanatic," of course, and that is a definition of disordered passion. And the less said about fan-talk-radio, the better, but that's where you'd find your slander, there and on the Internet, wherever that is (everywhere). Oh, football can be bad all right.

But you can also find encouragement in and around the game of football. I've heard men I know and respect tell me that football saved their lives, and I've heard from coaches how football gives kids from bad family situations a chance to believe in themselves and understand how to work productively with others. Michael Lewis wrote a book about that kind of story, *The Blind Side,* and it got made into an Academy-Award-winning movie, and its subject was Michael Oher, an offensive lineman who just happened to be playing in the Super Bowl in New Orleans as a Baltimore Raven. There are often-repeated legends of football seasons and games that turned the corner on integration (from Jerry LeVias at SMU in 1966 to Southern Cal's black running backs humiliating all-white Alabama in 1970, just to arbitrarily pick a couple of highly-celebrated examples). So the Good is just as real as the Bad in football. So be it resolved: this is a real examination of conscience, not the formal appearance of a question cloaking a forgone conclusion (which is what we have grown much more accustomed to in our public "deliberations"). Mission: seek to understand the Good and the Bad of football, judge for yourself what is Good and Bad, right and wrong, decode the game's myths and illusions and fairy tales to discover the truth and the lies behind them, to discern why football is such a big deal, such a *quintessentially American* big deal.

Is it time for me to say farewell to football? If I've learned anything in life, I've learned that important questions should be dealt with using a deliberate process, like military mission-planning, NASA flight-planning, NFL game-planning. Among my teaching colleagues, it was common to hear a version of that process-oriented philosophy: "I'm not sure what to think of that book, I haven't *taught* it yet." More to the point yet: Am I ready to say farewell to football? It all began with the Word, after all, so let me *write* about it and see how it comes out. Maybe I rattle my own cage and find out that my values are all out of line, like some character afflicted by Socratic dialogue, but maybe I can reach a point of clarity and form a vision of freedom, get myself right with football.

The Super Bowl in New Orleans fell right in the middle of the season called Carnival, which is a rough translation from the Latin for "farewell to the flesh." The idea was, in religious tradition, to take some time to indulge in the pleasures of the flesh prior to renouncing them during the solemn Lenten season. Like most things in America, however, this business has gotten a little out of hand, and in 2013 Mardi Gras season

Farewell to Football?

started on January 6, after 12th Night, and ran through Super Bowl week, culminating in Fat Tuesday itself (*Mardi Gras* in French—fat because it's the last day to indulge) on February 12. The way I see it, if the Big Easy can spend almost six weeks bidding farewell to the flesh, I can spend a year saying farewell to football—or at least contemplating the possibility, sifting, examining my conscience, deciding for myself if football is still worth it.

For me, it's all about football because the story of my relationship to football is inextricably intertwined with the mysteries and misunderstanding of fatherhood and love—sad confessions from inside the house of debased masculine identity as well as redemptive conversion narratives from the places I have successively if idiosyncratically understood as Houses of the Holy: public schools, rock concerts, Army posts, sports spectacles, universities, and church. I believe in writing, and I believe that when it comes right down to it, I can tell what's worth telling about my life by writing about a dozen or more football games spread out over five decades, coming to some sort of conclusion about American football, fatherhood, and love.

I got out a pad and made a few notes, working out what it would take. Now, here's a plan for an American examination of conscience: a life story told through fourteen football games that get to the heart of the matter, like that Giants game in Tampa the year I graduated high school ... the partying, my father's absence, the hovering, oscillating presence of Led Zeppelin, the deaths that followed hard upon. Fourteen games like that, where it all comes together, a handful of F-words (fatherhood, faith, fraternity, football, and free choice of the will) and that would be your story.

Or at least, buoyed by the food and drink that had accompanied the first half of the Super Bowl, until the lights went out and I went spiraling down the time-tunnel, that is what I resolved on February 3, 2013.

And then, whoever had to be paid off in New Orleans got the circuits squared away and the Super Bowl was back in business. And so was football, for at least another year.

CHAPTER 1. A.

— • • • —

Examen

"Why do you not judge for yourselves what is right?"

(LUKE 12:57)

• • •

IN THE DAYS that followed, I came to realize that the Super Bowl did mark a division between Before and After.

First there was my own Before and After: how had I, before the interrupted Super Bowl, gone along with this mass hysteria, one more sap in a sea of consumer saps preyed upon by the Powers That Be, the Owner/Ruling Class? Actually, the answer is simple: that's the ready and easy way, the whole thing is rigged for that to be the easy way, to go along and get along and pretend that this is freedom. Just let the market pluck out your liver and act as if you like it.

The bigger question, the better question, is what enabled the After to begin? How had I gotten into position to peer behind the veil?

The answer I must confess is Jesus. (For me; *is*, not was.)

Jesus comes not as a cause of peace but as a cause of division, dividing the Old Times of the Law from the New Times of the Free Choice of the Will.

Immediately after asking "why do you not judge for yourselves what is right?" in Chapter 12 of the Gospel According to Luke, Jesus seems to veer from an apocalyptic vision of ominous signs of heavy weather into a pragmatic discourse on juridical procedure. Try to settle your dispute before you ever get in front of the magistrate, He tells his audience, otherwise you will probably end up in prison, and "you will not be released until you have paid the last penny" (12:59). Jesus is really talking about the Apocalypse He comes to sponsor, the division he marks in human history, and the choice he will revitalize for us through his Passion and sacrifice. We can choose the old legal way, the way of the Pharisees, relying upon a moribund and serpentine legal code and cash nexus, and the result will be the endless grinding machinery of commerce and debt. Or we can choose to discern for ourselves, "to settle the matter on the way," to exercise free choice and to find true freedom.

We can be consumers of servitude sold as pleasure and freedom (the mobile phone that "allows" you to be reached by your employer around the clock—or that enables you to download pornography whenever you choose), or we can become producers of the freedom that comes from choosing what is right. That is the narrow way, the eye of a needle as the saying goes, but it is the only way.

I realized that I should take up the challenge of judging for myself when it comes to football, which had taken up so much of my time and energy and enthusiasm throughout my life. There are tons of books written in praise of football, usually mindlessly repeating the half-truths and outright lies, hyping the excess and illusion, often with a heavily distorted "religious" message. There are a few, and maybe a growing number, of books griping about what's wrong with football, arrogant with certainty about how to fix it and advocating a reform agenda as hopeless as any other stab at social engineering (the progressive political impulse that disguises the grab for power and wealth). I thought, instead, that I would seek to understand.

When the interrupted Super Bowl initiated this project, I had recently been advised by a convicted murderer to read Steven Covey's *The Seven Habits of Highly Effective People*, and in the spirit of a newly-adopted habit of what I hoped was a more effective person, I try to do what people of good will advise me to do. I found that one of those seven habits was "to seek first to understand, then to be understood." I decided I would commit my time, talent, and treasure to the pursuit of understanding my own relationship to football, and along the way seek to understand what football means to others, and how those meanings connect with major features and failings of American life. An American fan's examination of conscience, I came to envision the project, seeking to understand *why is football such a big deal, such a quintessentially American big deal, and how important should the game really be?*

In the days that followed that Super Bowl, I worked up a list of topics and questions for an extensive examination of conscience. I would spend years, if necessary, to track down answers to these questions, to understand, and then, if it please God, to write it up and seek to be understood.

$$\bullet \ \bullet \ \bullet$$

A Football *Examen*:

INITIATION: how does a young man matriculate into masculine institutions without the guidance of a father?

EDUCATION: what is the proper relationship between athletics and higher education?

DIVERSITY: can football create opportunities for powerful social transformations?

AMERICAN EMPIRE AND MILITARY: is football an extension of the military culture of the American warfare state?

ANTI-WAR: in a rhetorically busy fallen world in which the state is constantly urging expanded war powers, how does one discern right from wrong?

COACHING: does football provide a means for profound character development for the young men who play it?

FREE CHOICE OF THE WILL: what is the true nature of freedom, and what are the conditions for its exercise?

Farewell to Football?

RELATIONSHIPS: how do we overcome the impediments of our history to pursue unity in a broken world?

AMERICAN WAY OF WAR: how are techniques of emotional attachment and persuasion used to manipulate popular support for war?

DISORDERED ATTACHMENTS: how does football represent the common temptation to indulge excessive and disorderly passions?

NOT QUITTING: how do we endure in our commitments in the face of adversity?

SERVICE AND FAITH: is football, like military service, really antithetical to Godly life?

CHOICE: are the opportunities football creates for the young men who play it worth the risks involved in a violent and dangerous sport?

CHAPTER 2

· · ·

Houses of the Holy: My First NFL Game (1977)

"I had a dream—crazy dream
Anything I wanted to know
Any place I needed to go."

(Jimmy Page and Robert Plant, "The
Song Remains the Same")

· · ·

Sunday, November 13, 1977: New York Giants (4-5-0) at Tampa Bay
Buccaneers (0-9-0), Tampa Stadium. My first NFL game, in person, in the
stadium—one of the houses of the holy, *live*, turned out to be a pretty ugly
affair. At least my sorry Giants didn't lose to my old man's *expansion* Bucs.

The Giants won a sloppy game that featured 6 fumbles, 8 sacks, and
4 interceptions by a final score of 10-0. Joe PISARCIK played quarterback for the Giants—enough said with just that last name, as if all those
ill-sorted consonants in his name were getting ready to scramble off the
back of his jersey and hand that fumble over to Philadelphia's Herman
Edwards to run back for a touchdown a year later, November 19, 1978,
in what became, for the Eagles, the "Miracle in the Meadowlands." For
Giants fans, it was just more of the same.

I had grown up in central New York, between sojourns to Florida, so
I'd been watching middling Giants games on TV since the mid-60's. It
was what we had, like the weather, nothing you can do about it but gripe.

Farewell to Football?

The Jets were the happening football team in New York back then, with Broadway Joe Namath at the helm, but their games tended to go out to Long Island and the outer boroughs, while we got the Giants upstate. This was back before cable TV, back when you didn't have any choice in the matter and the NFL stood unchallenged like the Roman Empire, setting the terms unilaterally. In 1977, though, the Giants weren't even "next year's team," a loser's epithet with which the Dallas Cowboys had been saddled in the 60's and early 70's, when they could get to the play-offs but couldn't win the big games—no, the good times were even further into the future for New York. Phil Simms (1979) and Lawrence Taylor (1981) hadn't been drafted yet, and John McVay was coaching the G-men, not Bill Parcells (1983). It would take the three of them, among many others (Bill Belichick included), until the 1986 season to win the team's first Super Bowl.

The Giants won on that mild 50-degree Florida afternoon in 1977, which no doubt felt a whole lot better than the cold autumn rains I had left behind in upstate New York not long before, but their offense only gained 197 total yards in the game, a tally on the low side for a typical NFL quarterback's *passing* output for a game. The Giants' punter had more yards that day—by far (6 for 254). The punter has a big day when the offense repeatedly fails. It was ugly on both sides, and a bad, poorly-executed football game has a depressing tempo all its own, enervating the crowd and taking the air out of the ball for teams who are struggling through it, mistake building on mistake. Tampa Bay's quarterback, who the record shows was someone named Jeb Blount, coming out of Tulsa to play exactly one year in the NFL, was sacked 6 times and intercepted thrice. Those are awful numbers, a month's worth of misfortune for a quarterback. The Giants were in the midst of a long decline that really started with Frank Gifford's retirement a dozen years before, and they would end up 5-9 for the season, which only ran to 14 games in that era. The 1977 G-men were perhaps best typified by aging running back Larry Csonka, who in his ninth NFL season averaged only 3.5 yards per carry with a single touchdown on the year. The Bucs, on the other hand, were roasting in the depths of Expansion Hades in just their second year of life as an NFL team. They were "going for O" again—they had not won a game in their inaugural season—but didn't even achieve that distinction, finishing the 1977 season 2-12, failing to fail quite consistently enough to earn a punch line. Their only offensive star was rookie running back Ricky Bell out of USC, but he would never really live up to his first-round draft status, and in his inaugural campaign he fared even worse than old Larry Csonka, only averaging 2.9 yards per carry and scoring a single touchdown all season.

This was pretty much the bottom of the barrel for the NFL in 1977, and 1977 was a down year all around the league, with per-game scoring and touchdowns at their lowest since the 1940's. The big winners that year were in Denver, where the Broncos only lost two games all season, and Dallas, where the Cowboys would win the division they shared with the Giants (the Minnesota Vikings won the NFC Central, into which division the Tampa Bay Bucs had been inserted in 1977 after starting in the AFC *West* their first year, in spite of simple facts of geography). Denver and Dallas would eventually meet in the Super Bowl in the Louisiana Superdome in January 1978. That, too, was an ugly affair, a 27-10 Dallas blowout, though the power stayed on in the Superdome for the whole game.

But for all that ugly football in Tampa, it was still the NFL, the big time, America's Game. I had crawled to the top of a heap as far as my puny life was concerned, an NFL game and a Led Zeppelin concert probably the two peak experiences my life at age 18 seemed to require for perfection. Halfway there already, or really, one down and the other overcome by events. Towards the end of the game in Tampa I remember clambering down the stadium bowl from our high-elevation seats and getting close to the field, marveling at how big those players really were. For some reason I distinctly recall the uncanny sight of the back side of rookie linebacker Dave Lewis on the sideline, a 6-4, 240-pound beast of a man, his name sprawling big as the Hollywood sign across his impossibly broad shoulders in that Creamsicle-colored Buccaneers jersey. LEWIS. The name signified the American Dream: Dave LEWIS, football player, has made it in the NFL. I reeled a little as if with vertigo, as if I just couldn't get my eyes to focus, as if I were looking through that contraption at the eye doctor's, where they change lenses and ask you, "better or worse?" BIGGER. Unbelievable. The N F L! A scrawny and poorly conditioned 6-0, 135-pounder with an eight-letter surname that would never make it onto an NFL jersey, I probably celebrated Lewis's athletic perfection, and his pass interception that day, with another beer and Marlboro.

My dad's Bucs, this year's losers. Even though I was in Tampa to visit my father, spend some quality time with the old man, I hadn't gone to the game with him. No, he was, somewhat typically, out of town on business, too busy to do much fathering, too freaked out I'm sure by my long hair and rock-and-roll lifestyle, or just the unpleasing physical reality of his offspring, I don't know. I had his apartment to myself, with plenty of scotch and a few frozen dinners, and I went to the game with my high-school classmate Dan Perry, who was in school down around Orlando—living it up as a college man, with an off-campus apartment and, of all things, an Iranian roommate! Worldly! Oh, how far we Hawks had flown in a few short months.

Gonzo Chronicles, dateline 1977: We had graduated from little New Berlin Central School, ages ago in June (graduating class: 56; Iranian classmates: 0), seen our troubled friend Todd for what turned out to be the last time at a graduation party where my rock band played (and Todd had infuriated our drummer by repeatedly messing with the cymbals), and were now on our way to Miami to see our rowdy class-mate David (who had added to his authenticity in playing the judge in our senior-play courtroom-drama by sipping from a hidden bottle of Jack Daniel's onstage), an epic road trip that would unfold and entail: whole bags of choice sticky bud gone up in smoke, a monsoon deluge on a cross-Florida freeway when we would suddenly realize in the cloud-splitting fashion of manic comedy that we had just missed colliding with an 18-wheeler barreling up the down staircase on a divided highway, a Jethro Tull concert in a jai-alai *fronton*, stops in for rum with some handsome Puerto Rican women worldly David had been lusting after and hashish with these nerdy-cool college guys who listened to Steely Dan, guys stoned at 10:00 in the morning and talking some serious epistemology, dude, stoned *sharp*, diamond clear, ready to think about how we think. At least, I think that's what they were talking about. A road-trip worthy of 18-year-old rock-and-rollers set loose upon the face of the earth, illusions of freedom a little short on direction, some rambling concoction of Cheech and Chong's *Up In Smoke* and Elvis Presley's *Clambake*. High times, if not for long.

Both Todd and David would be dead before the year was through.

It was that kind of deal, hard times, scoring down in the NFL, the failure of fathers and the demise of our most devoted partying colleagues before the race was even fairly started. Really, Todd and David both suffered from *bad brains*, sad cases, allegedly the products of rough treatment in and around the home, abuse giving rise to perversion. Perry, on the other hand, had been brought up in a real family, and in church, but wasn't really making smart choices in 1977. He would drop out of college within a year. As for me, yes, I was susceptible to the disorders that killed our classmates. Count me in for acting out. I was dodging college for the time being, wasting my time on rock and roll dreams, wasting money I'd banked in an accident settlement back in seventh grade, money I could not afford to be wasting, not when I lived with my single mother, who hadn't been able to work much since a couple of heart attacks in the last five years.

What *was* I doing, and what was I doing my best not to do? I liked to drink and smoke pot and try whatever drugs might be available, and I was carrying around a few dark sexual secrets that I wasn't even particularly aware of at the time, but the drift of things led me in some unhealthy directions, tempted me to foolishness. It looks that way now, like a footnote to a chapter synopsis, mere words unambiguous in their signification. But none of that was clear then. We didn't know what was going on in that smoky cannabis cloud of ours back in our graduation year of 1977.

Farewell to Football?

We were just small-time guys from Giants country in upstate New York living it up, raging onto the frontiers of the Sunshine State with its college campuses and houses-of-the-holy *frontons* and NFL stadia, would-be worldly men evermore stupid and partying our brains out.

• • •

Graduation

Strange karma flowed all up and down the road that summer and fall of 1977, coast to coast, really, streams all connected by rock-n-roll and football. In early June, at that self-same Tampa Stadium Led Zeppelin started a show that only lasted about twenty minutes before a fierce Gulf-coast thunderstorm sent the band rushing off stage and occasioned a riot among disappointed fans. This was supposed to be the holiest of the holies, the very same Tampa Stadium where a few years earlier Zeppelin had broken the record held by The Beatles for the largest attendance of a concert by a single act—THE BEATLES! Like the decline of offense in the NFL, maybe the time was approaching when the curve would start to bend back earthward for the high-flying masters of light and shadow. From their origin in the ashes of the burnt-out Yardbirds, Led Zeppelin had soared to preeminence in the rock and roll world, becoming by the mid-1970's the top-selling recording and touring act, even if the music critics tended to treat them as secondary to the darlings of the scene like The Rolling Stones and The Who. Like being the biggest wasn't the best—critics!

I could be counted as a rock critic myself, having written a column called "Top of the Rock" in the *Hawk's Herald,* my high school newspaper, and I knew where things stood with all the bold certainty of an ignorant teenager. Led Zeppelin was by far the most important rock band to me, and rock bands dominated my life in those days. (I was so into Led Zeppelin, in fact, that I had my future laid out: because they made a big point out of crediting the "engineers" for all of their recordings, I had formed a vague notion that I would get an electrical engineering degree at the State University of New York at Buffalo and become a recording engineer.) Sure, ZZ Top had an ace lead guitar player (and went on tour with half the livestock in Texas on stage with the band), and The Who did that routine where they beat each other up musically on every song, especially live, and the Rolling Stones, well, I never got what was supposed to be so great about them. They certainly didn't have any really standout guitar solos, and that was what mattered most to make it to the Top of my Rock, guitar solos to evoke another world, a better place we could only imagine today but tomorrow we might inhabit. Zeppelin had that, the ultimate heroic guitar lead on the climax of "Stairway to Heaven," and a lot more to send a young imagination flying.

The first album I ever bought was *Physical Graffiti,* just as soon as it was released in the winter of 1975, and I feel like I have never really finished opening its complicated packaging and endless content, plumbing its depths with the diligence of the devout ever since—even unto this very day! A double album, assembled from both current material and the backlog unreleased on their first five albums, *Physical Graffiti* made clear how wide-ranging were the talents and interests of the band. How can a blues-rock howler like "Custard Pie" bubble forth from the same four-man source as the jazzily introspective "Ten Years Gone"? Some of these "songs" were better described as epic archetypes delivered from humanity's collective prehistoric unconscious: the woozy and protoplasmic "In My Time of Dying" (with its surprisingly organic evolution of a devastating locomotive rhythm section in its middle passages) and the simmering drone of "In the Light" and lazy looping of "Down by the Seaside." I can't count how many times I went to sleep with "Kashmir" fading away into its dreamy twilight, but I know it shaped some component in my unconscious, some region reserved for yearning, questing, journeying into the unknown. "Let me take you there ...."

I was bewitched by words, too, an avid reader of the rock press, of course, with Lester Bangs and *Creem* magazine particularly important to me. I loved how all of his stories were really about getting wasted and then incidentally listening to an album or going to a concert. I had read all about what an unbelievable live band Zeppelin was, how the music

Farewell to Football?

they played in concert was something totally different from the brilliant recordings they made, that they improvised and evolved live on the stage. But they had gotten so big that they could set their own terms as far as their touring schedule, and had reduced their visits to the US to every other year, and they only played the biggest venues—what they called "houses of the holy," the football stadia, Madison Square Garden, the Louisiana Superdome. It was tantalizing hit-or-miss whether the stars would ever align for me to make it to one of their concerts. But I followed the news and knew that they were on the road in 1977 (they played some landmark shows at the LA Forum the week I graduated high school), and had run into some trouble with the weather in Tampa (ultra-heavy manager Peter Grant hadn't gotten control of that—yet). There was plenty more trouble waiting down the road for them, but I had some serious business to attend to first in sedate old New Berlin, NY, a little crossroads village of around 1,000 in the heart of the Empire State. You could say it was about halfway between Utica and Binghamton, as if that meant much.

More Gonzo Chronicles: On June 25, I celebrated my eighteenth birthday, as I have come to prefer telling it in the grandiloquent style of the self-mythology (and influenced by gonzo-rock-writers like Lester Bangs and Richard Meltzer), by evolving out of the primordial sludge at a graduation-eve party, where I had passed a night of reptilian dreaming on the consoling ground at the foot of a mighty ancient oak tree, hitchhiking into town, there undertaking the next stage of ritual passage by graduating from high school inside the stone fortress of our three-story schoolhouse atop a terraced hill overlooking the forlorn little village (enjoying a sip of Yukon Jack on the stage with my classmate David—same stage where he played judge and I played prosecutor and he imbibed Jack Daniel's and I read from the script in lieu of actually learning my lines), and then playing rock and roll with my band at a fired-up party at the drummer's house north of town. As if it all just happened in one flowing cheerfully decadent sentence. Not so fast, gonzo. There was trouble on the way to quiet little New Berlin on the Unadilla, which river in centuries past once represented the frontier, where Indian country started. Trouble, trouble, everywhere.

31

That graduation party, which should have been the pinnacle of an endless series of parties—every practice at Bolek's was a party—was haunted by the unexpected, and ultimately unwelcome, appearance of my best friend, Todd, who had been in and out of mental institutions ever since his father committed suicide four years earlier. What was *that* all about? I never really knew, probably didn't know *how* to know that sort of thing at that age (which is what repression is all about, I guess), but you had the sense that sex and porno and other dirty secrets had their part to play, just given Todd's behavior and attitudes. He could be a smutty, pugnacious little rat, and there were some notorious smutty porno-hawking rats lurking about the remote environs where his family lived. *Do I have to deal with all of this on graduation day? Can I crawl back into that primordial sludge? Is this going to be one of those humiliating Lester Bangs partying-and-music pieces?*

How peculiar it all seems, looking back, how convergent, how all the rivers of trouble led somehow to the Unadilla. In 1975, as Todd began to seriously oscillate on the sickening wave of mania and depression that saw him flutter in and out of our lives throughout the high-school years, Pink Floyd released an album called *Wish You Were Here*, thematically centered on the misfortunes of their founder, Syd Barrett, who descended into madness, possibly exacerbated by excessive use of LSD, only a couple of years into the band's career. "Remember when you were young," one of the songs ran, "you shone like the sun. Now there's a look in your eye, like black holes in the sky." Shine on, you crazy diamond. I had me an anthem.

Fast forward to 1977. Todd showed up out of the blue before graduation, and sat with my family while I walked the stage with my class, my long blond hair hanging loose under my purple mortar-board cap with the gold Honor Society tassel. The first I knew about his appearance was after the ceremony, and I was flabbergasted, not ready to deal with something quite so heavy on a day that should have been celebratory. Not only was it graduation day, but it was my birthday, my *eighteenth* birthday, which in New York in those days meant I was legal to drink (not that I had been holding back for the legalities). My mother and I lived in an apartment over the Eagle Inn, a restaurant and bar at the crossroads of the little town, and we had arranged a family get-together to toast my big day, probably all three of my older sisters assembled (my father, of course, a world away in Florida). And here at our table in the bar lounge, where the bands played at night but where sunshine poured in during the afternoon, was this mysterious stranger in a well-cut mint-green suit whom we all knew and had never met before. The biggest problem, really, was the god-forsaken shape Todd was in. You couldn't look the young man in his sad dark eyes for very long before you were worried about belly-flopping into the cold pools behind his dilated pupils. Was he tripping? Heavily medicated with psychotropics? You could ask, but his replies had the circuitous squirmy logic of the paranoid. "I know they are all looking at me." Well, yes, they are, as a matter of fact. Shine on, you crazy diamond.

This man, like me only barely out of boyhood, had once been my most trusted colleague in the shimmering outer reaches of our imagined futures—witty, adventurous, tough, intense. We used to sleep over at each other's place and stay awake half the night just exercising our imaginations—he'd traveled a lot for someone so young, and he stirred in me that sense of the larger Elsewhere. Now he seemed to dwell in a self-containing shadow, and his clouded image loomed like Banquo's ghost for me, some dead phantom come back from the underworld with obscure lessons for me, but he couldn't spit out the lessons. *What? What?* I wanted to shout, but quickly came to realize he couldn't answer. The scene kept shifting, like incoherent cuts in a black-and-white foreign movie—we're sitting at the table with my sisters, we're standing cramped together in the corridor waiting to get into the men's room, we're crouched on the steps of the stoop outside—and still the dialogue maintained its monotonous pointless pursuit of an answer that wasn't coming. *What are you trying to tell me? What do you want?*

I thought his mother had come and picked him up from our apartment in town late in the afternoon, but after dark he showed up at Bolek's, a mile or so north of town on the way to Utica, and he ticked off our drummer and host, who whacked him on the hands with his heavy drumsticks when Todd started messing with his cymbals as we wailed away through our repertoire in the crowded second living-room that had always been our rehearsal space. We had fun in that band, a nondescript two-guitar-bass-and-drums outfit cranking out easy cover-tunes by the Doobie Brothers and ZZ Top and Bachman Turner Overdrive, and I guess Todd wanted to get in on the act as we played for a real crowd of our classmates. But it was a fellowship to which he didn't belong, hadn't earned a place through the tedious drudge-work of endless practice, playing those same three stupid chords over and over again, and Todd never should have gone after Bolek's drums. One thing about Bolek, his drums were his, *his* alone (I had voyaged with him and his mother in their powder-blue Nova to a music store in Utica, where Bolek, probably hectored by me in my John Bonham Led Zeppelin obsession, picked out a set of blue Vistalite Ludwigs—not amber, like Bonzo's, because Bolek thought amber looked like urine—and paid with cold hard cash, working-man's money—*his* drums, for certain). I've talked to people in later years who were at that graduation party, and not many recall that Todd was even there. Was he? Only Macbeth saw Banquo's ghost, right, and that because of his guilt? The night wore on, and eventually every detail was overcome by the darkness. In some ways it was only important that I imagined he was there, a faint hollow-eyed advocate for the secrets that threatened to vanish forever.

• • •

Cities on Flame with Rock and Roll

The summer got better and then the summer got worse, for me and for Led Zeppelin. I had scored tickets for the August 6 Zeppelin concert at Rich Stadium, home of the NFL Buffalo Bills (who would play almost as badly as the Buccaneers in 1977, going 3-11), but that never happened. On July 23 and 24, the band played concerts in Oakland's Alameda County Coliseum (home of the Raiders, who went 11-3 that year), the first punctuated by backstage ultra-violence from John Bonham and his "droog," Johnny Bindon, which would lead to lingering litigation against the band and its imperious manager, Peter Grant. A few days later, upon arrival in New Orleans Zeppelin's singer Robert Plant received the frightful news that his son had died back in England. The rest of the tour was cancelled, starting with the upcoming gig at the Louisiana Superdome (where the Saints would go 3-11, including a late-season loss to the Tampa Bay Buccaneers). Plant must have been wondering what was happening to him—and strong rumors smoldered concerning bad karma arising from Jimmy Page's occult dabbling, his purchase and study of esoteric works by the notorious Aleister Crowley, a prophet of the "Left Hand Path." Two years earlier, after a wildly successful tour, Jimmy Page and Plant and their families had gone on holiday in Greece, but Plant's car crashed on a remote road and he and his wife were badly injured. Bad, but nothing like losing a young son to a peculiar illness, a five-year-old dying from a stomach infection. Strange, like one of those Shakespearean ironies of a scene more redolent of war, a father mourning a fallen son, than the playful highways and the houses of the holy of a rock band's concert tour. All kinds of machinery ground to a halt that summer day in New Orleans.

In high school and college I dreamed unrealistically about rock-and-roll stardom (on the far left, with guitar).

Steven Liparulo

Led Zeppelin would never play the United States again, and there went my chance for the ultimate concert experience, a kind of dangling sentence fragment forever denied its punctuation in my life. I don't mean to put it on the same plane as the life or death of the singer's son, but that concert was a big deal to me, as it was to any true fan (short for fanatic). I had been initiated into the tribal ritual of the rock concert back in January, 1976, and it had changed my life. It all began with a triple-bill in Binghamton's hockey arena headlined by Blue Oyster Cult, supported by Bob Seger and Angel, and I could never get enough after that, after full-baptismal immersion in the wired energy of Seger's Silver Bullet guitarist and the muscular elegance of the Cult's lead guitarist, Buck Dharma, the evident camaraderie among the musicians onstage and the facile community of the faithful in the crowd, the communal body of the fan. That first show in the Broome County Veterans Memorial Arena, with the pyrotechnics and theatrics and light show of the Blue Oyster Cult, and that strange music and those esoteric lyrics, man, that really set the hook in me. "The clock strikes twelve, the moon-drops burst out at you from their hiding place." I had found a home in the world, and it was in the houses of the holy, the sacred realm of the massive PA and banked Fresnel lights and soundboards and follow-spots, where "Marshalls wail, boy, but Fender controls." Life in the tribe of the circulating joint, the village that reassembles itself every night and communes in strange, fiery rituals. Cities on flame with rock and roll.

If I had to venture a guess as to why rock and roll became my first religion (however false an idol it turned out to be), I suppose that I wanted, perhaps needed, a double life, and in some ways, despite the insecurities that probably every fatherless man finds draped heavily over his shoulders, I also imagined life on a grand scale, a reader's and a dreamer's scale, after the fashion of *The Lord of the Rings* and "Kashmir." Life as a good son and compliant little student was not quite enough, I wanted to be the cool intellectual who could handle the books and the math and the physics, and who knew the score and could navigate the big ideas and could sling the words. I also felt I had to have the wild-man, the transgressive fantasy of the rock and roll star, soaring high and free. I think I needed the consolation of an Elsewhere, too, the promise of a far-away Middle Earth or Kashmir. Even now, when I talk to people about religion—skeptical people who think it is nuts to imagine "some guy in the sky"—I have to ask, "do you really want to say that this puny human life is enough? Don't you have any imagination, and if you do, where do you suppose it came from?" The Holy Spirit is really not that hard a concept to get hold of. Anyway, for me it was simple: once I'd been to the Rock Show, I had to keep going back to find myself once again at the communion rail with the faithful, the people hungry to partake of the sacraments of the Faraway-Fantastic, Also Always Already Elsewhere.

For the next two years, my junior and senior years in high school, I made the scene as often as I could, and caught great touring acts like the Doobie Brothers, Journey, Tom Petty, and Van Halen in Binghamton and Utica. I worked after classes as a janitor at the school, and I spent my "disposable income" on stereo gear and albums and rock concerts. I'd gotten started on the electric guitar around the same time I started working for a paycheck, and I played in a band throughout high school, imagining myself one day wailing away in the spotlight at sold-out concerts. I saw Blue Oyster Cult several more times, including a few gigs with their now-legendary laser light show, in the "Godzilla" era, always mesmerized by the lead guitar of Buck Dharma, who all but glowed in the spotlight in his white satin stage outfit, a projection of every teen-aged fantasy.

For Halloween, 1976, in Utica, I got more than a rock show, I got a life-lesson as a group of us, led by Dan Perry, made the journey from New Berlin to see Lynyrd Skynyrd, the leading act of the Southern Rock movement. They had three lead guitar players who wailed for an hour and a half or however long they felt like on "Free Bird." Personally, I thought they were kind of boneheaded (they were named after cor-ruption of a gym teacher's name), and Lester Bangs really didn't like "torpid" songs like "Sweet Home, Alabama," so neither did I (but I liked words like "torpid" that he would use and I would appropriate), but you never knew when you might catch a great joint or some opium at a concert, so I was in. Dan was driving his old man's station wagon, and didn't realize at the time that he locked the keys in the car. We partied our brains out at the rowdy concert, and I seem to recall a few people passing out. That's how those parties went! *Wow,* you would shout when the band took a break between numbers, *I'm so wasted! This is awesome!*

It wasn't quite so awesome when we got back to the car and found out about the keys. It quickly became apparent that Dan was going to have to call his old man and work out a rescue. Dan's father was a bit of a legend in New Berlin, what you would probably think of as the Platonic Ideal of a Father if you were in high school in the late 1970's (and that's not entirely a compliment, these being the post-Vietnam days of "Question Authority"), a senior executive at the large insurance company that was the only major economic driver in the village. John Perry was a big figure in a dark business suit, spoke a little loud and with a city accent (a St. John's alumnus), all kinds of friendly, sometimes a bit obnoxious, maybe a glad-hander, but all of it right out there—on the back of his jersey, it would have said DAD. And I figured he was going to skin Dan alive for this car-keys boner.

What happened instead completely mystified me, in large part because I really had no idea what a father-son relationship might look like. My mother had left my father when I was three or four years old, taken four kids on the train from Florida to upstate New York, and I would estimate that I had seen my father a dozen times in those years, and when I had he hadn't made much of an impression, some short salesman in a car-coat. My mom had tried out a step-father for a while, but we the wicked stepchildren had killed him off back in Florida (for real: he died from complications ensuing from alcoholism, into which he sank as he probably realized what a dreary ordeal nuclear-family life could be), and we returned to upstate New York again when I was in the seventh grade. That was when I met Todd and Dan, neither of whom had lived in New Berlin the last time I served a sentence in what to me was a wretched burg, in fourth and fifth grade. So, it just seemed to me that Dan's father would act like fathers acted in my warped imagination—he would make an ugly emotional scene, belittle his son in front of his friends, blow up at all of us, come on like the fat guy in Laurel and Hardy.

Instead, he showed up after an hour or two, and treated us to breakfast. He wasn't wearing his business suit when he came through the door of the diner we'd settled into near where the station-wagon was parked, but he was obviously the Dad in the scene, making an inventory of who was at the table as he prompted us to give our food orders. He might very well have been a touch amused. He didn't seem overly surprised or concerned that we were all pretty elevated—obviously intoxicated and probably high on half a dozen different drugs. It was as if we had all agreed there was just nothing to say, no point in saying anything about our condition. There was a little tension around his mouth as he spoke in hushed tones that may well have represented him restraining stronger impulses, but isn't that the point? Real adult wisdom has something to do with restraint. I suppose I couldn't recognize it because this was a moment of grace, something I had not been educated to expect. This was really something I had to file away and come back to many years later when I had some additional experiences to help me sort this scene out.

• • •

Orientation

In August, I made my journey to Buffalo, not to be initiated into the houses of the holy but to visit the university where I was planning to start school in the fall. It was an unsuccessful trip for me if its purpose was orientation—if I'd gotten properly aligned I would have realized then that a college campus *is* one of the houses of the holy, maybe the most important of them all (I'd get there eventually). Instead, I came away disoriented, understanding all too well that I wasn't ready for college, that I was freaked out by big cities and big crowds of noisy kids from Long Island. I almost got ripped off on a bogus dope deal in the bus terminal in Buffalo before I ever even made it to the college campus, but somehow I had pulled off a double-reverse and got the cops to get my money back. Still, it had me rattled right from the start.

Once the orientation itself began in earnest on the SUNY Buffalo campus—a classic in public-university concrete architecture and eerily redolent of the apartment complex in Stanley Kubrick's *A Clockwork Orange*—I soon realized that the other freshmen had been in on prior *orientations* I had missed, maybe when I was sleeping off a Blue Oyster Cult concert. Since no one in my family had ever gone to college, and since my high school's "guidance counselor" considered students getting accepted to the two-year agricultural and mechanical schools all the success one could hope for, I had only the vaguest of ideas about things like majors and placement, the whole process of what you had to do to prepare for college. These other kids, who seemed to be hard-wired into coherent groups while I lone-wolfed it around from event to event in the concrete corridors and meeting rooms, they all seemed possessed of *esoterica* about the implications of declaring "EE," Electrical Engineering, which was apparently a tough handful, academically speaking. Wow. I recall my eyes glazing over looking at computerized class schedules and realizing that I didn't completely understand what the word "elective" really meant in this context. I hadn't gone much beyond imaging electrical engineering feeding directly into jobs in party-friendly recording studios, and here all these loud and aggressive *Lawn Guylanders* had already taken AP calculus and physics. This was going to be trouble. I was way behind, and out of my element, deeply disorganized. I couldn't sleep in the dorm room bed and felt like maybe this was going to be the place where I would fall into the black hole if I persisted in my plan of starting school here in the fall. I was fully capable of coming up with a plan much more irresponsible and stupid than that, and informed by my family's preferences for quitting things when they got hard, that's just what I did. Or what I started to do, before more trouble found me on the highway from Buffalo back to New Berlin.

I had arranged for my classmate John to pick me up at the bus station in Utica, and, normally as cheery a fellow as you could meet, he was in a peculiar mood as I threw my bag in the back of his Opel station wagon. He had joined the Army and taken "delayed enlistment," which meant he was loafing around all summer and part of the fall before reporting for basic training. (Steve Bolek, who was either the drummer in my band or I was the guitarist in *his* band, had enlisted in the Air Force, and a couple of guys from our class were going into the Marines. At the time, my rock-and-roll lifestyle didn't seem like a good fit with what military service seemed to be about.) Mainly, John was engaged in a notorious shack-up love-affair with one of the English teachers from high school. And she was an A-1 prime Elvis Presley fanatic. And the news I had missed in my sulking around on the Buffalo campus was that Elvis had left the building, shuffled off this mortal coil, the drugs prescribed by his sycophant doctors finally having caught up with him. The English teacher apparently resented my intruding upon her grief, and hence John's strange mood. He was a great friend, and he and I got on famously, had high times together. We had once left a party in that Opel station wagon and backed out directly into a deep drainage ditch, pitching up the nose of the car until we were staring straight up at a starry sky, astronauts about to lift off, and just turned to each other and laughed, observing the obvious that this wasn't in the plan. John was also ... let us say, *driven* by his passions and "relationships." What I was seeing, the dissonance in his mood, was him going through a conflict in masculine identity, a conflict between what he wanted and what *his woman* wanted. I thought it was a little silly, not least because I didn't think Elvis was such a special big deal anymore, but I was kind of "off" when it came to relationships anyway. More than anything, it was his affair, quite literally.

41

But Elvis was dead. The King of Rock and Roll—so maybe it is true, no one makes it out alive. Not even Elvis could stay the executioner. Wow. Trouble all up and down the highway.

• • •

Accommodation Address

It went on like that into the fall. After moping around for a while, hanging out on the street corner (there's only one in New Berlin), watching friends like John disappear into the service or college, going to a few high school football games (feeling totally out of place, as if I'd graduated in the 50's instead of in June), and getting stoned a fair amount, I headed down to Florida to spend some time with my father. This was probably a joint "great idea" between my mother and father, who agreed on nothing, another one of these "orientations" that proved counterproductive. At least I was flying instead of taking the bus, and the weather promised to be an improvement, unless I ran into one of those Tampa storms that shut down the Led Zeppelin concert earlier in the summer.

I found upon arrival that the living arrangements would have their complications. Gus had an apartment in the city, not too far from Tampa Stadium, in fact, but he didn't stay there all that often—it seemed more like an office (he was a sales manager for the Pabst beer brand) or what the spies call an *accommodation address*, someplace where you get mail and hide things. His main domicile was closer to MacDill Air Force Base, a 50's vintage ranch house in a 50's vintage upper-middle-class subdivision, and it belonged to his lover, who was an Air Force widow. Did this qualify as a pattern? I couldn't say, but he had done this before, found a service widow with a house and a pension, and I suppose a social circle, too. Crafty, some kind of ready-made thing, a turn-key life. The first time, he had gone the whole "relationship" route with the widow, getting married and even having a kid of their own. But then, like a serial killer growing into his work, he had refined the business, and now the old man was out and out "living in sin" with an Air Force widow who had a son in his twenties still intermittently living at home. I was welcome at either place, more or less, the welcome mostly coming from his lover, who was a gracious southern woman who had soaked up a lot of sun and gin in her time. The thing is, while Gus had enlisted in the Army right after Pearl Harbor, not waiting for the draft to get geared up, he wasn't much of a soldier and didn't take to military discipline, getting busted in rank several times. Drinking? Fighting? No doubt. Was there a special thrill now, all these years later, for him in sleeping with an officer's wife? It wasn't like I could ask, but I have to admit that maybe I was a little bit of the smug Socratic teenager who saw through the hypocrisy of the Pharisees among the "Greatest Generation" and picked up on something unseemly about the whole business. My father had some weird ways of loving.

The cool thing was, the intermittent son was a rocker, singer in a band and a big-time skydiver. My trip took the low road whole-hog when I went "on tour" with his band for a gig in Lakeland, in central Florida. It ended up like a real rock-and-roll tour in the 1970's, with groupies in the motel room and what you might call the "group scene," bodies all tangled up with bodies well beyond the normal inhibitory boundaries. I bet that wasn't what the parents were thinking about when they dreamed up this trip, but that was just more evidence that they really didn't know much about what they were doing. It was kind of a blast for me, another barrier busted through, but one *pranging* hangover the next day. I seem to recall calling Dan Perry the following afternoon from under the covers in my father's "accommodation address" and rescheduling our rendezvous based upon my faltering health. Rescheduling gigs, just like Jimmy Page!

Maybe delayed slightly, but not lessened in intensity, I made that gonzo road trip with Perry to see David in Miami and I went to the Giants game with Dan Perry instead of my father. I wish I could say there were some great moments of epiphany with old Gus, but it just didn't seem like he wanted to be there for me. He showed me how to mix a high ball—not a particularly recondite process—and we drank quite a few of them, and we ate any number of steak dinners. What we talked about, I couldn't tell you, and to be honest about it, I wasn't all that interested in what he might have to say, since he had already come through with the NFL tickets and wasn't in any position to do anything about the Led Zeppelin scene. What else could he offer?

I found out what he was really lacking when word came to me through my mother on the phone that Todd was dead. In some ways it was simply the conclusion of a sentence started in June, *Todd Is Dead*, he was dead when I saw him on graduation day, but even the inevitable, the already-true slams us in the gut when the sentence is finally and fully enacted. The details were sketchy—he had checked himself into the state hospital in Binghamton, and then had thought better of it, apparently, and gone over the fence in the night. The central fact of the narrative was he'd been hit by an 18-wheeler on the highway, and that was that. Now it's official, Todd is really dead.

Gus's response was to mix us drinks, highballs in tall glasses. I sat on the sofa and he sat in his chair in that other man's living room. Maybe *Lou Grant* was on the TV, a big console that was as much a piece of furniture as an electronic entertainment device, or maybe it was *M*A*S*H*. And he probably quoted the couple of lines from Shakespeare that he had learned through his community college education. And that, evidently, was enough for him. Obligation discharged. Before long the TV show had ended, and he'd finished his drink and was off to bed with that other man's widow.

It fell to Ivan, the intermittent son, to guide me through the ritual passage, which required quite a few more drinks, in the privacy of his room, which still featured his childhood bunk beds. Young Ivan, only a couple of years older than me but seemingly an open-hearted sort, sat with me and talked me through it. In some ways, my reaction was what you'd expect, first anger at the clown who would get himself creamed on a highway, and then sad mourning for a lost soul and crazy diamond. And then just blubbering, drunken *poor-poor-pitiful-me* self-indulgence, like no one had ever lost a friend before. The thing I recall as remarkable about Ivan was simply that it didn't embarrass him to see me go to pieces. He helped me maintain my dignity just by maintaining his. This was all OK. I would worry about what I'd learned about my father some other time.

If it hadn't already, summer ended right then. College was a bust, scoring was down in the NFL, the Led Zeppelin thing wasn't going to happen, Elvis was dead, and so was Todd. Call that the end of something, time to start over, I guess, so I headed back "home," back on the bus along those troubled roads to upstate New York and my mother, and who knew what else. I had to look it up to discover that Dallas beat Denver in the Super Bowl that season (in the Louisiana Superdome, where Led Zeppelin had last been scheduled to appear), although I'm sure I watched the game. Even football went out of focus for a while.

• • •

Winter (Wish You Were Here)
I hadn't been home all that long when word trickled north that David, whom we had visited on the beach in Miami like some scene out of an Elvis Presley movie, had died riding his motorcycle. That, my friends, was the sound of a chapter being slammed shut in someone's book of life.

It was the dark heart of winter, I felt like a gray-haired old man at 18, and I had to get something going, a job, some kind of direction. I started off by hitchhiking over the hill to work in the county seat, Norwich, first in a shoe factory and then at the hospital, where my oldest sister helped me get a job in housekeeping—second shift, basement porter. It seems like a ridiculous detail out of a horror story, but it's true that part of my job at the hospital was to burn the trash, and that sometimes included operating-room waste. On more than one occasion I stoked up the fire extra-hot to burn off an amputated limb. A couple of times a week I would come in early and empty the ashes, and I would get to enjoy a shower on the clock. I had won the Bausch & Lomb award at graduation for best overall average in science classes, and now I was collecting trash and operating an incinerator, peering in through the flames to make sure the arm was burning off properly. Shoveling ashes. My best friend was dead. I had no idea what I was doing, beyond working a routine job and living on my own in a cheap apartment. It seemed like something I had to do on my own, but I didn't really enjoy being alone. I got used to it, though, probably a little too well.

I rented an apartment in Norwich just blocks from where I had grown up during some of the most abject days of our single-parent-family poverty. I had a huge Peavey guitar amp, 6 x 12", and I would antagonize my neighbors trying to crank out tunes. I was finally asked to leave by my first landlord, an Italian barely fluent in English who pronounced my name like a German—"Schteef, I can't have'a the noise." What did I care, I moved—the guy worked in the landfill and always carried that overmastering garbage stench with him. I was circling around a primal scene and hardly understood what was going on, couldn't really see my own intentions or understand my inclinations. I liked rock and roll music, with a studious devotion, but I couldn't play it all that well (couldn't move up the Ritchie Blackmore scale from rudimentary "Smoke on the Water" to exotic "Gates of Babylon" or incendiary "Kill the King"). I drank a little, and liked to get high, but I wasn't dissolute nor was I in trouble with the law. I didn't date, and didn't really have any interest in "relationships." Obsessions were more my style. Sexuality basically took care of itself and didn't seem to make any trouble in my life or exert any pressure on my behavior, or maybe it would be more accurate to say I wasn't aware of it. That's the way illusions work, they make themselves invisible.

I just kind of drifted through the tail end of the first winter of my adult life.

On a few of those deep winter nights, maybe the darkest of them, when the moon would present its dark side to us and the clouds would block out the stars, I would indulge in a ritual of sadness, a cold sacrament of immersion from the church of rock and roll mysteries. I would put myself to bed with Pink Floyd's *Wish You Were Here* cued up on the turntable, and the icy tones of that melancholic album would reach out to me under the covers. "So you think you can tell heaven from hell, blue skies from pain."

In the 70's, Pink Floyd wowed the rock world with their album covers and graphics, featuring striking imagery from Hipgnosis and peculiar touches that represented the band's eclectic and esoteric interests (*Dark Side of the Moon* was all about triangles and pyramids, perhaps evocative of Freemasonry, and *Animals* featured absurdist shots of blimp-sized pigs in the skies over industrial London). *Wish You Were Here* even included post cards with some of the more distinctive pictures from the record jacket: the two business men shaking hands, one of them on fire; a swimmer emerging like one of Michelangelo's slaves out of desert sands; the post-modern Magritte man with no face and transparent wrists, carrying a copy of the album (like the huckster in the song "Have a Cigar": "we're just knocked out, we heard about the sell-out"). And can you believe it? I am pretty sure I sent Todd one of those cards when he was institutionalized. What a stunning lack of empathy and insight. Can you imagine getting a card, when you are in the mental hospital, that all but screams out, Shine On You Crazy Diamond, emphasis on CRAZY? I don't remember what I wrote on the card, but I know what was on my mind. *It's cold out here, you crazy rotten heartless little rat, cold and lonely and I don't know what I'm doing. Get your act together and get your crazy butt back here and help me hold back the tide of an insane world.*

Well, fair enough. Ambivalent love reaching out to ambivalent love across the years. The first I really knew of Todd was 1972, when we had moved back to town from Florida (again) when I was in seventh grade. I had gotten hit by a car in the depths of bleak mid-winter and he had sent me a card while I was in the hospital recuperating from a broken leg. Touching gesture, the only card I got that wasn't from a relative, until I opened the stupid thing. The message ran to the effect of "way to go, numbskull." Well, this was going to be a new kind of love, wasn't it?

And now, round three, trouble escalated from broken leg to mental institution to death: Shine on, you crazy diamond, in the outer reaches of your exile beyond the frontiers of human community and sanity, shine on through the cold and dark, and the sold-out and the broken, what is out of tune and what cannot be spoken. May we meet again somewhere down that road in the houses of the holy.

CHAPTER 3

• • •

The School of Athens: An Educated Life (1979-83/2013)

"Of Man's First Disobedience, and the Fruit
Of that Forbidden Tree, whose mortal taste
Brought Death into the World, and all our woe,
With loss of *Eden*, till one greater Man
Restore us, and regain the blissful Seat,
Sing Heav'nly Muse ...."

(JOHN MILTON, *PARADISE LOST*, I, 1-6)

• • •

SEPTEMBER 7, 2013. Athens, Georgia. Dr. Tim Loonam and I were walking toward majestic Sanford Stadium on a sunny Friday afternoon when I was suddenly overtaken by the memory of a painting by Raphael, *The School of Athens*, I had first studied as an undergraduate three decades earlier. How entirely that fresco captured the moment in our peripatetic conversation—here is Plato conversing with Aristotle, Dr. Steve and Dr. Tim, idealist and pragmatist.

I had made my way back to Georgia, where thirty years earlier I had spent the fall and winter and spring at Army schools as I began my tour of duty as an infantry lieutenant, to catch up with Tim Loonam. He was alive on that campus in Athens, mind, body, and soul, flesh and blood, too. As a student, he had earned his Doctor of Veterinary Medicine degree there, prologue to his reentry into the Army and eventual combat tour in Iraq. As an Army veterinarian, he had come back to that campus during his mid-tour leave from Iraq in 2004 and been honored by Coach Mark Richt as part of the pomp and circumstance of an SEC game-day. Tim's son was in his third year at Georgia, playing football as a walk-on and taking ROTC (Reserve Officers Training Corps) en route to an Army commission. His daughter was just starting her freshman year. Dr. Tim is in practice in Lexington, South Carolina, but he spends a lot of weekends in Athens. His email address is DawgDoc.

I spent the early part of that Friday working like a reporter on a long assignment exploring the Georgia campus, shuffling from one scheduled interview or site visit to another, always drifting North as if drawn by a compass needle, getting the lay of the land in Bulldog country, getting their stories from a variety of informants. In a lot of ways, it was just one more college campus, and I'd been on my share, earning between three and five college degrees, depending on how you count, and I worked at a research university for almost twenty years. You roll out the contents of a college-campus starter-set: a bunch of buildings—the more antique the better, some dorms, some libraries, some gyms, connected by a lot of sidewalks crossing a lot of quads. Sprinkle liberally with scooters and bikes. If you are lucky like here in Athens, the terrain rolls hilly and thick with trees, and plenty of colleges are lucky like that. But then again, this is an SEC school, a football factory, and smack-dab in the middle of campus, where it really has no earthly business because it serves no real educational purpose, stands this monstrous arena, Sanford Stadium, which rises up and towers above the campus like a colossus, or like something thrust down by aliens in the midst of an unsuspecting community, maybe a watering dish for a gargantuan extraterrestrial mascot dog—woof woof, Uga. On game-days, 92,000 and more fans make their way into that place and send up unearthly roars.

Tim Loonam and I were wrapping up the day, heading back down Sanford Drive on our way to the football complex to pick up his truck and head out, and that stadium started to unsettle my gyroscope, its incongruous size inducing a touch of vertigo in the steep-raking autumn sunlight. You keep craning up to see the top of the structure, and then when you look down you realize that the street is actually an elevated causeway that seems to hover about five stories above ground level—the stadium was originally built astraddle a river bed, taking advantage of the natural bowl the river's course had worn away.

And there was something slightly sinister in its Roman aura, down to the various gates for the sorted classes of Athenians. I had noticed in studying my maps—some things never change for an old Army Ranger—that there were segregated entrances to the stadium, gates for students, faculty, players and families, and Sky Club and Sky Suite patrons, in what I assume to be ascending class order (in the Roman Colosseum the gates would have read—in Latin—women and plebeians, intermediate class-es, equestrians, and Senators). That stadium seemed to me—prone to entertaining the worst of thoughts, I guess—to encrypt the dark secrets of segregation and slavery and brutal violence of the Roman Colosseum at the heart of the otherwise idyllic Athenian campus, so cute, so quaint, so many tousle-haired Georgia boys in button-collar oxford shirts and long-legged Georgia girls in denim shorts and cowboy boots, so quint-essentially *collegiate.* It was as if I were encountering the clash of Rome and Greece, the bloody ghost of Spartacus haunting the ethereal midst of the very *Platonic form* of a college campus (in the heart of the bloody old American South, too—on the way in from my distant motel I saw the turn-off for Winder, Georgia, hometown of legendary Senator, and de-vout segregationist, Richard Brevard Russell, who earned his law degree here in Athens—woof woof, Uga).

Something was rushing in my head, thoughts like roller-coaster cars careening and swooping and rattling at fearsome speed. I knew what I wanted to say—I wanted to explain how it all comes down to a fresco painted by Raphael in the Vatican.

I was gesturing to Tim, pointing to the stadium and trying to explain the painting, pointing skyward just as Plato suggests to Aristotle that our thoughts must arise and seek their home in the heavens. "That's you and me, Tim, that is how our lives add up, the essential productive dialectic tension between us. That's why we are here, educated men. A Doctor of Philosophy and a Doctor of Veterinary Medicine."

I was trying to say something like that.

Dr. Tim Loonam and I recreated the old "Raise Up, Buffalo" gesture of our infantry battalion (1-17 INF), when we were reunited in Athens, Georgia, for an SEC football game, September 2013.

In that moment I was fully in the presence not only of Tim Loonam, my old friend nearly as youthful and handsome and fit in his appearance as football legend Doug Flutie, trying his best to follow my manic signifying, and not just in the presence of Raphael and the Western tradition in art, but in communion with the whole living body of an educated life, present laminated on top of past and animated with vital figures like Plato and Aristotle, inhabiting ancient Rome and Sir Thomas More's early-modern London, reviving in some very real sense the School of Athens. In my mind and in my writing, in the research that motivated my trip to Athens, I was engaged in a dynamic dialectic, the Socratic dialogue of my life questioning the value of and relationships between institutions like education, religion, family, the military, and government, seeking to understand what was really important. I was there on that green undulating campus to watch a football game, and how sham-important was that, how likely to be the very intersection of excess and illusion? This whole community, the university plus the town plus the diaspora of alumni who reassemble for games equaling the School of Athens, was undergoing a transformation and by the time I arrived back on campus tomorrow morning, Athens would become Rome, 92,000 in that stadium, the Circus Maximus of Football, the game all that was going on for the day. Already, ESPN trucks were lined up outside the stadium, crews crawling around like ants wiring the venue for a big national telecast bouncing off alien satellites to a waiting world. What kind of college is this?

The school where I took my undergraduate degrees and studied Plato and Aristotle and Raphael and Milton didn't even field a football team, and neither did it host an ROTC detachment.

• • •

Educated Conversation

February, 1981. Binghamton, NY, could get hopelessly gray on winter days, between the endless clouds in the sky, threatening snow any time from October to April, and the concrete buildings of a Utilitarian Ugly Public University campus, all the charm of an Air Force missile base in Nebraska. But inside those buildings the colors of an educated life at a "Public Ivy" school shone. In we would slog wearing heavy coats and boots, leaving snail-trails of slush and road-salt in the tiled corridors, finding seats in the carpeted lecture hall and continuing to unwrap, tucking hats and gloves and scarves into backpacks to replace the textbooks and notebooks dislodged. And then our eyes would light up, or at least mine would, because by the Spring 1981 semester I had given up the illusion of a biochemistry major and was drifting through the humanities.

Art History. Onto the massive screen lowered from the ceiling in the lecture hall Dr. Mayo would throw the image of Raphael's fresco or Michelangelo's sculpture with the help of a slide projector, but the real color came from the talk, the professor professing that art had stories to tell. The content was often narrative. Jacob and Esau and the whole conflicted routine of the hirsute sons of Isaac and Rebekah, for example, was the subject of one painting I distinctly recall for the engaging familiarity with which the professor, whose name was of all things Penelope, spoke about the two brothers, as if maybe they were *her* brothers. It didn't really occur to me then that for a lot of people, the stories of the Bible are like family stories. There were stories, too, in the work of the artists, tales of technology in pursuit of the spirit. *Somehow with this paint and brush I'm going to touch people's souls*, these artists must have reckoned, *with this metal and clay and stone I'm going to evoke the human quest for divinity. I'm going to figure out how to rig this scaffolding so that I can paint the hand of God reaching out to Man on the ceiling of the Sistine Chapel.*

Rembrandt, working on his own variation on *chiaroscuro*, painting canvas after canvas to perfect the full humanity of light coming out of shadow. Caravaggio, his paint brush more like a knife, an edged weapon, his paintings explosions of violence, none better than when representing the conversion of Saint Paul as if by a kick in the head from a horse.

These weren't pictures, they were *works*.

Scholarship was work, too. I could dig that. After a semester or two deluded about making a career of rock and roll and indifferent academic performance in a major I wasn't prepared for, I was starting to come around to that realization. Work hard, get something out of the deal. Spring 1981 would be a good semester, my only 4.0.

So here came "The School of Athens" up onto the screen, which was obviously going to be a handful. Clean colors and crisp rendering of the setting and figures. It was a crowd scene—who *are* all these dudes in their togas? Philosophers, all the big-name philosophers of ancient Greece. And you knew we were going to have to talk about its use of perspective, with vaulted ceilings receding back toward the vanishing point, while the foreground figures seemed about ready to leap off the wall (not the canvas—this is a *fresco*, painted on a wall in a palace in the Vatican, you had to write that down, along with the title and date and artist). A lot of it is just mechanical, admiring the colors and figures but mostly just concentrating on writing down what the professor was saying to prepare for the exam. This would clearly be on the exam, not as an ID question, which would be a little obvious, but more likely a short-answer question, and maybe as a choice of topics for the essay.

Then the professor cut to a detail that framed Plato and Aristotle—*I know those guys, I'm reading those guys this semester, those are heavy dudes.* And now they have risen from the page and taken human shape, and they are dynamic, walking and arguing some point, vital contentious men. Plato looks like Moses, hefty and grave, while Aristotle favors my physics professor from last semester—it's as if they don't exist in the same time frame, and that's part of the design of the work, the contrast between the two great men. Plato has the edge on looks as far as I'm concerned, and the professor tells us that his finger points skyward, where we should seek the truth in the perfection of forms in the heavens, while Aristotle exhorts his fawning students to find truth through observation of the natural world (though, like all disciples, they seem prone to finding truth through writing down what Aristotle says). I write that down—you always want to have a good two-parter sentence ready for the essay, one of those "While BLANK does X, we see OTHER BLANK do Y." That's what we're doing here, beyond studying for the exam, we're learning how to talk like educated people. And I guess eventually you talk that way long enough and you become an educated person. Maybe that's the way a Utilitarian Ugly Public University goes about its business. I don't really know. In my early life I didn't meet many educated people.

After fifty minutes of that, we're trading books for hats and scarves and retracing our snail-trails into the corridor, and in my case, heading across a wind-blasted quad, in and out of the library lobby and into the lecture hall complex to a class where I'll learn how to talk about ... Plato and Aristotle, with Professor Roberts.

Larry Roberts was a good man and a good teacher, and he was indirectly responsible for me "backing into" the Philosophy double-major. I'd taken courses with Roberts three of my first four semesters in college. In my last semester I would take a two-hour practicum in college teaching as his TA for Plato and Aristotle.

Early in my college career, I knew I needed help and sought counseling concerning my relationships with people. When your best friend dies, likely of suicide, and prematurely ends a complex, ambivalent, vaguely homoerotic love-hate relationship, it's obvious you're going to have problems opening yourself to love and friendship. I knew I missed him. I knew that Pink Floyd album still made me sad, and that I still needed to go there to that sad cold place with "Wish You Were Here," and I learned to play it on the 12-string guitar and sing its doleful melody, which didn't require much in the way of pipes. I wasn't quite as aware of one of my other problems, my sense of fatherlessness, but looking back I can see that I sought out father figures in teachers in high school and college.

For six years in New Berlin I was blessed to take science classes with three of the best teachers and best men that anyone could hope for. Wayne Aldrich once blew out the flames from an overturned alcohol burner in the lab with a single *whooshing* breath like Superman—no students were going up in flames on his watch! Pop Everts taught you statistics the old fashioned way: collect one hundred rocks, weigh them and measure their displacement by dunking them in a beaker, and then run a bunch of equations on your columns of results. Pat Vartuli handed out a half-page physics reference guide the first day of class and told you that by the end of the year you'd know how to use this. Man, he was like Vince Lombardi spending an eight-hour workshop on a single play, the Packer sweep. In fact, Vartuli was a football coach, and I'm sure a really good one. They were all great teachers—got the most out of their students, had us laughing all the time, and never left a moment's doubt about who was in charge. Inspired by them, I won the award for best science student in my high-school graduating class. (Unfortunately, we weren't quite so blessed with math-teaching talent, or maybe I just burned out those brain cells at Blue Oyster Cult concerts, and I wasn't prepared for the math needed for college science courses at the highest level.)

College was a different type of a deal, way bigger, a less intimate community, but when I did find good guys I tended to try to stick with them, and that was how I wound up double-majoring in Philosophy. My second semester I took a symbolic logic course with Larry Roberts and found him to be personable, low-key, and intellectually supportive, which doesn't exactly sound like a Father's Day card, but it does say a lot about my reserved emotional nature. So, the next semester I looked for him in the course listing and hit the jackpot—he was teaching a course on the philosophy of religion that concentrated entirely on Saint Augustine.

The funny thing about my undergraduate education, as I look back on it, is its declination diagram, how everything was actually located five degrees away from where it should be, how everything was displaced a little from what Plato would call its eternal form, or Marcus Aurelius its essential nature. Here we were getting Old Testament stories from the history of paintings, reading Sir Thomas More, Renaissance man and author of *Utopia*, instead of Saint Thomas More, "the King's good servant and God's first" (that conjunction *and* the subject of considerable controversy). We were reading Saint Augustine, Doctor of the Church, as philosopher, looking for arguments.

This intellectual approach left my reading of the *Confessions*, especially, incomplete and dissatisfying, since it was written as a conversion narrative, not a book of arguments, and I was as yet unconverted. *On the Free Choice of the Will*, on the other hand, would hold up better as philosophy since it was intended to present arguments, a response to the Manichaean heresy of the day. I can't say that I would read the right work by Saint Augustine properly until at least 1997, when I studied *On Christian Doctrine* and its place in the history of rhetoric, and then a dozen or so years later returned to it as ... theology, its intended purpose all along. Round and round and slowly up the seven storey mountain. Better a misreading of *On the Free Choice of the Will* early in my intellectual formation than none at all.

I did understand that Augustine was dealing with the problem of evil and how it arises. That's a good problem to confront. His answer was actually simple enough, that evil comes from the misuse of God's great gift to us, the power to choose freely. God gives us this gift to allow us the freedom to attain perfection, Augustine writes, for "without [free will] man cannot live rightly" (Two.I.5). Evil amounts to this one thing, this one bad choice, over and over again, in all its worldly variations. "All sins are included under this one class: when someone is turned away from divine things that are truly everlasting, toward things that change and are uncertain" (One.XVI.116). The seeming paradox of sin arises, however, because God loves us too much not to give us this great gift of choice, and also loves us too much not to subject us to the consequences of our choices. This idea of how we sin becomes known as the doctrine of *concupiscence,* embodied in the Garden of Eden narrative as the choice that Adam and Eve make (what Milton calls "Man's First Disobedience"), which results in the inclination we all struggle with even today—original sin.

In 1980 I read it, took down the notes from Professor Roberts' lecture on the arguments, and wrote the papers and exams required to demonstrate understanding of the philosophy, got my "A." But I can't say that I fathomed the depth of what I was reading or what it was offering me. I was just lucky, I guess, that I took a course that got me to buy a book that years later I would come back to for some real answers to this very real problem of evil and sin, which turned out to me to be a whole lot more important than Augustine's argument for the existence of God.

That was just dumb luck, finding a course that connected a professor I liked with subject matter that touched on a need I was only dimly aware

Farewell to Football?

of. By the time I looked up Dr. Roberts for Spring of 1981 and found him teaching Plato and Aristotle, I was starting to think maybe I ought to do something with these philosophy courses I was piling up. Plato and Aristotle was a required course for the double-major in Philosophy.

The course was fun because it started out with the Pre-Socratics, some of whom were kind of nutty. They all seemed blissfully pithy, in large part because the record was incomplete and all that came down the ages were tart fragments. One of them said something about hedgehog only knowing one thing, one big thing. Everybody laughs. Heraclitus said "war is universal and justice is strife." That stuck with me.

Then came Plato, who I found out later didn't have to be considered a philosopher. He certainly didn't write like one, taking up the dialogue form always centered on the same dramatic character—Socrates, who rarely "won" his arguments outright. His general procedure was to engage fellow Athenians in conversations about some topic, like love or happiness or persuasion, and how important it should really be or what one should do to achieve it. Most of these Socratic dialogues explored what some specific Athenian claimed to believe, and Socrates usually found that his interlocutors were either inconsistent and contradictory in their beliefs or else didn't really know what they believed. While apparently an affable guy and admirable citizen, who comes off as pretty funny and witty in Plato's rendering of him, Socrates as an examiner of consciences also rubbed a lot of people the wrong way. He believed that the unexamined life was not worth living, but for many of his friends and neighbors, examining their lives was an unpleasant task they'd rather avoid. This is in ancient times, so different from today ....

The end is in the beginning: courses on Plato always read *The Apology* (sometimes called *The Defense*) first, and it depicts Socrates' unsuccessful defense against charges of corrupting Athenian youth. He takes the hemlock rather than the alternative of exile, since for Socrates life without disputation is worse than death. Another way to put it is that for Socrates, Athens is life and anything else is death. In another dialogue, the *Phaedrus*, a very important treatment of lovers, audience, and persuasion,

Socrates and Phaedrus both joke about how out of place Socrates is in the countryside beyond the city. If a dialogue about choosing a virtuous death over exile from civilization is your starting point, you realize that Plato's project is more subtle, or maybe just more obscure, than straight philosophy. He was exploring questions about how life should be lived.

Aristotle, for all his brilliance, seemed to "do" philosophy the way a handyman does chores. In one book he was a biologist, observant of nature. In another—and these "books" were all really notes taken by his students, not works of his own hand—he theorized on the poetic and dramatic arts. His analysis of the tragic hero, whose character flaw leads to a downfall that inspires pity and fear in the audience in order to discharge these vivid emotions in a catharsis, is still the basis for how we tend to think about characters in all forms of narrative. On he went, the diligent handyman, to ethics and to rhetoric, a powerful mind at work on all the major problems. You tended to plod through reading the translations of his works and end up with systematic notes on philosophical topics, the gems produced from the pressure of his fearsome analysis. With Plato, you tended to find yourself abstracted from yourself and deeply absorbed in the conversations Socrates initiates, and then when you've finished the story often reflect—*wait, what?*

That shivery day in class, almost everyone sweater-clad since the heat in that lecture hall tended to be spotty when it wasn't just meager, we went over the assignment for an upcoming paper, dealing with arguments for the immortality of the soul in Plato's *Phaedo*, which depicts Socrates' last conversation, as the hemlock takes effect. I was careful to clarify what was expected in the paper. I've always liked to write, but I went through a major tussle with my first English professor over a paper the year before and didn't want any misconceptions to slow down my march to GPA perfection this semester.

In my Introduction to Literary Analysis class I had let slip to the professor that I worked as a journalist during the two years I took off after graduating high school. Admitting that to an academician, especially as in his case a librarian posing as a literature professor, was like declaring open season on my writing, and he bore down hard, making every effort to extend and complicate my sentences. I didn't help matters by misunderstanding the context rather severely. Full of myself, and fed up with the professor's obsession with the works of Harold Pinter, which I found tedious and pretentious (almost as much so as his other favorite, T. Eliot's *The Waste Land*), I had submitted a final paper in the form of Pinter's dialogue, full of verbal ticks and obscurities and ... pauses. That wasn't going to fly—"a creative option wasn't offered to the rest of the class," I recall as his exact words, tactically stated in the passive voice—and he slapped me with an "Incomplete." After some wrangling, I gave in, wrote the stupid paper his way, having seen his point. *Who am I to think I can decide what counts for good writing in this class?* I still can't stand Pinter or Eliot (whom I took to calling Pompous Poeticus), but I did learn to adapt to the context of the writing situation, humble myself before the task at hand, so now I wanted to make sure I knew what kind of paper Larry Roberts was assigning. I wasn't going to essay a Socratic dialogue for this assignment.

By the time I got out of class the day was already fading. The sun goes down pretty early during winter afternoons in those latitudes, and it was always tempting to stop off at the campus pub for a few drinks before heading home to an evening of reading and studying. Better not. I was taking two English classes on top of Philosophy and Art History, and there was a lot of reading to do (not that I minded much, since one course included some fascinating and downright funny novels by Walker Percy and Flannery O'Connor). Work hard, get something out of the deal.

Consider it a successful day for education, however grim the weather, another step on the road to the School of Athens. In about two hours, I'd gotten a fix on the major philosophers, could now put them in a picture, knew that Plato pointed upward to the sphere of the heavens where the forms achieved perfection, knew that Aristotle pointed to the ground of observation and analysis. And just as the mastery of perspective enabled Raphael's figures to all but step off the wall where they were painted, in time education would allow me to step into the picture, take my place in the educated conversation. There's your essay-exam starter sentence.

• • •

Pretty Good Deal

September, 2013. Here in Athens the athletes—football players, at least—live in a world that struck me as both elite and glossed over with the kind of false patina of class that characterizes big-dollar scams like Scientology (maybe that's just my own dear personal psychosis, but a vibe is a vibe). What a tour I'd had that morning—the Butts-Mehre Heritage Hall and Football Facility. No one would ever call that place a *gym*, no cinder-blocks, no I beams or exposed trusses. It was all burnished metal and lightly-greened laminated glass, as if maybe it was bullet-proof, and where there weren't windows the walls were covered with gigantic photo-murals of Georgia Bulldogs in action and endless repetitions of the red-black-and-white oval G emblem. The head coach occupies a corner office half-way up into the sky, whence like the unseen giant with a hundred eyes in the Panopticon he can see *everything*. Weight room, trainers' facilities, the small indoor practice field, the two full-scale outdoor football fields … Coach Mark Richt's gaze penetrates every space to see them all. And here in this realm of endless wealth they talk as if they are deprived wards of the state because they don't have a full IPF—indoor practice facility. Prince Nick Saban in the city-state of Alabama has a full IPF.

The locker room was carpeted and it was hard to imagine those timeless athletic smells of sweat and dirty cotton socks and Ben-Gay rub and bleach here. There were no scummy tiles in sight, and I'm certain the shower heads never dripped. The "student athletes" were probably issued individual bottles of "body wash," and there was undoubtedly an endorsement deal involved in supplying the goods. In big-time college football, there was undoubtedly money to be made in keeping clean. Jut to look at one source of income for the Bulldogs, the Southeast Conference (SEC, fitting enough initials for such a big-money operation) disburses about $20 million per year to member schools like Georgia, their share of the revenue generated by television contracts for SEC sports, and that number is likely to go up sharply as the conference launches its own TV network. That's a lot of body wash.

They gave me a tour, just like I asked for—what did Martin Sheen's character say in *Apocalypse Now?* They brought it up to me like room service, tremendous southern hospitality. A tour of the jock facilities and then a tour of the academic facilities for the jocks. Unbelievable. The former owner of the NFL Atlanta Falcons, Rankin Smith, made a gift to the university that translated into a $6.7 million Student-Athlete Academic Center (I was half-expecting the faux-English touch of a "Centre") so generous and comprehensive that I had to wonder (I'm not alone in this), "with all this support, how do *any* of these scholarship athletes *not* graduate?" But that's really a variation on the real question: what is football doing on campus?

Why is "college ball" considered the routine stop for the elite player between high school—which he attends because the law says he has to—and the pros, where only one in 50 scholarship college football players make it (Easterbrook, p. 132)? There's your answer. College ball does the dirty work of sorting out the prospects, and I think an economist would say the NFL "externalizes" the cost of that sorting onto whomever it is that pays for college football. It would take a *forensic* economist to sort out who all that includes, but it's not just the ticket-buying fans—many schools, though not Georgia, subsidize their athletics departments, and some, including the University of Houston, rely heavily on subsidies. On the intake side of this sorting process, "college programs" like Georgia are all about recruiting, keeping talent on the field and in the pipeline. My tour of the academic center was one of maybe a dozen that day, but the rest were all student athletes and their families being recruited, being sold on how the Smith

Center would help them stay eligible to play. On the output side, they sort out the prospects for the NFL, and they *produce*. The Georgia Bulldogs are in the top 5 of all American college football programs in putting players into the NFL.

It's all about the deal. Georgia alum Matthew Stafford makes over $13 million per year as an NFL quarterback, and Coach Mark Richt earns "only" about $3.3 million as a college football coach (that ranks him 13th in the country in his profession at the time of this writing). Socrates, that gadfly of the Athenian city-state, would be certain to ask an irritating question like, "what was NFL owner Rankin Smith investing in with his Student-Athlete Academic Center? Pipeline, keeping the players eligible so the school could do its work and sort out the players for the NFL?" Socrates, rewarded with a cup full of hemlock. I'm here to inquire, too, and I'm wondering how it became the job of higher education to sort out football players for a $9 billion-a-year business. At the time of my visit to Athens, I had been at the University of Houston for more than sixteen years, and I'd seen the whole "business model" of the university drift from an economic structure that supported research and instruction to something more like a for-profit business that included education somewhere in the middle of its priorities. There's probably a cup of hemlock in my future, too.

After lunch at the Georgia Center, whose hotel was already fully booked for this game-day weekend when I started making my plans for this trip six months earlier, I continued my drift north along Lumpkin Street and into more familiar terrain. Located next to the Fine Arts building, the home base for Military Science seemed a lot less sumptuous and therefore a whole lot less deceptive than the Football Facility, just a two-story structure called somewhat obviously the Military Building. It was a modest brick building refitted with some discomfort to its present purposes, classrooms and common areas and offices "re-purposed" from whatever the layout was before with the violence and random geometry of hasty carpentry and tons of paint, and that was suitable. Here they prepared college students to become military officers, a career that's all about adaptability on the fly, a career that frequently entails living in substandard or ill-suited quarters, not in the crystal palace of football that I'd toured before lunch (Tim Loonam and I lived in Quonset huts in Korea back in the day). The Professor of Military Science doesn't have a Panopticon office suite like Mark Richt, just a painted-brick room with a desk and some flags and military mementos. Regular doors, regular windows.

This was where Jack Loonam's deal was being transacted. He was, like his dad (and me, for that matter), going to school on an Army scholarship. Football was just something he really wanted to do, and he knew he was lucky that he even had a chance to make it onto the team. His locker was located in a side-wing with the other walk-ons, but at least he was dressing for this weekend's game against South Carolina—part of his football deal was that sometimes he traveled with the team and sometimes he didn't, sometimes dressed for games and sometimes didn't. We all make our deals, and Jack's seemed like a pretty good one at the time. After all, he got to use that weight room in the "facility," got to use that academic center for student-athletes, got the bag-of-bling when the team went to a bowl game. Of course, I'm sure that when Tim Loonam was going to veterinary school on the Army scholarship and living it up like the second coming of Joe College, going to football games and taking care of Uga, the Georgia mascot, he thought it was a pretty good deal. There had just been that little bump in the road called Iraq.

We all make our deals. Mine included an ROTC scholarship, but not right away. My road to Athens had so many zigs and zags and backtracks and false steps that if you drew it on the map it would probably spell CHAOS.

• • •

Declination Diagram
September, 1982. Binghamton, NY. My senior year of college got off to a great start when I returned from ROTC Advanced Camp at Fort Bragg, NC and plunged into an Honors seminar devoted to the epic. I

had performed well enough in the classes I took for my English major that I was invited into the Honors program, substituting two seminars for English electives and writing an Honors Thesis. I was up to the challenge and took the first seminar in Spring 1982, where I found myself seated at the table with a select group of high-achievers. For the second seminar, in Fall 1982, we started with the *Odyssey*, the story of that wily captain and all those strange adventures on his long voyage home from the protracted Trojan war, then followed up with the *Iliad* and the *Aeneid*, a couple more bloody tales of antique heroes. The destination, though, was puzzling: Milton's *Paradise Lost,* the tale of how Adam and Eve blew it for the rest of us, a more intimate scenario, rated R for nudity and not for violence. How were we going to get there from here?

We needed a mentor, and we had one of the best, Mario DiCesare, one of Binghamton's faculty stars. He had his Ph. D. from Columbia and was widely published on the epic and the religious poets, especially George Herbert. DiCesare would stride like a Colossus from the polytheistic There of Homer and Virgil to the Christian Here of Milton and we would be good little students and follow with our scholarly baby steps. He was famous on-campus for team-teaching a high-profile introductory course with John Gardner, in one of those iconic set-pieces of contrasting big-ego academic identities—DiCesare the bearded classical scholar, erudite and maybe a little out-of-it; Gardner the long-haired pipe-puffing creative genius enamored of pagan mythology, unkempt and wild, Tolkien without the restraint of Catholicism. Gardner was also important to the creative-writing world as the author of *The Art of Fiction*, in which he described fiction as an extended dream. Gardner died in a motorcycle accident in September of 1982, the beginning of my senior year.

These were going to be action-packed semesters to end my career at Harpur, as we called it, for Harpur College of Arts and Sciences. (Originally, what became the state university at Binghamton was just Harpur College, but had since grown to include all the other major colleges of a research university: engineering, business, education.) I had to take five courses in fall and six in spring to complete my double-major in English and Philosophy with Honors in English. A pretty tall order, and I had to do those all on Monday, Wednesday, and Friday, because during my junior and senior years, Thursday was ROTC day at Cornell University and I started and finished my day on the bus to and from Ithaca (the one in New York).

Odysseus on the bus was a strange combination of ambition and detachment, the epic and the quotidian. To say the least, it was grandiose to think that I, who hadn't played any team sports in high school and started college at a scrawny 6 feet and 140 pounds, neither fit nor fleet, a smoker of Marlboros and a drinker of what-have-you-got, would earn an Army commission and become an officer, a battle captain, a leader of men. That would be some odyssey. But things had been changing, and I'd taken on another life beyond the borders of SUNY Binghamton, another fantasy but maybe less of an illusion.

My military adventure started with the most unlikely of mentors. Back a few illusions, when I was horsing around with plans to start college as an engineering major at SUNY Buffalo, and then calling off the plans in my panic upon encountering the wider world I would have to navigate in college, my friend John was getting ready to go into the Army as an enlisted man in a communications specialty. John the epic war-hero! Nah. His hair wasn't quite as long as mine, but it was a whole lot fuller (if we were in the Eagles, he would have been Don Felder to my Tim Schmidt), and he was even scrawnier than me. What kind of warrior was he going to make?

The answer was "not much of a warrior," no "thing of blood" like Shakespeare's Coriolanus, and thank God for that. John was a sweet-spirited guy, definitely a lover and not a fighter, with the notches in his belt to prove it (it wasn't just the conquest of a high-school English teacher or women from out of town, it was the easy way he had with women, sincere, a little shy, but very seductive in his own way—a complete mystery to me how you do that). I guess we probably exchanged a few letters during his tour overseas, but what I really recall is that by the time I got myself aligned to college in Binghamton, in my second year, John had completed his three-year active duty contract and was a civilian again and in school himself at a community college.

Like his father, John was a fairly serious amateur photographer, and when I visited him one time in the funky little half-trailer he was renting, he showed me slides of his Army days, a lot of nice full-color shots of him visiting picturesque spots, mountains and forests and waterfalls in Germany, Belgium, France. I'd never been any place like that. Lots of the slides were group shots, young Americans partying it up on good German and Belgian beer, French wine. I liked to party. I liked good beer, I could learn to like wine. The thing was, John was smiling in all those pictures, that same slightly cockeyed grin that's in most of his yearbook pictures, not some baby-killing fire-breathing blood-soaked man-of-war. John was smiling when he was showing the slides and telling his funny little Army stories. He was still John the good guy everybody liked. The Army hadn't made a monster out of him, which was something I had worried about a little. Maybe all that stuff about making a man out of you was overblown, another one of those widely-held illusions. Maybe the Army was just something you did for a while and then got on with your life. I'd been wrong that way about football, thinking it was something well beyond me when it was, really, as we say today "just a thing." Maybe I'd better not miss out on this thing.

Something started to click, *tick tick tick* like the starter on John's old Dodge Dart trying to kick over on a cold morning. Why not see the world after college, get in on all that partying and travel and fellowship? The rest of the boring routine would still be here after a few years in the Army. Hmmm. It wasn't like we were at war—after that ten-year disaster in Vietnam I couldn't see America making that same kind of mistake again. I started to seriously consider this thing, and then went to work on improving the concept. I couldn't see going in like John as an enlisted man. Under his various disguises, Odysseus can be a very ambitious fellow. College guys don't enlist, they go in as officers (Odysseus is

Farewell to Football?

usually referred to as a captain), with more pay and more status. That would be cool, to give the orders! Play quarterback, calling the signals, the guy in charge!

Tick tick tick, maybe the old Dodge slant-six is going to fire up. More serious consideration. How do you get commissioned as an officer? One way is college ROTC. Turns out Binghamton didn't have an ROTC detachment, an after-effect of the school's left-leaning politics and the Vietnam War. Where's the nearest school with ROTC? Cornell University, in Ithaca. Now you're talking! Odysseus's destination was always Ithaca. High upon a hilltop! The Ivy League!

That engine finally turned over with a sudden rush. The summer after my second year of college started off pretty lazily. I took a summer class to get a loan for living expenses. I planned a long weekend in Ithaca to celebrate the Fourth of July, with a visit to the ROTC detachment on Friday, just checking things out. My lazy summer shifted into high gear that day, though, because I found out that if I wanted to get a commission I would have to do what they called Basic Camp this summer, and that if I wanted to do Basic Camp this summer I would have to get ready to go in about a week. Last-train-leaving kind of a deal. Adrenaline, excitement, maybe a little anxiety. Camp was six weeks long, and the last cycle would be starting in mid-July so that it would be finished in time to get cadets back on campus for fall semester. Somehow the summer telescoped and we were already planning for the fall. The tempo and horizon for planning was rapidly changing for me.

"Cadets." I was contemplating becoming an ROTC Cadet. It sounded goofy, not a real rank. Space Cadet.

Well, why on earth not? In the few moments I had to idle before a decision was required, I mulled it over. The way ROTC worked, you didn't have to sign your contract until after Basic Camp, so in effect I could check it out, see if it was right for me, and then make a decision. *They* were recruiting *me*, free choice was part of the deal, officers were always recruited, never drafted. And we would compete for scholarships at camp, too, which would definitely help sort things out for that contract decision—get paid to go to college, with a guaranteed job upon graduation? Who got that kind of a deal? NFL prospects? What the heck? Why not go to Fort Knox, Kentucky, for six weeks and check out the Army?

They called it Basic Camp because while it was held at a unit that did regular Army basic training (the unit, in fact, where they had filmed the movie *Stripes* the year before), it was mainly a provisional summer operation run by ROTC, with a lot of the trappings of a college campus temporarily attached to an Army post. So there were drill sergeants, but it wasn't the full-Monty cliché of NCO's in Smokey-the-Bear hats hollering profanity at you night and day. That's not discipline, anyway, just abuse—discipline is something you develop inside, maybe in response to external challenges, but it's not something that can be hurled at you, not with any expectation that it will stick. So at Basic Camp you got a little dose of that comedy, a dosage the Army calls "familiarization," along with some of the basic military instruction that all recruits get, from drill and ceremonies to communication to land navigation and basic rifle marksmanship.

The Army trains its soldiers assuming that underneath whatever specialties they may take on, all soldiers are first of all *infantry* soldiers, foot-soldiers and ground-pounders, capable of the fundamentals of the infantry: shoot, move, communicate. The mission of "basic" is initiatory, to turn civilians into the raw materials of soldiers.

I loved a lot of it, including the prevailing ironic sense of humor, knowing and sarcastic enough to appeal to one of my family traits. I loved doing things you couldn't do anywhere else, like the grenade assault course, the most grim and serious of our combat training, acting out a fantasy of maneuvering close enough to your enemy to kill him with a hand-grenade. I found transcendent synthesis in land navigation and map reading, the best of our bifurcated fallen world, the abstract-mathematical and the concrete-practical, like solving calculus problems and then finding your way through the world based on your figures. I was fascinated to discover that magnetic North and map North weren't the same in all parts of the world, and that maps have a little decoder section called the "declination diagram," where you were given a number of degrees to offset your compass in order to line up with the map. That just seemed like exactly the sort of *esoterica* a man needs to get through this cock-eyed world.

This was a kind of a camp, too, rustic and outdoorsy, though more like football training camp than Boy Scouts summer camp (honestly, I was a little disappointed it wasn't more monastic). You were trying out under stressful conditions. The program included assessment of the cadets' leadership potential—not everyone who completed the camp would be offered a contract, and fewer still scholarships. Of course, not everyone would complete camp, as some weren't in shape to pass the physical-fitness test (I barely could eke out enough push-ups, but was good-to-go on the run and the sit-ups) and some ended up with injuries or previously existing physical problems that disqualified them. Some might flunk out on basic training soldiering tasks, like assembling and disassembling radios and weapons, although that was pretty rare. Even if they could hold up under the modest physical stress of a watered-down basic training (in the summer, in Kentucky, it did tend to get miserable as the day wore on), not everyone could handle the mental demands of leadership, which in this setting just meant getting a group of your peers organized to accomplish simple tasks when they were hot and tired and frustrated. You might have to line up your platoon for first formation in the morning, or march them over to the athletic field for Physical Training (PT), or get them in line for chow. Basic stuff. ROTC units back at your schools were going to have another two years to get you up to speed on the more demanding elements of leadership (plans, schedules, orders), and then you would go through a branch Officer Basic Course, too, before you were ever really in charge of troops, so in camp you just needed to meet the minimum requirements. "Close enough for government work" was one of those funny-sarcastic phrases I learned that summer.

I survived and succeeded, if not always with distinction, struggling to march and bridling a bit under the pressure of Army "discipline," still a rock-and-roller at heart even though my long hair was long gone. I can't say I enjoyed being called "Frankenstein" by a drill sergeant for my inability to synch up "left" and "right" to a regular cadence, though sometimes I found it pretty funny, too, having been a gangling goon all my life and rarely in the groove with my mediocre rock bands. As always, though, I did well on the tests, and I got offered a scholarship, a decent deal. Two years of ROTC, full tuition, books, and a monthly stipend, and in exchange I would commit to four years of active duty as an officer. It wasn't the NFL, but it was a long way from New Berlin, New York, just the same.

What the deal really meant to me was Odysseus on the bus, an Army of one every Thursday for two years on the bus to Ithaca, a backward odyssey that instead of leading home led to even greater adventures.

On the bus, those Thursdays of junior and senior year were epic in themselves, more than one bus, actually, starting with pre-dawn rising in a one-room student apartment and a city-bus trip to the BC Transit hub in downtown Binghamton. Walk a few blocks to the Greyhound station, toting travel-bag loaded with books and Army uniform and boots, then that hour-plus ride to Ithaca, up and down the sides of glacier-cut valleys in central New York, sometimes blazing glorious in autumnal colors, sometimes grim and flat in the scant light of midwinter. Off the bus at a Y-junction on the hill near Cornell, not an actual stop, just a favor from the driver to the Army of One (cut about a mile off the walk from the bus terminal). Walk to Barton Hall, the big stone armory with its indoor track and drill hall, offices upstairs in what looked like castle towers, vintage 1914 architecture that always put me in mind of Marshall and Eisenhower and Bradley early in their careers. Get into uniform in that World War I men's room, train the training on the training schedule for ROTC (sarcasm from *Stripes*, the Bill Murray comedy popular back then, "*Army training*, sir"), go back through the bathroom costume change, from WWI dough-boy back to scrawny civilian. In those days we wore the "pickle suit" uniform, olive drab shirt tucked into olive drab trousers with bloused boots and olive drab baseball cap, fake soldier with fake cadet rank (they call cadet insignia "pips," of all things), fake all the way. Glad to get out of that for the day. Walk down the hill to the bus station (two-mile hike), ride back to Binghamton, try to get my ROTC homework done on the way home, eat dinner at McDonald's, and then catch the bus back home—and the thing is, no one knew what I was doing, no one from home understood all the moves it took to get all of this done, none of the ROTC cadets were undertaking anything like this odyssey—it was my solitary adventure, something I'd dreamed up and was trying to make work, something kind of dramatically over-complicated.

I was an outsider everywhere, and looking back I have to think that was my free choice of the will, where I wanted to be or thought I should be, though I don't know that I understood then why—I don't know that I understand now why, not entirely. There might have been some element of self-punishment in putting myself on the edge and in isolation, setting myself an almost impossible task which, while a great invigorating challenge, also created opportunities for ill-founded resentment as well as—in failure, should it come—self-pity. In some sense, I think that my incongruous self-image was as a con, a three-time loser, a prisoner of something I wasn't fully aware of, something half-forgotten in my past, something that had been stirred up by my encounter with Todd, but not articulated, and then rendered taboo by his death. Sin, unconfessed, unforgiven because unacknowledged, hiding in shadows and looming in aspect like that cartoon villain Mr. Big.

Out of place everywhere. The ROTC thing made me seem right-wing on the ultraliberal Binghamton campus, and caused some tension with the pro-Sandinista lead singer in the last rock-and-roll band I ever played in. At Cornell I was an Army of one from Binghamton; there were other schools in Ithaca and Cortland with formal Military Science relationships connecting them to Cornell, but I was an undrafted free agent, making this up as I went along, no institutional support. Everywhere I was the man without a car. Fatherless, unchurched, no wheels … Odysseus on the bus.

Steven Liparulo

Back in the classroom in Binghamton, September gave way to November and Homer gave way to Milton, and here I was in strangely familiar territory. *Paradise Lost.* Free will and concupiscence. We each had to write a seminar paper, narrowly focused and tied tightly to the text, New Critical style, and I chose to fall back on the philosophical concepts I'd learned almost accidentally from Larry Roberts to address what we might call our Human Family Primal Scene, the shame and secret and origin myth of our fallen world. Adam and Eve in the Garden of Eden, "the Fruit Of that Forbidden Tree, whose mortal taste Brought Death into the World, and all our woe, with loss of Eden." We've all been there, especially Americans, who live in a country dedicated to making up elaborate myths to explain all the exceptions we claim to our otherwise admirable values (we are a peace-loving law-abiding society of free people, except when we aren't).

John Milton was a clever poet who worked the way screenwriters do today when adapting "source material," inserting backstory to develop character. Here Milton "adapted" Genesis, and whereas there the snake was simply "the most cunning of all the wild animals that the Lord God had made" (3:1), the English poet depicted Satan himself, a fallen angel burning with resentment at Adam and Eve and their "pleasure not for him ordained" (IX.467), entering into the body of the serpent. Thus Eve was tempted not just by a snake but by the father of lies. In screenwriter terms, that's called "punching up the drama" of the scene.

For my honors seminar paper I wrote what I later learned is called a "rhetorical analysis" of Eve's temptation and fall. How did Satan create a persuasive appeal to overcome the prohibition God had imposed on the first couple not to taste the fruit of the Tree of Knowledge of Good and Evil? I thought that was a good question to explore. Of course, I used the techniques of literary analysis to confront essentially religious questions—why did man fall from grace? Why are we stuck in bodies of sin and death? I was seeking to answer a spiritual query with analysis of metaphors and repetition and amplification/diminution. I might learn

Farewell to Football?

more about the mind and practice of the poet than the state of the collective human soul.

But still, the story—the Christian epic, *Paradise Lost*, in part an act of linguistic and patriotic pride on Milton's part, a demonstration that English can be the language of epic just as much as Greek and Latin—sets out to show that we are truly free, free to choose good or evil. Not free if not free to fail. God truly loves us and has truly given us the gift of free will. Adam and Eve really do have the freedom to choose. But the bad news is that the very first people chose the lesser over the greater, and we inherit that Original Sin, that *concupiscence* down to this very day. And more bad news that's also good news: God loves us too much to let our transgressions go unpunished, and so we live, east of Eden, outside the garden, in a corrupt and fallen world, "territory held largely by the Devil," as Southern Gothic/Catholic writer Flannery O'Connor calls it. But the good news is that we are still free to choose, just as Eve could have chosen to listen to God but chose instead to listen to the serpent, and just as Adam chose instead to listen to Eve, we have all we need to choose the greater good, even the greatest good, but it requires free choice of the will—it still does, it always does, evermore. This choosing goes on in an eternal present, or what we might call *simultaneous* time (the same startling sense of simultaneity that we experience when Christ claims that "before Abraham came to be, I AM" in John 8:58). There's nothing antique about the allegory, however out-of-date the diction may seem. (I believe this now, profess this faith out loud every week in the presence of others, but in 1982 I'm not sure I even understood it, and if I did, might only have hoped it were true, and certainly would not have said so out loud.)

Here was and is our Original Sin, our Paradise Lost—MY paradise lost—thinking we want what we don't understand, or wanting what we think we understand, disordered in our thinking, wanting regardless of consequences. I was once more a few degrees off, observant but adrift in the world, vaguely alienated—the declination diagram, as I had learned in the Army, called for a little compensation from compass reading to map reading—reading John Milton's poetry instead of scripture, and approaching the question with the techniques of the literary scholar instead of the spiritual director. Still, I was rooting for Adam and Eve and hadn't fallen in with the party of the serpent.

I hadn't followed Jimmy Page down that "left-hand path" with Aleister Crowley and all that esoteric lot, who essentially adopt Satan's envy and seek to "be like gods, who know good and evil" (Genesis 3:4). Led Zeppelin was in the rear-view mirror, and in a lot of ways, rock and roll would never mean as much to me as it did in the mid-70's when I was in high school. Football, too, was at least temporarily in repose; Binghamton had neither ROTC nor college football, and I had boycotted television in my apartments starting sophomore year. By the time I was studying *Paradise Lost* and on my way to graduating with Honors, Zeppelin had been broken up for years, the end coming with the tragic, scandalous, senseless "death by misadventure" of the genius drummer, John Bonham. Whether or not any karmic debt was being paid off for Page's dalliances with the occult, as some believe, the fact is that Page and Bonham gave in to indulgence far too deeply and frequently, and the consequences were inevitable (Bonham died after drinking 40 shots of vodka in one day). I would face temptation, too, just on a very different path, chasing different illusions.

• • •

May, 1983. My last trip to Ithaca wasn't on the bus. My youngest sister masterminded the operation and was at the wheel the whole weekend, which began with my Phi Beta Kappa induction and Honors recognition ceremony in Binghamton, followed a day later by commissioning at Barton Hall in Ithaca. The symbolism was entirely appropriate as my mother pinned on my lieutenant's bars. I might gripe that I grew up without a father, and it's true, but I did grow up with a mother who did the best she could, and I didn't get where I was, whatever modicum of achievement I could claim, on my own. My sisters, all three, supported me, quite literally, fed me, housed me, drove me places I needed to go as I wandered through the first few years after high school. So it was entirely fitting and proper that my mother pinned on my bars and my sister masterminded the trip. We would repeat this ritual almost a year later, when I graduated from Ranger School at Fort Benning, Georgia, only then my father would attempt to join the celebration, a bit like Banquo's ghost, not quite legitimately and fully present. Still, he had gotten there, or as Horatio says, "a piece of him." That's really all I would ever get from him. In some ways every man's mission in life is just getting there.

My mother pinned on my lieutenant's bars at ROTC commissioning, Cornell University, May 1983.

On the other hand, I had seen it the other way, father-forward: one of my classmates at Cornell was the son of a Major General, which seemed like a heavily Faulknerian burden for a young lieutenant to try to get out from under at the start of his military career. The commissioning ceremony had to include special arrangements to handle the presence of a general officer according to military protocol. By way of contrast, who my dad was, or wasn't, would have no impact on my military career. That's one ghost that wouldn't be bothering me.

I would be free to rise and fall on my own choices of the will.

• • •

CHAPTER 4

"Five in a Row Dome Show" (1968/1982/2013)

"Now in these dread latter days of the old violent be-
loved U.S.A. and of the Christ-forgetting Christ-haunted
death-dealing Western world I came to myself in a grove
of young pines and the question came to me: has it happened at last?"

(WALKER PERCY, *LOVE IN THE RUINS*, P. 3)

• • •

FEBRUARY 3, 2013. Houston, Texas. Super Bowl Sunday. Before I watch
the tattooed bodies of Ray Lewis and Colin Kaepernick proclaim in
inked skin and kneeling prayer and howling attestation their devotion
to their Lord Jesus prior to battling for brutal supremacy of the NFL,
I receive the body and blood of Christ at St. Thomas More Catholic
Church in Houston.

Going in for 7:30 Mass, I greet the lay ministers lined up in the nar-
thex with their backs to the floor-to-ceiling windows that look over the
nave, a shallow bowl that seats around 950. In particular, I have to check
in with one of the Mass Coordinators, Milton Morgan. Milton bosses
the lectors, as well as the ushers and other ministers, and I am his "go-
to" substitute lector. If the person assigned to read for Mass doesn't
show up, my man Milton puts me into the line-up. Sometimes he sidles
up to me after Mass has begun and whispers in my ear that I'll have to
take either the first reading, which is generally from the Old Testament,

or the second, which is always an Epistle. Ordained ministers, deacons or priests, read the Gospel.

After we shake hands and offer greetings, he smiles broadly and lets me know that he's good to go. He will be reading the Old Testament passage, a robust game-day pep-talk from the Book of the Prophet Jeremiah, and the other lector is already here, too. I'm clear to go into the church and take my place in my customary pew a few rows from the front on the side of the church closest to the ambo, which is on the left side of the altar. I kneel and say a few prayers, joyfully aware of the sun coming in through the stained glass windows above and to my right of the altar.

The church is laid out as a canted rectangle. Actually, from above it is designed to resemble a dove with its beak ahead of the altar, its wings spread out to embrace the congregation. Stained glass windows run the length of the upper half of all four walls below the perimeter of the soaring arched ceiling, depicting the life of our patron saint, Thomas More. He is generally known in current usage as "A Man for All Seasons," the title given him in Robert Bolt's biographical play, so here in the stained glass More's life is divided into color-coded sections by the four seasons. On the north side, to the left of the altar, More's family life is depicted in the golden hues of summer and the symbolic elements of wedding rings and the wheat and grapes whose fruits eventuate in the elements of the Eucharist. To the right of the altar, mature autumnal colors of red and gold help depict More's public life, while in the back are the renderings of spring and winter, with its deep cold-blue depiction of More's imprisonment in the Tower of London and execution by beheading via double-headed axe.

The sun glows mellow and bright today, a mild gorgeous Texas winter morning whose bleached-cobalt skies somehow remind me of the same season I spent decades ago in Special Forces School at Fort Bragg, North Carolina, as if the sun connects the far-flung episodes of our fleeting lives and renders them occasionally accessible. Perhaps it is the Holy Spirit, mobile across the ages. Depicted in the stained glass illuminated by that winter sun, literary Sir Thomas More stands out as a welcome minister of words from my academic past, the author of *Utopia* and one of the main subjects of Stephen Greenblatt's landmark work of literary criticism, *Renaissance Self-Fashioning*, wherein More is depicted as the ultimate good host and family man as well as a crafty writer and enthusiastic religious polemicist. The literary ironies of my church run even deeper for me, inasmuch as one of my all-time favorite novels, *Love in the Ruins*, by Louisiana writer Walker Percy, depicts the "adventures of a bad Catholic at a time near the end of the world." That bad Catholic is Dr. Thomas More, who invents a "*lapsometer*" enabling him as a psychiatrist to diagnose and treat ruptures and disorders of the soul, a handy tool in dread latter days whenever they come. In a moment of fraught confrontation with a Satanic figure disguised as a federal bureaucrat in a "bi-swing jacket," Percy's Dr. More invokes the name of his kinsman, St. Thomas, and the day is won for the good guys.

I had been introduced to Percy in an undergraduate class that also featured fiction by Flannery O'Connor, both writers identified more as "Southern" than as "Catholic." Over the years I had re-read *Love In the Ruins* time and again, not as a *lapsometer* (a notional instrument that measures the divisions in man's soul due to the lapse or fall from grace in original sin) so much as a lap-meter, marking the cycles of my spiritual quest, searching, finding, searching again, round and round the seven storey mountain. At first the book seemed very funny, though cluttered with a lot of confusing religious stuff. Later I realized that the religious stuff was the main story and that the book was pretty elegant and spare, if occasionally over-ripe in the "adventures" department (Dr. More drinks like James Bond but never really gets the girls). So for me, this church commemorates three Thomas Mores: Doctor, Sir, and Saint. More and More and More.

Our pastor presides over the Mass. He is a small, compact, middle-aged priest whose rather dour and sarcastic character is exacerbated by some recent physical ailments. He is assisted by Deacon Ed Stoessel, a retired BP executive with a Ph. D. in theoretical physics. Deacon Ed has been instrumental in my Catholic formation and I always feel an extra sense of belonging in the church when he's present. Among other things, his example assures me that there is room for intellectual complexity in the faith.

As the Mass proceeds into the Liturgy of the Word, Milton Morgan reads the passage from Jeremiah, his gentle East-Texas cadences in marked contrast to the bold prophetic message: "They will fight against you but not prevail over you" (1:19). Milton always takes his time with the Word of the Lord, leading me to think that maybe he knows some of the inside story. The second lector is a very large fellow who reads from First Corinthians with angular and incisive inflections, the edges Paul put on some of the key words intact in his delivery. I am struck by one much-quoted passage. "When the perfect comes, the partial will pass away. When I was a child, I used to talk as a child, think as a child, reason as a child; when I became a man, I put aside childish things" (13:10-11).

In America, in these dread latter days, I muse, much in the company of Dr. Thomas More and his diagnostic *lapsometer*, childhood can be extended almost indefinitely, such that one "progresses" only from infancy to childhood, and then unto death, round and round the mountain but never ascending above the first storey. We are tempted to devote our lives to children's games. In a land dedicated to freedom of choice, the paths to becoming a man are all optional: one can choose an education or not, one can choose military service or not, one can choose initiation into a church or not, and so on. I've chosen all three of those, some to the highest degree of initiation, but like many American men I might say that my ascension into manhood is incomplete. Have I put aside any childish things? Is it time to say farewell to football, the ultimate American childish thing?

In today's Super Bowl, any number of players will claim Christian faith. Ray Lewis has been spouting some war-like words from the Old Testament ("no weapon that is formed against thee shall prosper" Isaiah 15:47), while Colin Kaepernick's arms are tattooed with verses from

Farewell to Football?

Psalm 18 ("You armed me with my strength for battle; you humbled my adversaries before me" 39). Does that sanctify the game? Or is Super Bowl NFL football just another instance of a national tendency to glorify violence through symbolic displacements, to wrap up displays of our disordered passions in the flag or tattoo them with the cross? A good tip-off would be to count the tie-ins between the NFL and the military leading up to and during today's game. (On this Super Bowl Sunday in 2013, oddly enough, Chris Kyle, author of a memoir of a Navy SEAL sniper claiming over a hundred confirmed kills, was found shot to death at a Texas firing range. Dread latter days.)

Deacon Ed reads the Gospel, and the pastor offers the homily, a sales pitch for the Diocesan Service Fund instead of preaching. The pastor opens with a somewhat despairing "homage" to February (good thing it's short) and closes, as he did last year, by mistaking the sense of Shakespeare's "now is the winter of our discontent." I personally dislike these business homilies but recognize that the church has to do some of its work in the fallen world. (The pastor mentions the Super Bowl in passing, making a dismissive comment to the effect of "why should the Patriots even show up, it's apparently a done deal," possibly mistaking Patriots for Ravens—or is this last year's homily? Our priest is not well.)

The Eucharist is the source and summit of all Christian life, and as the action of the Mass proceeds, I marvel at the large team of men and women, diverse in age and race and profession, who work together each Sunday. The priest and deacon sit on the left side and behind the altar, as seen from my pew, while the altar servers sit on the right. It always strikes me that they are like a family seated in their car, two in front, two in back. Volunteers bring forward the gifts, and the priest makes the body and blood of Christ sacramentally present, transcending time and place—the real presence—under the species of bread and wine. A Mass Coordinator leads a group of a half-dozen or more Extraordinary Ministers up to the altar to receive communion, and then they all are given body and blood to distribute to the congregation, a Houston-diverse mix of Anglo- and African-Americans, Hispanics, Vietnamese, South Asians, Africans, and whoever else has chosen to answer the call.

I process down my row, down to the front of the church where I receive the body and blood, and then back to my pew where I kneel. I try to look as many of the congregants in the eye as I can as they wheel through the Communion Rite. This sacrament joins us all together in the Mystical Body of Christ and I want to see who's been joined to me.

At St. Thomas More, under the sheltering wings of the dove, I am joined together in this sacred mystery with men and women, children and adults, black, white, red, brown, and yellow. For a few moments each week, at least, the American dream of a community of equals is achieved under conditions of humility in the presence of the Lord. In doing His will, we leave behind however briefly our race and class and age and gender.

I pray for my continued conversion.

And then we are all standing and the Mass is ended. Go in peace, glorifying the Lord with your lives.

On my way out, I always get my copy of the weekly bulletin from Milton Morgan. If I have read, he is always ready with a compliment. He is an old football coach, and you can tell he understands how praise functions as the daily bread in the life of a team.

Today I compliment him. He really brought that dignity necessary to proclaim the word of the Lord's reassurance to Jeremiah that He will deliver him. It would have made a pretty good pre-game speech, with that line about how He has "made you a fortified city, a pillar of iron, a wall of brass."

• • •

August, 1982. Beaumont, Texas. After church every Sunday throughout the football season over thirty years ago, Milton Morgan would spend the rest of the day at the field house, the new one, the one that still seemed blessed with the new-car smell. Beaumont West Brook, a name the kids had voted on. A name from out of nowhere, like that whole season.

Farewell to Football?

Coach Morgan faced a monumental task in 1982, and not just in breaking down film on the upcoming opponent and putting together his parts of the scouting report and game plan (adjusting his fronts to take away the opponent's strength was always the key to his defensive plan). He'd stepped up the coaching ladder to defensive coordinator, but this was going to be a whole new ball game for him and for all of the coaching staff. The school for which he would be coaching was being forged together from two formerly segregated high schools of the South Park school district in the steamy East Texas port city of Beaumont, and Morgan would be coordinator of a defensive staff made up mostly of white coaches from Forest Park. Morgan had been a defensive assistant at the black school, Hebert High, and had been rushed into position as the defensive coordinator for the new school, Beaumont West Brook, when his former defensive boss took a coaching job in Houston. The head coach for West Brook would be Hebert's head man, Alexander Durley, a dignified, calm, authoritative leader, who advised Morgan that he would probably want to use a little more tact than he was used to. Coach Durley tended to understate things like that.

Durley faced his own challenges. It was one thing for the black coach from Hebert to be named head man for the new, bigger school. Durley could stand by his success—he'd won a state title in 1976, and his Hebert teams had a far better record than those of Forest Park, including a pretty amazing 37-3 in the last three years. Those were great numbers, but as standout fullback and defensive lineman Jerry Ball said at the time, the most important number would be 22, everyone would be counting to 22 to see how many of the starters were black and how many were white—opening night it would be 14 and 8, minority become majority (Winningham, p. 159). In this tense racial situation intensified by the latest judgment in a long-running series of court battles that started in earnest in Beaumont in 1970, the head coach would have to take his shot at balancing fairness and winning.

For some people it came down to simple counting, simple division, just black and white. In his outstanding 1983 treatment of this season in *Texas Monthly*, Geoff Winningham conjures up a dialogue between representatives of the opposing positions. Since the landmark 1954 Supreme Court ruling in *Brown vs. Board of Education*, the question had been how to enact school desegregation—or maybe, as an attorney recently suggested to me, how to avoid it. For Bill Womack, head of a group called Freedom of Choice founded in 1976 in response to that year's ruling in Beaumont, *Brown vs. Board* "was not really a decision that separate is not equal, as most people think. It was a decision that you, all of us, have the freedom to choose" (p. 236). Ed Moore, head of the Citizens Action Committee, saw the exact opposite: "Go read the *Brown* decision. It doesn't say that we all have freedom of choice. That's a bunch of bull. It says segregation deprives minority children, is therefore harmful to all of us, and must be done away with." Count to two, make the call: freedom of choice or desegregation.

That 1982 season in Beaumont was really but a late chapter in a very long saga of counting and dividing. To recount the story about racial identity in America, we can trace a conflict back to the Constitution, which included a "three-fifths compromise" to appease slave-holding states, counting black men as "three-fifths" of citizens for the purposes of apportioning Congressional representatives and levying taxes (not that they had three-fifths of the rights and privileges of a citizen, nothing of the sort). The Civil War was in part fought to resolve the issue of slavery, and the Thirteenth Amendment wrote the bloody resolution into the book of law. The consequent question of racial equality was answered in *Plessy vs. Ferguson* in 1896 with the onerous formula, "separate but equal." *Brown vs. Board* revised that definition, and Texan Lyndon Johnson at the height of his power as president pushed through the Civil Rights Act of 1964 to start putting federal muscle behind that redefinition (against the opposition of segregationists within his own party, including the formidable Senator Richard Brevard Russell of Winder, Georgia).

If it's a question of race relations in American sports, the timeline drives through different checkpoints, but includes at least one stop in Beaumont prior to 1982. Paul Brown in Cleveland, along with the coach of the NFL Los Angeles Rams, actually integrated pro football a year ahead of Jackie Robinson's high profile debut as the first black major-leaguer for Brooklyn in 1947, but baseball's prestige as "America's pastime" overshadowed football at the time, and the Browns were playing in the upstart All American Football Conference in 1946, not the NFL. In fact, not just one but four African-Americans played pro football that year, one of whom, Woody Strode of the Rams, later took up acting and faced Kirk Douglas in the gladiatorial arena in Stanley Kubrick's 1960 *Spartacus.* The ongoing football saga featured NAACP protests of segregated seating in Houston's Jeppesen Stadium for Oilers AFL games in 1960 and 1961 (Carroll, p. 101), and then ironically enough, encompassed the forced migration of the January 1965 AFL All-Star game to that same Jeppesen Stadium in Houston when black AFL players called and won a vote to boycott overtly-racist New Orleans, where the game was originally scheduled to be played.

Jerry LeVias and Milton Morgan, who played
and coached at Beaumont's Hebert High School,
on the occasion of their induction into the
Prairie View Interscholastic League Coaches
Association (PVILCA) Hall of Fame, July 2015.

1965 was a big year for racial advances in Beaumont, as Hebert High School's speedy flanker Jerry LeVias committed to Southern Methodist University in Dallas as the first black scholarship football player in the Southwest Conference (SWC). In his own context of big-time college football in the mid-1960s, LeVias faced a lot of the challenges that Jackie Robinson endured in baseball in the late 1940s, including rabidly racist fans, spitting opponents, and even death threats. Looking back on the 1982 reorganization of the South Park schools that erased Hebert and created West Brook, LeVias told me recently that he was "kind of confused—why would they want to take Hebert away from its long tradition? Why did we have to lose our school, in our neighborhood, that had long had success athletically, academically, socially?"

LeVias's principal at Hebert, James Jackson, saw something similar at the time. "When the 1970 court order came, we were torn apart by wanting to be treated fair but wanting to keep the legacy of Hebert intact" (Winningham, p. 237).

In 1982, Coach Durley was put in the tough position of balancing the legacy of Hebert—the 37-3 tradition of winning ball games—with fairness to kids coming from Forest Park and looking for an opportunity to compete on the field. So were all of his coaches.

Coach Morgan, Durley's new defensive coordinator, hadn't won anything on his own, and this would be his first stint as a coordinator—boss of his side of the ball—and one of his subordinates would be the defensive coordinator from Forest Park, a white coach many years his senior. Durley stood by his choice. Morgan planned on spending a lot of time on his knees Sunday morning to get prepared to stand up to the challenges that started fresh each Sunday afternoon in that field house when the head coach would arrive from his trip to the bus station to pick up the VHS game-tapes ("film") of the week's opponent. They would begin the process of breaking down their opponents' tendencies, the nuts and bolts of scouting and game planning, charting play frequencies by down and distance, identifying which plays the upcoming opponents ran out of which sets, their blocking schemes, pass patterns, fronts and coverages.

That new car smell was rapidly being replaced by football's answer to Chanel No. 5, the scent of hard work and sweat.

Houston Astrodome, November 20, 1982. Beaumont West Brook 7, Baytown Sterling 7. If that 1982 season had a peculiar, polarized cast to it leading up to the playoffs, it went through the looking-glass entirely when the Beaumont West Brook Bruins won a second-round playoff game 7-7. The whole season was summed up in the fourth quarter, when the Bruins turned the game upside down, and it took the teamwork of black and white counting to 22 to get the job done.

With three minutes left to play and up 7-0, the Baytown Sterling Rangers were looking to salt this one away, attempting a field goal that would put the game out of reach for the Bruins at 10-0. Milton Morgan's best player on defense—the best player on the field that day—had other ideas. A year later, Jerry Ball described his technique: "I lined up in the gap, keeping my eye on the holder. When he moved his hands for the snap, I go. I knew I had it. Took it in the stomach" (Winningham, p. 244). Ball's teammate Clem Coleman ran with the blocked field goal for 60 yards, but was tackled and fumbled the ball near the Sterling 20-yard-line. And then to complete the through-the-looking glass absurdity of the play, here came Dan Kroesch to recover it for West Brook. Three plays later, tailback Terrance McCarty, one of those Forest Park kids looking for a chance to play for Coach Durley, took the ball into the end zone to tie the game.

The rules for settling a tie in a Texas high-school football playoff game are almost as arcane as the rulings that forced the desegregation of South Park schools. First tie-breaker: how many times each team had penetrated their opponent's 20-yard line. With 2:13 left in the game after McCarty's touchdown, those stood even at 2-2, telltale evidence of a tight defensive struggle. Second tie-breaker: how many first downs each team had made. Those clearly favored West Brook, 12-8. But the game wasn't over yet, and the Rangers had several paths to victory.

Baytown Sterling rolled the dice on a Hail-Mary pass play that had Coach Morgan cursing on the side-line, as one of his Bruin defensive backs was called for interference. Ball on the West Brook 25. Even if they didn't score, the Rangers were only five yards away from a game-winning penetration. Here was your ball game: the West Brook Bruins needed a stop or the playoff run was over.

In a season marked by polar-opposites, Hebert and Forest Park, black and white, desegregation and freedom of choice, the fearful symmetry of the game brought the play to Jerry Ball's doppelganger, linebacker Layne Walker, the Forest Park kid who played with such an edge that he forced the coaches to move Jerry Ball to the defensive line.

Eight months earlier back in Beaumont, Ball and Walker had approached each other with the wary intensity of a couple of Alpha dogs considering whether to fight it out. There were 180 kids on the field that first day of spring practice, but more likely there were really just two kids repeated many, many times, two kids like Ball and Walker peering at each other across divisions of expectations and perceptions, history and performance, old dividing lines of race and class. Ball said in 1983 that he and his old Hebert teammates were figuring the Forest Park players "to be a bunch of rich kids, you know. We expected to see a whole bunch of limos dropping off white kids" (Winningham, p. 158). From the other side, Forest Park lineman Keith Zoch said that "we'd been hearing for years about all these black studs from Hebert and how good they were and how fast and how mean they were." All that peering across the line, "it was real strange, just being out there with those guys."

In the decisive moment of the playoff game that crystallized that 1982 season, which had begun with so much uncertainty, linebacker Layne Walker shot across the line of scrimmage to stop Sterling's quarterback for no gain on a sneak, sealing the strange West Brook "victory" in the tie game.

Farewell to Football?

The team that boiled down to 47 players at the start of the season, 27 black and 20 white, had to count on every one of those players to win a tie ball-game in the friendly confines of the Houston Astrodome.

• • •

Houston Astrodome, December 31, 1968. SMU 28, Oklahoma 27. The Astrodome looms in sports folklore like some fabulous mythic destination, Shangri-La or Xanadu or the moon, a place about which the story keeps changing depending on the storyteller, many things to many people. Ask an architect about the massive enclosed stadium, completed in 1965, and he might start talking about the world's largest daylight failure, how the glass panels in the roof made it impossible for baseball outfielders to find and track down fly balls. A groundskeeper—or orthopedic surgeon—might lament the advent of Astroturf, the artificial surface developed when the daylight failure of the glass roof led to painting the panels, which led to the failure of grass to grow indoors and the substitution of a "rug" that would put a lot of groundskeepers out of work in stadia both indoors and outdoors over the next decades, and almost certainly supplied a lot of knee work for orthopedic surgeons, too.

Over the years, football players have also given voice to a few observations about the great domed stadium. Alex Karras, the acerbic Pro-Bowl lineman for the NFL Detroit Lions of the 1960s, said that the turf in the Astrodome made a squishing sound when you ran on it and the place was fairly empty (in Plimpton 1973, p. 400). Rocky White played there in the 1980 Astro-Bluebonnet Bowl on a North Carolina team that featured legendary linebacker Lawrence Taylor, and he remembered the seams in the turf and the "sliding pits" in the baseball diamond, where the turf overlaid plywood—it might have been the worst field he ever played on. Ketric Sanford, who played most of his home games there as a running back for the Houston Cougars from 1996 to 1999, describes the atmosphere as a peculiar combination of surreal and dangerous. It felt like it would take you all day just to make a first down in there, especially when the place wasn't full—and it generally wasn't in those lean years for Cougar football (they had a head coach who hosted a radio show as "the Love Coach"). If you were tackled on some of the painted spots on the field, he told me later, you'd come back to the huddle with a lot of skin missing. By the advent of the new Millennium, the Cougars had moved back onto the University of Houston campus full time, the Oilers were long gone to Tennessee, and the Astros moved to a baseball-only stadium downtown. The Astrodome was dark, long before the last payments were made on its construction (Gast, p. 180).

Legend has it that Judge Roy Hofheinz, the self-proclaimed "huckster" who put together the group that built the stadium, came up with the idea for the Astrodome when he was visiting Rome and heard about how the Romans used the *velarium*, a sail-like canvas awning strung up on massive cables, to protect spectators in the Colosseum from sun and rain (Gast, p. 52). The Romans apparently avoided the daylight failure by making the *velarium* retractable—an innovation that would come to NFL stadia only in the 21st century. Of course, the Romans didn't "play their games" on a grass surface, choosing instead a sand floor, which better absorbed the blood of dead and dying gladiators and Christians.

The Astrodome. Eighth Wonder of the World. On New Year's Eve, 1968, packed with well-dressed partiers and the crowd was going wild, especially at the very end of the game, when the Oklahoma Sooners and Southern Methodist Mustangs combined for four touchdowns in the last seven minutes. Not a great night for Oklahoma's running back Steve Owens, though. All season long, Owens had only been tackled for a loss once, but in the Bluebonnet Bowl—re-christened the Astro-Bluebonnet Bowl as it debuted in Houston's Eighth Wonder—he was set back five times. SMU defender Rufus Cormier had his number that night, throwing Owens for a loss twice. Cormier, Jerry LeVias's teammate at Beaumont Hebert High, had followed him to SMU a year after LeVias "broke the ice" for black players. The undersized (6' 220 lb.) nose tackle Cormier was credited with a whopping 16 tackles in the game and recovered a fumble early in the second half. That Astroturf provided a fast track favoring SMU's stunting defensive game plan, and helped Cormier earn defensive player of the game honors.

The Mustangs came back from a 14-6 third-quarter deficit with 22 points in the fourth to beat the Sooners 28-27 in a rollicking game that saw both teams rack up gaudy yardage. Oklahoma gained 470 yards of total offense, while SMU put up 353. A crowd of 53,543, the largest to date for an indoor football game, found the Astrodome an ideal place to count down to the New Year and watch some frenzied football, but SMU quarterback Chuck Hixson sounded a familiar theme right after the game. "I didn't think the turf would be so hard," the leading passer in college football for 1968 told a reporter from the *Houston Post*. "These are the greatest playing conditions anywhere, but that turf is just like cement. My forearms and elbows are just raw."

1968 was some kind of a year for the old violent beloved U.S.A., and December 1968 was a heck of a month for the Space City of Houston. The year started with a bloody set-back for the American war effort in Vietnam, where the rebel Vietcong celebrated Tet—the lunar new year—by launching a coordinated offensive throughout South Vietnam. Blood was spilled at home, too, with the spring assassination of Martin Luther King and the summer shooting of Robert Kennedy. The Democratic convention in Chicago went bad, with the whole world watching—"huckster" Hofheinz had hoped to attract the convention to the Astrodome and was no doubt glad that hadn't worked out for Houston (Maule, p. 41). In November, Richard Nixon (whom gonzo writer Hunter Thompson described as "a god damn stone fanatic on every facet of pro football," in MacCambridge, p. 300) was elected president. The Apollo space program pulled off a great fourth quarter comeback of its own in December when the mission of Apollo 8 was revised to send it hurtling out to the moon, resulting in one of the most spectacular theatrical moments of the entire epic of manned space flight: three heroic astronauts reading from the Book of Genesis on Christmas Eve as the world watched the first television broadcast from lunar orbit, including the revelation of earthrise. In the descriptions of astronauts Frank

Borman, James Lovell, and Bill Anders, our blue planet was the only color they could see as it rose above the forbidding surface of the Moon. This triumph of engineering and daring redounded to Houston's greater glory as the astronauts' radio transmissions frequently began with the salutation, "Houston," short-hand for Mission Control at Houston's Manned Spacecraft Center, later renamed the Johnson Space Center, which had risen from the flat coastal plain of east Texas simultaneously with the Astrodome.

1968 is often portrayed in histories as the passing-over point, the dawning of the Age of Aquarius, and on its final evening dreams and dread hovered over Houston and the old violent beloved U.S.A. and the earth and the moon besides. The tide was turning for the better for America's dreams of a lunar landing when just a week before the New Year's Eve game in the Astrodome those astronauts aboard Apollo 8 helped rehabilitate NASA's public image, which had suffered a horrific setback when three astronauts died in a launch-pad fire early in 1967. Conversely, the impact on the military situation in Vietnam of the January 1968 Tet offensive and the follow-up escalation of American combat operations, which brought the war into American living rooms each night on the TV news, was debatable, but it clearly helped turn the tide of public opinion against the American war, leading to years of turbulent protest as the government slogged on in pursuit of "light at the end of the tunnel." Protest against the war often stood in for the more generalized conflict in the late 60's between the "Establishment" and the "counterculture" of sexual liberation, widespread drug use, and rock and roll.

All the convolutions in this conflicted 1968 America showed up on network TV: the Monday before Thanksgiving, when The Beatles' "White Album" (alleged inspiration for Charles Manson's grisly murders the following summer) was released in the U. S., 52-year-old Frank Sinatra hosted young African-American pop-stars The Fifth Dimension on his NBC special "Francis Albert Sinatra Does His Thing." Together, they sang 21-year-old Laura Nyro's "Sweet Blindness," a lyrically-ornate ode to wine-drinking. The Fifth Dimension also sang their hit version of Nyro's "Stoned Soul Picnic" on the special, and a year later would have another hit with "Age of Aquarius." Wasn't this the essence of 1968, to see and hear Francis Albert, who long ago sang a TV commercial for John F. Kennedy's 1960 presidential campaign against Richard Nixon, crooning Nyro's "please don't tell my mother, I'm a saloon and a moon-shine lover" in living color with a pleasant middle-of-the-road black vocal group? That turbulent summer, Nyro had written and recorded "Save the Country" in response to Robert F. Kennedy's assassination, a song expressing an essential 1968 zeitgeist: "In my mind I can't study war no more."

You could see a tide turning in the racial complexion of college football in that New Year's Eve game in Houston, too. While SMU's LeVias and Cormier were among the first black players in the SWC, Oklahoma's Owens would be the next-to-last white running back to win the Heisman Trophy, when he followed O. J. Simpson in receiving the award in 1969—the last would be John Cappelletti in 1973. In a college game increasingly dominated by black players, Andre Ware of Houston, playing his home games in the Astrodome, would become the first black quarterback to win the Heisman in 1989. And the arc of history bends on over East Texas, however slowly: Rufus Cormier, who followed his undergraduate career at SMU with a law degree at Yale, where he was a classmate of Bill Clinton and Hillary Rodham, and service on the House Judiciary Committee as it prepared for the impeachment of Richard Nixon, was reportedly the first black member of Houston's exclusive River Oaks Country Club—in 1997.

And while New Year's Eve 1968 was a night to remember for Cormier and LeVias and 53,543 fans in the Astrodome, it was a night to forget for me. More precisely, I suppose, a nightmare to repress. I was in fourth grade at the time, my mother married for the third time (my father was her second husband), to a man who drank himself to his death in the early 1970's. I used to love to watch sporting events from the Astrodome on TV because of that scoreboard, what seemed like a million lights displaying pictures and even moving images on a massive "Astrolite" screen. It reminded me of my Lite Brite, a toy with which you could form glowing color images and illuminated words by plugging colored Lucite pegs into a grid with a light behind it. I used to love to set it up neat and orderly like that Astrodome scoreboard, and no doubt had the Oklahoma/SMU matchup plugged in that night. I'm quite certain I didn't stay with the game to tote up that final score, though. In the spirit of the times, I suppose, my mother and step-father decided that it would be all right if I joined them and some neighbors in celebrating the New Year with a few drinks. A few too many, in my foolish case, as I became the blabbering capering entertainment for a party that still reeks of humiliation to me, when I bother to exhume the depressing memory. Oh, sweet blindness.

While I dealt with my first hangover, New Year's Day 1969 started with some unfinished business in Southeast Asia, as alongside SMU's bowl-game triumph the *Dallas Morning News* announced the liberation of US Army Lieutenant Nick Rowe, a Special Forces officer who had been held captive by the Viet Cong—in *South* Vietnam, no less—for five years.

• • •

Houston Astrodome, December 18, 1982. Beaumont West Brook 21, Hurst L. D. Bell 10.

In the 1982 state title game, the last of Beaumont West Brook's miraculous run of five playoff games in the Astrodome, Milton Morgan's defense held the Blue Raiders of L. D. Bell to only 170 yards offense (a meager 17 passing). The Blue Raiders, representing a school from the Ft. Worth suburb of Hurst, had averaged 360 yards per game through the season. For their part, the Bruins of Beaumont West Brook rang up 397 yards (265 rushing, 132 passing). Coach Durley seemed to find his Golden Mean, the ideal balance between the Hebert kid, Jerry Ball, who ran for 104 yards, and the Forest Park kid, Terrance McCarty, who ran for 134. They each scored a rushing touchdown. After the game, McCarty underlined the balanced approach the offense took, telling a *Houston Chronicle* reporter: "I don't know if I was part of the game plan or not, but the coaches knew Hurst Bell would be keying on [Quarterback Gerald] Landry and Ball. And they forgot about me."

After the game, everyone reflected on the unreal journey that began with a very rough start and ended through the looking glass with a championship.

Alex Durley struck up a familiar refrain, noting that "the media didn't help us early in the season with all they were printing and saying about us. We're talking about young kids out here. The eye was on us a little too much. And that's a lot of pressure to put on them"(Stickney). With all the emphasis on racial politics and court orders, it's easy to forget these were high school students playing football part-time, but that sensitivity to the human scale of the ordeal and triumph may have been a big part of what made Durley a championship coach.

For his part, Jerry Ball talked about how the team turned the adversity around. "Motivation and caring for each other brought us through all of that [losing 4 of their first 5 games]. At the beginning the team wasn't together, the school wasn't together. But our principal (Jerry Mallett) talked to us and told us we, as a football team, could bring the school together" (Stickney). The principal's name really was Mallett, and he was a commanding presence at 6'6", and he knew a little something about sports, having played pro baseball for six years.

They came together at least long enough to win that title. The road is long, with many a winding turn, is how the Hollies sang it in those far-out Age-of-Aquarius days of 1969. The center cannot hold, is how the esoteric poet W. B. Yeats wrote it just after the end of the apocalyptic First World War. Different eras, but maybe not-so-different readings on the old *lapsometer*. Football may seem to change the world, to erase perceptions of color, to bring the black kids and the white kids from

Beaumont together, but no one should expect a game to heal those rifts forever. Turning and turning in the widening gyre ....

Jerry Ball comes from a football family, and probably knows better than most that a football life is a transitory life, or maybe more optimistically an evolutionary life, marked by frequent changes. His uncles include Mel and Miller Farr, and his cousins include Jerry LeVias and D'Marco Farr, all of whom played college and NFL ball. His father played some serious football, too, though not in "The League." The younger Ball followed Rufus Cormier to SMU, and made the same shift from fullback to nose tackle, a step down in the pecking order of football, from ball carrier to trench warrior. Unlike Cormier, he made a 13-season career of football in the NFL, playing for the Lions, Browns, Raiders, and Vikings from 1987 through 1999. Defensive line in The League, a tough way to make a living.

Cormier didn't follow the developments in Beaumont in 1982 very closely, working hard at the Houston law firm where he became its first black partner, but reflecting on his own earlier experience with football and racial integration, he described the basic dynamics. "In the south, football is so significant in the social fabric, the fact that integration resulted in a lot of black athletes making significant contributions to their respective teams probably resulted in acceptance of integration in periods when it would have been resisted more were it not for that athletic contribution." Football was "something that mattered to a lot of influential people" and as far as Cormier was concerned it enabled relationships between influential people and black athletes. No guarantee of how those relationships would turn out, but football could open some doors.

Layne Walker comes from a political family, a family of lawyers in the Democratic stronghold of Jefferson County, where his grandfather and grandmother served as County Commissioner, and his father as County Judge. In Walker's case, Jerry Ball's image of the white kids being dropped off by parents in limos might not have been all that far off the mark. Long after he and Jerry Ball had faced off on that practice field the spring before the 1982 season, both trying out for linebacker (Milton Morgan moved Ball to the line so that they could be on the field together—they *had* to be there to win that weird tie game against Baytown Sterling), Walker served as Jefferson County 252nd Criminal District Court Judge from 2003 until 2013. As Beaumont's *12News Now. com* reported, he chose not to seek a third term amidst substantial political controversy, including allegations from Houston's New Black Panther Party leader Quanell X that Walker had established "a pattern of giving African-Americans harsher punishments." Turning and turning ... law and politics in East Texas can be a tough way to make a living, too.

The coaches, Alex Durley and Leo Nolan and Milton Morgan, held the team together for an unprecedented season of high school football, conjuring order out of chaos. There was a little magic in the air in the fall of 1982, and Milton, with his deep roots in the Baptist church, was the go-to guy for the pre-game speech and the post-game quote, the gift of the Holy Spirit anchoring the center for the time being. After that victorious title game in the Houston Astrodome, he told the *Houston Post*, in words evocative if mysterious: "We had a welcome wagon, hoping to instill Bruin spirit. The plan worked, so Christmas came one week early. After a five-in-a-row Dome show, we'd like to see another first-year school duplicate it."

• • •

December 31, 2013. Thirty-one years later, in the midst of college-football bowl season, over lunch on New Year's Eve in Houston, not too far from the now-decrepit Astrodome, I bring my inquiry about football—how big a deal should the game really be?—to Milton Morgan, my Mass Coordinator at St. Thomas More Catholic Church. I ask him about those glory days of coaching champions in Beaumont. Whenever I talk to the

---

real football men, legends from the past like LeVias and Cormier, or lesser-known but deeply respected coaches among the fraternity like John Pluta and Carlin Lynch, it's almost as much of an encounter with a great mystery as when we all fall silent and take our seats after the Gospel and the minister begins the homily. I don't want to aggrandize football or trivialize my faith, but there is something I don't quite understand—but seek to understand—in both of these situations. I seek a plentitude of blessings from father-figures, I guess.

I'm wondering if Milton could preach me one of those pre-game barn-burner speeches, right here over his baked chicken and my grilled fish.

Not exactly. All these years later, Coach Morgan couldn't really remember the text, not with any vivid detail or flow. He knew how the speech generated itself throughout the week, starting with the scouting report, with practice, with meetings, with what the kids said, what the captains said, what the coaches said. If they left it up to Coach Durley, he'd just say "headgear and shoulder pads and knock it in the dirt." Milton tried to give them some of the old fire and brimstone.

That's what he told me, that and little more, as if he couldn't divulge the secrets to me. He could tell me this fact or that—how they mimeographed the scouting reports so that each player knew who would be lining up against him in the game that week—but it was like he couldn't give up the whole story. You probably had to be there.

What *was* it like to be a part of bringing together a community across age-old dividing lines for that brief shining moment when a common commitment—motivation and caring for each other, as Jerry Ball said back in 1982—enabled the deepest possible human connection?

Maybe I do understand. Maybe I've been there, and done that. I have to figure that Milton's reading at 7:30 Mass on that Super Bowl Sunday in 2013 could stand up as a pretty strong pre-game speech. It's what we have now, having put aside childish things, having effected our conversions.

Farewell to Football?

But do you gird your loins;
stand up and tell them
all that I command you.

....

They will fight against you but not prevail over you,
for I am with you to deliver you, says the Lord.

(JEREMIAH 1:17-19)

CHAPTER 5

— • • • —

Monday Night Football: Everybody Wants to Rule the World (1985)

WILLARD (V. O.)

Everyone gets everything he wants. I wanted a mission,
and for my sins, they gave me one. Brought it up to
me like room service. It was a real choice mission, and
when it was over, I never wanted another.

(FROM MICHAEL HERR'S NARRATION FOR
FRANCIS COPPOLA'S *APOCALYPSE NOW*)

• • •

OCTOBER 21, 1985: Chicago Bears 23, Green Bay Packers 7, Soldier Field, Chicago. In the autumn of 1985, I watched a boring NFL football game with Lieutenant Tim Loonam. Tim's hometown Chicago Bears were on the way to the Super Bowl that year, even threatening to equal the 1972 Miami Dolphins' undefeated season record until the Dolphins got their revenge in a Monday Night Football game in December. The Bears' recipe for victory featured a conservative offense focused on the rushing attack led by Walter "Sweetness" Payton and a crushing defense masterminded by buffoonish and outspoken coordinator Buddy Ryan. The "46 defense," a complex set of pressure packages nicknamed for the jersey number of a safety who played up close to the line in the manner of a linebacker, confusing to quarter-backs as they "read" coverage, was so dominant that it even started sending a representative over to the offense to run the ball. The Bears got in the habit of putting massive first-round draft pick defensive line-man William "Refrigerator" Perry onto the field as a running back in goal-line situation, as they did against the Packers in this Monday Night Football game.

After Green Bay got off to a quick start with a touchdown pass to speedy Pro-Bowl receiver James Lofton in the first quarter, the Bears answered with three short touchdown runs in the second, Perry taking in the second of them from one yard out. Dave Duerson, a third-year player out of Notre Dame who was developing a reputation as a smart businessman off the field and a vicious hitter between the lines, had one of three Bears interceptions and also ran back a punt. The defense even provided the closing punctuation, sacking Green Bay's second-string quarterback in the end zone for a fourth-quarter safety, making the fi-nal score 23-7 Chicago.

For prime-time Monday Night Football, this game came up short as entertainment, the Bears just crushing the Packers, a once-glorious team mired in a decade-long slump. For me, thought, the setting gave the game an edge that the play on the field otherwise lacked. We watched the broadcast, which featured the indescribable three-player announcing team of Frank Gifford, O. J. Simpson, and Joe Namath, tape-delayed on the Armed Forces Korea Network, huddled around a little black-and-white set in Tim Loonam's room in officers' quarters on the American army base at Camp Casey. The telecast served me as an NFL appetizer for upcoming home-cooking. I was counting down the days until I would leave the 1-17th Infantry Battalion (the Buffaloes) in the Republic of Korea (ROK), heading back to the States for a vacation after an extended 18-month tour of duty on the "frontiers of freedom," and then on to Special Forces (SF) school in North Carolina and a choice assignment as an A-team leader with 10th SF Group in Massachusetts.

There were four of us junior officers watching that game, as we were four for many purposes and occasions. We were an organic tetrad, four lieutenants somewhere on the spectrum between family and rock band, four lieutenants with the stability of the square, a quartet that could have been The Beatles or Led Zeppelin, or maybe more appropriately The Ramones, who sang with gleeful sarcasm that *we're a happy family, we're a happy family!* They weren't related, The Ramones, weren't even named Ramone. I was thinking a lot about the adventures of rock bands in those days because just as I was heading overseas for my tour of duty in the Second Infantry Division, my musician friend Jimmy Frech (with whom I'd first seen The Ramones back in 1978) was heading out on the road as bassist in the band opening for a couple of legs of Van Halen's 1984 North American tour in support of the album that featured "Jump" and "Panama." I think we both hoped we would be competing to see whose road-trip wound up most debauched, how many deadly sins we might commit. *Might as well jump!*

We Buffalo lieutenants were musical in our own ways, each of us attached to a theme song, at least in my memory. We were certainly all spending plenty of our disposable income on hi-fi gear at the PX to blast our tunes. Tim, the medical platoon leader, seemed to have stepped out of the MTV video for Glenn Frey's "The Heat Is On," attractive and energetic as that signature saxophone riff, one big ongoing snap of the fingers. Pete, the wiry battalion chemical officer, was forever bonded to Tears for Fears' "Everybody Wants to Rule the World" because he brought that album *Songs from the Big Chair* along with all of his other pop-culture machinery, the Macintosh computer and the video camera and the TV we were watching. The mortar platoon leader was a lanky creature known only as Snake—as Willard says in that movie, I was unaware that he had a name nor would I be disposed to reveal his name if I knew it—and oddly enough, he was a big Rush fan and obsessively played that *Signals* album with "Subdivisions" on it through his monster Bose 901 speakers in the room I shared with him. *Any escape might help to smooth the unattractive truth,* the singer intoned portentously over the hypnotic droning synthesizer wash, occasionally jarred by the complex veering of the superb drummer. How could this be the anthem of a towering Aggie? *No comprende, it's a riddle!* In those days, having schemed my way to leading the scout platoon—the plum job for a lieutenant in an infantry battalion, especially if it was mechanized—I was mighty fond of Led Zeppelin's "Nobody's Fault but Mine" for its crack-of-doom drumming and apocalyptic blast of harmonica (and maybe, too, for its hint of contrition and guilt, that singer Plant was paying the karmic price for guitarist Page's dabbling in the "Left Hand Path" occult). Yes, we were a happy musical family, happy and loud.

We even created a music video using Pete's camcorder. You might say we shared an ironic sense of humor, maybe a little more than that, a rebellious sarcastic streak perhaps endemic to young men who volunteer for the profession of managing violence and representing the American Way of War in the overseas branches. We selected Wall of Voodoo's instrumental "On Interstate 15" as our soundtrack, techno-pop as postmodern and ironic as it comes (they had their MTV hit with "Mexican Radio," lines from which I frequently crooned out of one side of my mouth: *wish I was in Tijuana, eating barbequed iguana*). Our video documented the hygienic start to everyday life in the Bachelor Officers Quarters (BOQ), which I had dubbed, for a sign that must have puzzled the Koreans in the base paint-shop, "Chateau de la Montagna de la Rivieria English Country Manor Estates." There on screen went four Buffalo lieutenants, marching in tempo to the pseudo-spaghetti-western strains of Wall of Voodoo, into the showers, brushing our teeth, shaving our faces. Happy, happy family, clean and minty-mediciney, preserved forever on video tape. *I hear the talking of the DJ, can't understand, just what does he say?*

Steven Liparulo

Four young Buffalo lieutenants, near Camp
Casey, Republic of Korea, circa 1985.

We cooked up adventures worthy of The Monkees, like the time the four of us decided to spend a Sunday afternoon climbing the towering hills behind our barracks at Camp Casey. Korea, sometimes dubbed The Land of the Morning Calm for its frequent fogs (nicknamed The Land of Almost Right by one of our acerbic brigade commanders for the knock-off shops downtown where you could buy "Bolex" watches), is a very hilly country, but in the South, at least, few of the hills achieve "mountain" status. So our happy family Sunday outing wasn't quite a walk in the park but it wasn't really mountaineering, either—there was an entrepreneurial Korean guy up at the top of the hill taking pictures to sell to us, as I'm sure there was an older woman with a cooler, selling RC Cola and Moon Pies—frequently referred to by the semi-honorific *ajumma*, she was everywhere Americans went with their money. In some ways, it might have better resembled the surreal album cover photo from Led Zeppelin's *Houses of the Holy*, naked children climbing on rocks. Well, we weren't naked, but we were out of uniform and off the reservation, so to speak. If we were children, we were climbing the stones of adolescence and our destination was ultimately the peak experience of killing our fathers. There's no other way to put it—for all of our commitment to an orderly democratic society and military hierarchy (and that commitment a thin crust, really, because beneath the superficial talking points and recruiting commercials we mostly got into this business to pay for college and maybe see the world and party it up like we were going out on tour with Van Halen), what really set blood coursing through our veins was the possibility that we could topple authority figures and, in the end, kill our fathers.

Our rage was formally encoded in an initiatory ritual called a Buffalation, a kind of military Carnival, a night to celebrate military discipline by indulging in its breach—transgressive revels that let the Lord of Misrule loose for one night, paradoxically keeping him in his place. Seen from one perspective as nothing more than the ceremonial induction of new officers into the fraternal order of our infantry battalion (as part of the 17th Infantry Regiment, it had quite a distinguished history, including suffering intense casualties in the Civil War debacle at Fredericksburg, a high-water mark for life-is-cheap infantry tactics), the Buffalation was from our subordinate point-of-view a chance to invert values and subvert the senior officers in all their false enlightenment (the majors and colonels were mostly veterans of the Vietnam war, and we knew how that had turned out, like Fredericksburg spread out over a decade). They had their unholy catechism to try to catch us up, their ritual inquisition that amounted to Trivial Pursuit for Numb-Skull Infantry Officers.

INQUISITOR
How many MDL markers are there in the DMZ?

NEOPHYTE
1,292, sir.

INQUISITOR
How many steel balls are there in a Claymore mine?

Steven Liparulo

NEOPHYTE
Approximately 700, sir.

INQUISITOR
Is Boss Buffalo's butt black?

NEOPHYTE
(awkward silence)

Revenge was swift. The lieutenants were required to put on entertainment as part of the program, after the questioning of candidates and
before the climactic rite of fetching one's Buffalo nickel with one's teeth
from the "sacred chalice of the vaunted Buffalo pee" (a pewter mug
holding vile liquor punch). Our mandatory revels usually devolved to
skits that I took a heavy hand in preparing, derivative of or straight-out
ripped off from *Monty Python* and *Saturday Night Live* sketches, lampoon-
ing our officers, whom I viewed as pretentious, or undereducated, or
uncultured—you name it, James-Dean style, I held it against them. Our
"entertainment" frequently bordered on insubordination, and for me
was just one of several outlets readily available for disordered passions.

When you think about it (when I think about it, now, a somber
adult), there was something fishy about the whole legionary business,
serving in the US Army and deployed to a foreign land (our unit crest included a symbol for a Cuban fort, and the "Buffalo" symbolism reflected
the nickname of a regimental commander during the Korean war), the
melodramatic cult of death and honor and history (putting a symbol of
Fredericksburg on your unit crest amounted to a paean to blundering
bloody incompetence, like adopting Ambrose Burnside as your patron
saint). Maybe this Korean tour was turning out to be a tragic Oedipal
nightmare—having thought to flee an imminent disaster, had I blindly
headed straight into the very heart of catastrophe? Maybe I hadn't avoided the Left Hand Path at all, that *esoteric* Satanic Majestic Rock-and-Roll
Rebellion, when I signed on for a four-year scholarship contract with

the Army, but instead had crossed the International Date Line, gone through the looking glass, and landed smack-dab in the Realm of the Serpent. My friend was off slapping his pink bass and snorting coke with Eddie Van Halen and the bearded guys from ZZ Top and I was downing *chalices* of Buffalo Pee in the Land of Almost Right. My room-mate here in the Hermit Kingdom was called The Snake, and this Dali-nightmare is true of him: he once stripped completely naked, donned his protective mask, smeared chem-light juice all over his body until he glowed bright as landing lights at the airport, and then proceeded to douse himself with Lindane powder, muffled screams emerging from his gas-mask, something about curing himself of these confounded crabs. Something needed curing.

• • •

Subdivisions

A few years after my service in Korea, as a graduate student in litera-ture, I started hearing about this concept of history and national des-tiny, American Exceptionalism. As an ideology, it's a whopper, and has lately become something like a litmus test for aspiring political leaders (*everybody wants to rule the world*, just like the song says, but American poli-ticians claim it as a right), asserting that America is the exception to the general rules of historical development and decline, a nation destined to rule the world with its democratic values and personal freedoms. America the Exceptional would avoid the second-half trajectory of the Rise and Fall of the Roman Empire, would not blow a first-half lead and spiral downward into decadence and decay, instead defying the laws of physics and remaining ever ascendant. Politicians seem to love that idea just about as much as deficit spending.

When I first heard the term, I thought it meant something slightly different: the tendency among Americans to claim exceptions to other-wise firm articles of faith—"I really believe in telling the truth, except in this case it's better if I lie." You string enough of these exceptions together and it starts to look like systematic denial and a culture of hypocrisy, and I think some people from other parts of the world see Americans this way. I know it's a little easier to imagine if you've lived in another country for a while. That outsider perspective, that sense that other people put the world together differently from us, was part of the appeal for military service and world travel I picked up from my friend John, who came back from his Army tour of duty in Germany and started noticing how *cute* our culture is (the poet and social critic Robert Bly tends to prefer the word *puerile*), America a never-ending plentitude of largely-inessential consumer products advertised with puns and word-play, a country that makes a big deal out of replaying the *commercials* from the Super Bowl.

Certainly my life as a military officer in Korea was conditioned upon these dualisms, these exceptional *subdivisions*. I was a soldier in a "peace-time" army, and yet here I was serving in a war zone, the Korean conflict having never been concluded by treaty, only suspended by a cease-fire agreement. Americans are a peace-loving people, runs the article of faith, yet our government is constantly involved in wars, either fighting them or encouraging and supporting them materially among our "allies." We spend more on "defense" (one of those Orwellian euphemisms—the Department of Defense used to be called the Department of War) than most of the rest of the world combined, and our arms industries sell to the rest of the world everything they need to keep the wars going, lethality a pretty lucrative business model. America is a society putatively free from the rigid class-boundaries of decadent old Europe, and yet here I was in the middle of an essentially feudal caste system in the military, with strict subdivisions between enlisted men ("private soldiers"), non-commissioned officers (NCO's—sergeants), company grade officers (lieutenants and captains), field grade officers (majors and colonels), and general officers (essentially, political appointees).

The most controlling subdivision for the experience of the soldiers and officers of the combat arms battalions of the 2nd Infantry Division was the distinction between life in garrison at Camp Casey and life in the field, either in winter maneuvers after the rice had been harvested in the frozen countryside north of the "ville" of Tongduch'on or in operations along and in the Demilitarized Zone (DMZ) separating North and South Korea. The five infantry battalions rotated through 73-day mission cycles on the DMZ, and for the Buffaloes, this took place in the first half of summer. I had arrived just in time for the mission in 1984 and then extended my 12-month tour of duty to 18 so that I could lead the scout platoon during a second round of the mission in 1985.

The DMZ mission was a chore endlessly subdivided, with major functions rotating between the rifle companies of the battalion: patrolling the DMZ, occupying and operating two guard posts in the DMZ, and serving as the ready-reaction force in case, as they say, "the balloon went up." The scout platoon, in our ongoing role as the "eyes and ears of the battalion commander," ran patrols throughout the ten-week mission, and as the platoon leader, I could take patrols as often as I wanted, since I was relieving my squad leaders from the duty every time I went out. The patrol process is demanding, so it was no small favor to give my sergeants an occasional break, but it was also the best practice for an insecure young leader looking to increase his skills and experience in small-unit-tactics. I was already looking ahead to leading a Special Forces A-team, so I eagerly took out as many patrols as I could. Each patrol was really something like a three-day event (a short game-week, in football terms), all the stuff you spent the eight weeks of Ranger School learning how to do, only now with live ammo and a live enemy somewhere just the other side of that line. Graduate school, you might say. The DMZ patrol was the ultimate performance of the Army's Holy Five Paragraph Operations Order, acting out its sacred script like a thespian taking on a role in a five-act Shakespearean drama. Situation, Mission, Execution, Service and Support, Command and Signal. Lay on, MacDuff!

The first day, you would receive your single-sentence mission from the S-2/S-3 Intelligence and Operations shop on a slip of paper with the essentials—time of departure, time of return, time on target, checkpoints, command and signal data—for both a daylight reconnaissance and a nighttime ambush patrol. You would plan, put up all the data in grease-pencil on a big acetate-covered board, work out the route on your map, deliver orders to your squad, memorize the times and azimuths and distances and radio frequencies and passwords, and rehearse immediate action drills and actions at the objective. Day two you would draw your weapons and ammo and gear and go through inspections and run your recon patrol, getting a look at the ground where you would set your ambush the following night. Day three would be the ambush, which meant heading out into the dark in the demilitarized zone. A spooky place, especially when you carried live ammunition and your sniper went out with one round in the chamber and the Claymore anti-personnel mines you carried were live, too.

When the Korean War ground to a halt and the cease-fire was signed in 1953, the battle front hardened into the border subdividing the two warring countries and a four-kilometer zone was "demilitarized," two kilometers either side of the Military Demarcation Line (MDL), a 248 kilometer boundary marked by 1,292 identical signs on irregularly-spaced posts without a fence—a perfectly insane invitation to provocative border crossing. "Demilitarized" is another one of these through-the-looking-glass euphemisms, since that zone is actually highly militarized. Both sides basically built up fortifications and stationed forces just outside the DMZ, waiting to resume the fight, and they send armed patrols into the zone on a regular basis (the patrols are, putatively, "policing" the enforcement of the cease-fire, and patrol members thus wear "DMZ Police" brassards on their arms). On occasion, the two Koreas will exchange fire across the MDL. In the American sector, a small fraction of the border but highly important since it encloses the Joint Security Area at Panmunjom where negotiations to end the long-stalled war still occasionally take place, military personnel are *required* to be armed.

During the DMZ mission, running patrols on a regular rotation, living in one of the big canvas tents pitched on concrete slabs at Warrior Base as if the circus had come to town, focused squarely on the mission 24/7, my life was nearly monastic, a great way to stay out of trouble. The patrol schedule told my life story. The same cannot be said for garrison life. While the US Army in Korea was, in the early 80's when I was there, on a near-war footing, conducting regular alerts in addition to maintaining the activities on the DMZ, working a five-and-one-half day week, life in garrison was still not that much different from any other job. Catch up on the paperwork, perform maintenance on the weapons and vehicles and equipment, do some training, keep regular hours. We ate lunch in the Officers Club almost every day, often enjoying ice-cream sundaes for dessert. Then evening would come and havoc would reign.

Korea was what the Army called an "unaccompanied tour," meaning that duty was so rigorous that spouses and families were not invited and their expenses were not covered by the Army. A few soldiers and officers paid their own expenses for family, but mostly it was the single life—in a male-only combat arms battalion, the *bachelor* life. For that reason, among others, garrison life took on a Wild-West aura, as soldiers and officers stepped out the gate of Camp Casey into "the ville" of Tongduch'on (abbreviated as TDC), a carnival for disordered passions. While there were certainly plenty of good restaurants and a few decent shops and tailors, the typical menu for an evening in "the ville" was heavy with GI clubs, where copious amounts of alcohol and a plenteous variety of prostitutes were readily available. A lot of GI's went on sick call for venereal diseases.

Here is another of those subdivisions or hypocrisies or manifestations of the more-recent American Exceptionalism: while civilians in the post-9/11 world love to idolize our warrior class (you can't watch a football game anymore without an earnest ceremony of devotion to the military, often accompanied by a standing ovation that builds out of nowhere like a subconscious wave, no matter how inconsequential the honored "hero" might be), most have no idea of the often-squalid lives these "warriors" live and corrupt values they frequently live by. Stateside military bases are typically surrounded by pawn shops, bars, and strip clubs, where soldiers, sailors, airmen, and marines choose to waste money and get drunk and fight. Especially since we started fighting open-ended foreign wars over a decade ago, subjecting service members to frequently-traumatic levels of violence, the American military struggles with domestic violence, drug addiction, depression, and suicide (as I write this, the figure is 22 American veterans committing suicide every day). Overseas, you can add essentially-legal prostitution to the mix, and pornography is a big part of the lifestyle, too, at home or abroad (one of my fellow former Army officers recently told me about the massive supplies of porn American forces brought with them to the most recent Iraq war, while another told me about the great lengths to which the Iraqi officers he was training would go in order to lay hands on American porn). The article of faith proclaims that we are a Christian, god-fearing nation of laws, but if you look at our military "heroes" you tend to see a lot of debased outlaw behavior. Exceptions to the rule, no doubt.

I readily confess that at the time, with the pretzel-logic of that Orwellian year of 1984, I thought I was having the time of my life in "TDC." I particularly loved The Moon Club, in part because it was not a front for a house of prostitution (I found my way into plenty of those) but instead a haven for hard-core hard-rock music fans. The proprietor was an ex-Korean Air Force sergeant and his unique selling proposition was his extensive record collection. You would fill out a slip of paper with your song request and he would play them in the order received, blasting out from his excellent sound system. Part of the fun was the anticipation of what raving tune would come up next. My all-time favorite for these purposes was Deep Purple's "Highway Star," a metal anthem for speed-freaks that featured the exquisite multi-tracked guitar work of Ritchie Blackmore on an extended up-tempo solo orchestrated with a blues-based introduction followed by cascading Baroque triplets over four cycles through a pounding chord sequence, elevating and escalating toward the peak whammy-bar climax in the history of heavy-metal guitar. The specialty of the house at the Moon Club was a drink called Lig Mill: Soju, the Korean equivalent of vodka; Seven-Up or similar Korean knock-off; and a milky drink they called yogurt, though who knows what it was. A good clean cocktail, the Lig Mill also happened to glow radium-luminous in the black-light. Awesome.

I had a major crush on the proprietor's sister, Jina, and that whole affair worked out as ominous evidence of things not seen, not fully clear to me, disordered passions submerged into the unconscious and only visible under the Moon Club black-light. Something had happened in the long-ago shadows to deform me as an unusual man. It should have been easy just to get to know Jina, open up to her, see if we had common ground for pursuing something more than my lust for her (or whatever it was that stirred in my soul in her presence—I hadn't really mastered that Platonic/Aristotelian discrimination of the various movements of the soul). She was quite stunning in her unadorned beauty, short, well-proportioned (19" waist!), with radiant bronze skin, and she wasn't a "working girl." But I became aware of a whole bank of circuits faulty in the wiring of my personality—I could not go from A to B to C when it came to women, could not process those signals. I could pay the price and find that brief yield of pleasure, but I could only get so far down the road to ordinary love, the kind of simple flirting and courting millions of Americans with a whole lot less education and refinement than me managed every day, before an internal "No" clanged mysteriously in my mind, sabotaging my best intentions. "No, this is not for you." I didn't really hear it so much as it functioned like white noise, seeming to cancel out other more positive signals. This pattern had emerged when I was in college and started up a romance that quickly bogged down, leaving me with a paralyzed sensation that I wasn't in control of my own feelings and actions, a threatening sense that things were about to exceed the boundaries of simple, puerile sexuality and present insoluble challenges to my idealized and remote sense of romantic love. I got some counseling that suggested that the suicidal death of my friend Todd probably was to blame. It would turn out that there was more down there in the repressed holding tank—really, more to my relationship with Todd than friendship, in addition to other sources of suffering—but that would take ages to work itself toward consciousness. In Korea, during the seemingly-normal stretches of garrison life, I tended to get mired in dark fugues of unhappy introspection, and looking back I would have to discern a connection between this problem and my aggressive sub-version of my senior officers whenever I got the chance, and also my frequent over-indulgences down in "the ville,"the drinks that glowed like radium and the working girls sadly imprisoned by the debt of their par-ents. I probably would have been better off spending all 18 months on the DMZ.

• • •

"Periods of Limited Visibility"

The monastic life on the DMZ meant I had time for reading, and potent texts came my way through strange and mysterious channels. My first tour, I found a copy of Walker Percy's second novel, *The Last Gentleman,* under the flip-up front seat of a Jeep—what was *that* doing *there?* It had to be a sign of something, coinciding as it did with the *Reader's Digest* I hap-pened upon a week or so later with a wry father-of-the-bride piece written by my old college professor, Richard Pindell, a self-mythologizing Dixie wild-man who had assigned me Walker Percy and Flannery O'Connor when I was an undergraduate at Binghamton. Coinciding? Hmmm. Percy novels always featured a main character waiting for some kind of sign, while in the O'Connor stories someone always seemed to be vio-lently beset by whatever they most fervently seek to avoid.

My second tour, I worked my way through T. R. Ferenbach's 1963 *This Kind of War,* which I discovered was passed from hand to hand among the thinking officers, the mutedly cynical and Stoic descendants of the Roman centurions commissioned to lead the American legions. They read it as their preferred history of the Korean War, and it reflected what you might call the *ethos* of the American officer, post-Vietnam (though its author had only drawn upon a similar post-Korea *ethos*): critical of the politicians, cognizant of the mistakes of preparation and leadership by the officers, and loyal to the combat soldiers. Something on the order

Farewell to Football?

of an Aristotelian examination of conscience concerning the relationship between the military and a liberal American republic of the post-World-War-II era, the book dispensed the wisdom of Zen-on-the-Imjin: "Only those who have never learned self-restraint fear reasonable discipline" (p. xi).

In between chapters, I ran patrols with the scouts.

Tim Loonam decided he should go along on some of my patrols as the medic, based upon his incisive reckoning of leadership. As the medical platoon leader, he was responsible for the training and disposition of all the medics in the battalion, each of whom got attached to a platoon in the line companies during deployments. Every DMZ patrol had to include a medic, which put them into an intensive rotation, and Tim believed that he should fully understand what his troops were required to do in order to properly train and lead them. It made sense, but it also ran up against a line of military "thought" arguing that no medical platoon leader had done this before and therefore neither should Tim (med platoon leaders tended to be what we called "pogues," chairborne leaders habituated to their desks). Then there was the "problem" of rank, a threat to the whole feudal caste system—if Tim, as a second lieutenant, went out on a patrol led by a squad leader, a sergeant, he'd find himself in the unacceptable situation of an officer taking orders from an NCO. That's where my practice of taking out scout patrols came in handy. I outranked Tim, so we wouldn't have any risk of insubordination.

Tim was enthusiastic about his chance to get into the thick of things with the scouts, and he proved adept at processes like memorizing the route by legs and helping the scouts memorize call-signs and frequencies and code words to use when reporting via radio. He would enthusiastically run through mnemonic drills with them. Tim was patient with these soldiers, some of whom, let's face it, had signed that Army contract because they weren't academically competent enough to go to college to learn how to write essays. I think he had the right touch, maybe because inherently he liked people (I'm not sure that's true of me, and I know I was impatient with the soldiers who struggled with the "mental reps"). Tim kept his good humor further into the process, when both of the inspectors (the company commander or his delegated substitute, the battalion commander or his delegate) really teed off on him as the "fish out of water," hammering him with all manner of arcane questions.

INSPECTOR
Medic, what would you do if this lieutenant got hit with a hand-grenade on your patrol?

LT LOONAM
I would apply the ABC's: clear the airway, start the breathing, check for bleeding and dress any wounds, and then treat for shock.

INSPECTOR
Would you take command of the patrol?

LT LOONAM
No, sir, the Assistant Patrol Leader would be next in the chain of command.

INSPECTOR
What would you do if Kim Il-sung stepped out of the tree-line and approached this patrol?

LT LOONAM
(awkward silence)

We made it through the recon patrol just fine. Tim showed he could deal in the field—operating as part of a unit, following the script for moving and stopping without the need for talk, knowing what was worth observing and reporting and what was just routine, staying oriented to the map at all times, knowing the pace-count and compass heading, using hand and arm signals as necessary, keeping all of the details under control in a tense environment. None of that is easy if it's not your regular job. The real test would come the following night, when we set up our ambush. Night time in the DMZ turns into a real freak show.

North Korea was one of the last of the great cult-of-personality communist dictatorships, and in the 1980's was still led by the original personality, the Great Leader Comrade himself, Kim Il-sung, Korean by birth and communist by dint of his life's journey. The 1950-1953 war had never formally concluded—as Fehrenbach writes, extending an ongoing metaphor linking America and Imperial Rome, "MacArthur was told to hold the frontier so that the tribes of the interior could continue to organize, and to forget about carrying the war to the barbarians" (p. 276), and then Dugout Doug got sacked for not listening anyway. The country had been artificially subdivided by outsiders, and North Korea kept up active measures to subvert the Western-aligned and financially-prosperous South. They maintained one of the world's largest standing armies, dug tunnels under the DMZ, and engaged in near-psychotic propaganda histrionics. For example, on the other side of the MDL from the American sector of the DMZ, they maintained a Potemkin-village façade where laborers "lived" in a model workers'-paradise community in plain view of the DMZ outposts (but then retreated out of the DMZ under cover of darkness). That was supposed to demonstrate … something. They jockeyed back and forth with the South to see whose flagpole was taller at that same region of the DMZ. And at night, they tried to freak out the Americans on patrol in the DMZ with propaganda broadcasts on a network of loudspeakers aimed across the MDL (just the phase-differences of so many speakers spread out unevenly made it sound pretty freaky, and then they frequently threw in brief snatches of dissonant music, overloaded and distorted, like outtakes from a King Crimson album). Combined with their practice of turning on and off lights along the fence-line, it could make for an unsettling night for an American experiencing it for the first time. How would Tim handle that?

In my arrogance and ignorance I thought maybe Tim was the Nick Adams type, the Michigander protagonist in a number of the landmark Ernest Hemingway stories. Nick was always losing his innocence—when his father delivered an Indian baby by Caesarean section, when killers came to town to get Ole Anderson—but then somehow regenerating it so that he could lose it again the next story. That's why Hemingway was the great American writer of the 20th century—America was like Nick Adams, always losing its innocence and then having it again to lose in the next episode. Pearl Harbor, Kasserine Pass, Korea, Vietnam.

We ate our pre-game meal at the dining facility on Warrior Base and then started suiting up for the ambush patrol. Tim and I reviewed the game plan as we got into uniform and applied camouflage, going over our route and actions at the objective. He had played high school football in Chicago, and even made it as far as a prospect camp for college ball at Colorado, and that experience with teamwork probably made this whole process easier for him. I hadn't played any team sports, and I always felt like an imposter trying to make up for that deficit. I'd gotten plenty of good Army training, of course, up to and including Ranger School, and now had run more than a dozen of these DMZ patrols, 60-plus paragraphs of Operations Order drama, so I felt OK about my ability, but still, none of it came naturally. I didn't really know what I would do if Kim Il-sung stepped out of the tree-line, either.

We made our way over to the inspection tent, where our equipment was laid out. This time, the inspectors were in no mood for horsing around with Tim. We were going to be patrolling out in the dark on the DMZ, setting up an ambush, carrying live ammunition, and I would set out live Claymore mines the detonators to which were at that moment residing in my pockets, tied with parachute cord to my belt. Very close to me. We would be in a position to start the next world war if we chose to screw up our mission, and the inspectors were determined to ensure that we didn't screw up.

I could smoke my last cigarette of the night as we rode in the back of a "deuce-and-a-half" truck from Warrior Base to the Tactical Operations

Farewell to Football?

Center (TOC), a little tent-city just outside the DMZ. That was always a great smoke. The year before, I had been a green lieutenant working the radios at the TOC, and now I experienced what I imagined the varsity felt on game-day, coming in painted up and wearing all that gear, M-16 clutched in one hand the way a running back might carry the football in the open field, checking in with the Intelligence Officer (S-2) for final updates on the enemy situation. It was all routine, but nobody took anything for granted. I was always aware of the S-2, a pretty keen, soft-spoken officer, taking a moment to look me directly in the eye, probably scanning for any signs that I was off my game in any way. It was his job, too, to make sure I didn't screw up and start the next world war. I was tight, but my breathing was slow and under control.

The whole process of getting underway with a DMZ patrol runs just the opposite of pre-game festivities leading up to kickoff of a football game. Instead of emotions rising as the crowd roar throbs, things get quieter as you motor through the DMZ gate, lights out on the truck, and then approach dead silence as you slither off the truck, take prone positions off the side of the road, and wait for the truck to disappear. You wait, silent, listening for anything out of the ordinary. It was my job as patrol leader, when I was assured that we were good to go, to get up and start to move in the direction of the first leg of our route. That was it. The patrol's job was to move out in concert with me, just like we'd rehearsed. We'd gotten off the truck in our moving formation. This was no game. We were heading to our ambush site.

The trick that most civilians don't get about military operations at night is that it's almost never really dark. In fact, the military favors the expression "periods of limited visibility," which beautifully captures the relative nature of light and dark. Minus man-made artificial lights, night may still be illumined by moon and stars, and even minus the moon, starlight adds a certain "visibility." Only on moonless and cloud-covered nights away from civilization do you really approach total darkness. The key to operating in the limited visibility is getting your eyes adjusted and keeping them adjusted, pupils dilated to let in maximum light. That's why from the time we left the TOC until we were dropped off at a numbered pole on the side of the MSR we didn't use any flashlights and the truck was operating only using "black-out lights." By the time we were starting our patrol route, we were dilated enough to get on with the operation.

A strange thing, though: we are so visually oriented, most of us, that even with a million abstractions and numbers to keep our mind focused—in my case, the azimuth, the pace-count, the head count, what the North Koreans are doing with the lights on the fence-line— in the absence of something to look at, our minds tend to wander. In my case, I found my mind subdivided, the main part still counting and checking the compass while one subdivision tended to drift to memories of similar situations, with that sticky associative poetic logic of dreams. Tonight begets another night as I return to ponder how far off its bearings my mind wandered when I was in the mountain phase of Ranger School last winter, patrolling the hilly country of northern Georgia. *Mountain Laurel*, I remember how much trouble the mountain laurel made for our night-time movements, always tangled up in that low shrubbery. The gyroscope of my luck had gone swinging wildly throughout the early stages of my tour of duty in the Army. First it was the sickening yaw of failing a PT test and being cut from orders for the much-anticipated Airborne and Ranger schools, then an unexpected pitch up into a miraculous second chance due to a screw-up at headquarters, and finally to a climactic roll— a Pass on my first patrol at Camp Darby, something almost no one does because it comes early in the syllabus of Ranger school and it's hard to master all the details of patrol leadership. Who would have thought that I'd be the guy to keep my bearings in that situation, a night-time occupation of a patrol base? Then I lost the gyroscopic platform altogether when we got to Camp Merrill in those Georgia mountains and I started screwing up, literally screwing up and around, gyroscope twisting around and up inside my head, hands dropping things, feet moving out when the rest of the patrol was at the halt, forgetting my rucksack and losing my head and then one night on patrol I am pretty sure I felt my eyes twist up inside of my head as I hallucinated. It was too dark to know for sure if I knew for sure. I had gotten an infection on a small cut on my thumb, a little initiatory wound through which the educational process drew its sacrificial blood, and it turned into blood poisoning and I really was losing the executive functions of my mind when—

—*WHAP!*—

Something exploded in my chest, and I was fixing to start the third world war in the DMZ. No, not in my chest, but near it. I quickly patted my uniform blouse and found no blood nor tattered fabric from a gunshot or grenade blast. No. Now that I thought of it, I had felt a little skitter, almost like getting brushed in the face by a cat's tail, and then had felt the explosion. No, not a cat, a pheasant, and not an explosion at all. A ring-necked pheasant taking wing right in front of me, bursting into flight and scaring the crap out of someone in the patrol, who had violated noise discipline and shouted out.

I figured I had better check in with the rookie, since Tim was right next to me in the order of march. The patrol had halted, frozen, then taken a knee according to our Standard Operating Procedure (SOP), weapons at the ready facing out from the line of march, so I just took a couple of steps to kneel right beside Tim, where I could whisper in his ear. I figured I'd better settle him down and let him know that it was OK if he had inadvertently blurted out.

"Did you hear who said that?" I asked, favoring the indirect approach.

"I did," he whispered back.

"It's OK. It can happen to the best of us."

"No, I mean, I heard who said that."

This was a lot of whispering for the DMZ at night, but once started down this track I figured I'd better wrap it up.

"Who?"

"You did."

I did. Crap.

"All right. We're moving out." I whispered to the patrol.

Getting myself centered again, I did a little math in my head and sidled over to Tim Loonam again.

"What's the pace count, medic?"

"Two hundred meters from start point, sir."

"Attaway, Buffalo."

For several long, tedious hours of this particular period of limited visibility, we were lined up in ambush formation, soldiers in the prone position with maximum cover if not concealment, weapons aimed and ready to fire, disposed to start the third world war if it came down to it.

In this strange crepuscular realm of Almost War and Almost Right, a foggy world of propaganda and illusion and mixed metaphor, we were pawns in a Cold-War game of chicken. The North Koreans were rumored to occasionally send infiltrators across the MDL, seeking to provoke an embarrassing response from the US forces, and so our role was two-fold: to be here to detect any infiltrators, and to keep the situation under control if it happened, exerting discipline in a chaotic situation.

In fact, there had been one of these "Spot South" incidents the night before I arrived on the DMZ for my first tour in 1984. It was shrouded in mystery, at least from me as a newbie, but I could tell it had rattled the battalion commander and his staff—when I was introduced to them on arrival, they had the sleep-deprived hair-standing-on-end look of men who had survived a plane crash. The scout platoon leader's patrol had picked up on something approximately human-sized moving in the sparse vegetation of a field to their front, alerted to his heat-signature in the limited visibility by the thermal night-sights that the scout patrols took on ambush missions in those days. The world stopped turning for the battalion until the phantom finally disappeared—the scout had wanted to maneuver his squad to force the issue, but the battalion commander in his first night on the job was not inclined to pull that particular trigger. So nothing really happened. Had a North Korean played us for suckers, slipping in, stirring the pot—they were undoubtedly aware that a new battalion had just taken over the mission—and slipping out?

Farewell to Football?

Had a lucky possum gotten away with its life, having avoided being targeted by a command-detonated Claymore anti-personnel mine, which would have shredded its hide with 700 stainless-steel balls propelled by 680 grams of C-4 explosive? A strange mystery everyone would have to live with. A great story for that scout to tell over endless drinks the rest of his life, like the pompous Commander McBragg. "There I was, ready to start a third world war but the Boss Buffalo wouldn't let me shoot ...."

Mainly, the job on these patrols was to try to stay awake, to try to pay attention even though the odds said you wouldn't see much of anything. They gave us Essential Elements of Information, things to notice and record—which fence lights came on and off, and when, mostly, since these were thought to be signals to infiltrators working their way across the MDL. We brought along a "Korean Augmentation to the U. S. Army," or KATUSA, a soldier from the ROK Army fluent in English, to translate and transcribe the propaganda broadcasts. The patrol would be deployed on line, facing the kill zone of the ambush, with rear security a dozen yards or so out back. The KATUSA would sit between the main line and the rear security, often with his back to the kill zone so he would listen and not watch. He carried a notebook to write down what he heard.

The Great Leader-Comrade Kim Il-sung deployed specialists to travel the fence line, climbing up into the guard towers to take over the live microphones and lay it down like rap artists. They would get on the PA system and holler propaganda into the night for hours on end. From time to time I would crawl back and check in with the KATUSA as he translated the rap. *Can't understand, just what does he say?*

The night that Tim Loonam went out with me as medic, I recall asking the KATUSA what was the message, since the rap artist had adopted a mellow tone, like he was imparting a narrative instead of the usual ideological rant (I got so I could recognize the Korean word for "running-dog lackey" pretty readily). The KATUSA told me it was a long story about the Great Leader-Comrade Kim Il-sung feeding the multitudes, feeding vast hordes of the starving people during the war with

Japan, feeding thousands with just a few loaves of bread. "He really said that?" I asked quietly, not sure how much of the allusion the KATUSA was on to. "Did he mention anything about fishes?" The KATUSA replied, "no, sir," but I think I heard a little smirk in his voice. Oh, my. I'd heard that story before somewhere. What an insane madman up there, sending seething rant-artists all along the watchtower to holler parables at us. There's nothing *cute* about the Great Leader-Comrade's culture, his starving people and his standing army. It was more like something out of the paranoid science-fiction movies America loved in the 1950's, alien perils and brain-washing evil-genius dictators, out to feed on our gray matter.

That was as far as we got toward starting the third world war that night. We got told a bed time story about a monster manipulator with one of the world's largest collections of field artillery, who runs a side business feeding the multitudes.

I was nagged by the partial recall of an enigmatic phrase from Fehrenbach, something about the bones of the legionnaires, but couldn't remember the exact wording. Funny how you obsess over little things like that, the same way your tongue can't avoid the rough edge of broken tooth.

Well, I also got something a little more personal. I think. In that hypnogogic trance of a night, while disparate parts of my body fell asleep from lying prone on damp ground as the temperature dropped off, as my eyes wondered if they were open or closed, looking or only imagining they were looking, I thought I heard something very different briefly come flying out of those arrayed loudspeakers, prefaced by an extended piano arpeggio that often dramatically signaled a change of programming on this weird DMZ network. It was an American voice, a farm-boy Wisconsin type of voice (or was it Nick Adams from the Upper Peninsula of Michigan, shocked at what he'd stumbled onto north of the MDL?), proclaiming "I want to tell you …," but then abruptly cut off, not revealing anything. Had the henchmen around the weird evil genius Great Leader-Comrade invented a soul gyroscope, a distant-early-warning *lapsometer* that made it clear that *I wanted someone to tell me something*, like a character in a Walker Percy novel?

I hear the talking of the DJ, can't understand just what does he say? I'm on a Mexican radio.

For our efforts, after we packed up our ambush site and made it back to the MSR, clambered onto the trucks for a quick stop at the TOC where we debriefed the S-2 on the whole Leader-Comrade story, as the sun started to invest the fog of the morning-calm with milky light, we got to enjoy French toast dripping with hot maple syrup in the Warrior Base mess hall. Man, that tasted good. And then, after a very satisfying smoke and a few paragraphs from Fehrenbach, finding the passage I'd thought about in the night ("This was the kind of war that had bleached the bones of countless legionnaires on the marches of the empire" p. 59)—ah, such stuff to dream on, this kind of war—I would drift off to sleep as the world around me began to stir awake for another bustling summer day. By the time I woke again, dripping with sweat, I would have another mission.

• • •

November 18, 1985: New York Giants 21, Washington Redskins 23, RFK Stadium, Washington. By mid-November, I had completed my voyage home from the frontiers of freedom, and on Monday night I was welcomed home with an event equal parts family reunion and ritual humiliation. A gaggle of sisters and nieces and nephews were crammed into the living room of my mother's small apartment in Norwich, NY, and I was the guest of honor for dinner and dessert, an unusual man both admired and ridiculed for his ambitions. My father had enlisted in the Army right after Pearl Harbor, and my mother earned a nursing degree through the Cadet Nurses Corps, but he got busted for fighting every time he made sergeant and with the post-war demobilization she never got to serve out her commission. Neither of my parents earned college degrees. None of my sisters had gone to college, but they had all married—more than once—and had kids. I was the family freak-show, the worst combination of "book-smart" and lonely-heart single. Still, they had all loved me and supported me, so I was obliged to put up with their aggravation.

In those days, the kids liked to put on shows (not so different from our antic Buffalation entertainments), and they made good use of my military props, especially the black-framed "TED" glasses (Tactical Eyewear Device), evolving goofy characters, and nobody was paying too much attention to the Monday night game playing on the Trinitron color TV I had shipped home from the PX in Korea. The Washington team was hosting the Giants, with whom they were tangled in a three-way race for playoff spots in the NFC East that also included the Dallas Cowboys. Somewhere along the line, though, the horsing around in the living room petered out as all eyes were drawn to a replay on TV. Early in the second quarter, with the game tied at 7, Washington tried a trick play to exploit quarterback Joe Theisman's mobility—a flea-flicker, which entailed a handoff to the running back, who plunged straight up into the middle of the line, only to turn and pitch the ball back to the quarterback. Theisman was in trouble right away, since the Giants' linebackers were notoriously fast, smart heavy-hitters. Harry Carson thought he had the wiry quarterback, but Theisman wiggled free, only to be brought down for good by Lawrence Taylor, who came skidding into the play from off the edge, driving his knee into Theisman's lower leg and—

—*WHAP!*—

Something exploded and Lawrence Taylor came screaming out of the pile like a man possessed. Like everyone watching that game, whether they said it out loud or under their breath or in the silence of their hearts, all the family gathered together for my reunion gasped, "oh, dear Lord." Theisman's leg had broken in two, and spear-tips of the bone protruded out from his bloody sock striped with team colors. Taylor had heard the shotgun blast of both lower-leg bones snapping and had screamed to the sidelines to get help out to Theisman, who was writhing in pain.

Farewell to Football?

The game was stopped for a long time as medics reassembled the leg enough to wrap it in an air-cast so they could put Theisman on a stretcher. In the three-man ABC Monday Night Football booth, as they repeatedly ran the replay, you could hear something catch in the voices of the ex-players, who had all been there with injuries, some more serious than others. O. J. Simpson was relatively lucky by NFL standards, "only" requiring two knee surgeries but suffering from arthritis after his playing days were over, a fact brought up in his later trial for murdering his wife. Joe Namath's middle name might as well be "knee injury," so famous was his robotic Lenox Hill knee brace and gimpy drop-back gait from under center. Frank Gifford as a New York Giant had been carted off the field, some thought dead, after sustaining a concussion on a vicious tackle by "Concrete Charlie" Bednarik of the Philadelphia Eagles in a November game in 1960 between those two long-time rivals. Gifford had sat out a full season of football before returning for a couple more productive seasons.

Theisman would never play football again.

I think maybe my mother suggested we turn off the TV. I wonder how many TV's across America were shut off that night. Theisman's injury seemed to function like some sort of Return of the Repressed, revealing in a strobe-like flash that when we made an entertainment of football, prime time, Monday Night Football, a national TV spectacle—more than that, a *worldwide* phenomenon—we had repressed the violence at its core. I remembered something I hadn't thought about in years: I used to shoot baskets with this guy from New Berlin, Jeff Ackerman, whose dad sometimes came out and shot with us, in between his work as an undertaker and part-time mail carrier. His father walked with a pronounced limp, but he cut no one any slack on the basketball court. He had lost his leg playing football when gangrene set in after his leg was broken in a high school game in the mid 1950's. Jeff had grown up a rabid Green Bay fan, to the point that his nickname was Packerman, and initially his parents hadn't given him permission to go out for football. In Jeff's sophomore season, though, he prevailed upon them with the logic that emergency medicine had improved and that an injury like his father's wouldn't result in such a catastrophe today. Jeff had made a good career of it as a high-school running back, and even played a little ball in college before giving it up to concentrate on his studies, then giving up on his studies to join the Navy, in which setting like Paul Brown he found his way back to football. I had to wonder what his father thought of this horrid spectacle on Monday Night Football.

I had just come back from one of the outposts of the American Empire, where the legionnaires' bones were supposed to be bleaching, and I'd watched the Packers get creamed by the Bears on Monday Night Football in Korea. The mighty NFL, its symbol a heroic shield redolent of warriors and legionnaires, strides the world like a Colossus, almost as much as the American Empire (and the NFL shield features white stars in a blue field, just like the American flag), and these two dread monstrosities share that repressed violence at their core, occasionally poking through like the bones of the quarterback's broken leg. Maybe bubbling even further below the surface the night of Theisman's gruesome injury was this dim awareness that my military adventure was, ultimately, a journey into the essence and function of violence, something essential but unpleasant that I had largely avoided through most of my early life. Watching something as exciting, expensive, and violent as Monday Night Football may have been enhanced by the tingle of having learned a truth written in invisible ink in the Book of the Cultural Repressed—that sometimes the empire must be subdued by violence or its threat. Why else would the "American" army have half or more of its duty stations outside of the country? In the Platonic dialogue, some character would answer, "there are monsters at large in the world, and nothing cute about the threat that Kim Il-sung presents from North Korea," only to be rebutted that it wasn't like the Great Leader-Comrade was menacing the Canadian border with his fence-lights and rant-artists. And then, if neither character was Socrates, you would have to figure out for yourself whom to support, what would be the consequences of supporting either one. *Why don't you judge for yourselves what is right?*

Farewell to Football?

Is it the definition of empire or exceptionalism to imagine your shores everywhere in the world? Isn't that megalomania?

I had earned my college degree in English literature, could rightly claim the title of a Word Man, and I took a close look at the words here. The Giants were playing the Redskins that night—the *Redskins*, a scandal of a moniker, like calling a team The N-Word, a name dripping with the Trail-of-Tears history of imperial violence. Maybe that's how the NFL worked, just like the American Empire. Even the name of the Washington NFL franchise carried that threat.

Ah, well. "The problem is to understand the battlefield as well as the game of football," Fehrenbach had written, Zen-on-the-Imjin wise and inscrutable, recognizing how much more willing Americans were to sacrifice for team sports than to prepare for war (p. xi). "The problem is not to see what is desirable, or nice, or politically feasible, but what is necessary." He might as well have thrown in "cute" along with "nice." So there's nothing "cute" about a name like *Redskins* associated with the capital of the American Empire and representing one of the old-guard franchises of the NFL (and the last to integrate its roster, and then only when a cabinet officer from the federal government threatened to evict them from their stadium if they didn't), but what is *necessary* about such a public obscenity?

That kind of question, which ambiguously invites us to travel or escape the Left Hand Path, seems like just the kind of vexation the Serpent spends his days slithering across the face of the earth to track us down and pose to us.

CHAPTER 6

• • •

Free Fallin' (1991)

"War must always be for a cause, a transcendental purpose: it must not be to restore the Union, but to make
men free; it must not be to save the balance of world
power from falling into unfriendly hands, but to make
the world safe for democracy; it must not be to rescue
allies, but to destroy evil."

(T. R. FEHRENBACH, *THIS KIND OF WAR*, P. 181)

• • •

JANUARY 27, 1991: Super Bowl XXV. New York Giants 20, Buffalo Bills 19,
Tampa Stadium. Things aren't always what they seem and memory can
reshape our sense of what happened. The story of Super Bowl XXV is
often reduced to: "Scott Norwood misses a 47 yard field goal to lose the
game for Buffalo." And according to the credo that "the story is whatever
happened," this is true enough, Norwood misses that kick. But no single
story covers *all* that happened, let alone what could have happened.

For Bill Belichick, the Giants' defensive coordinator, that story was
written the week before, when he started studying the film of Buffalo's
"K-gun" offense, so named because quarterback Jim Kelly ran a high-
powered up-tempo offense mostly out of the shotgun formation, backed
up off the line where he could get a good look at what the defense was
presenting. The Bills had led the league in scoring that year. The Giants

had beaten Joe Montana's high-flying San Francisco 49ers by holding them to a single offensive touchdown and scoring a bunch of field goals to win the NFC title, 15-13 (a triumph of gritty Jersey Springsteen and the E-Street Band over slick bay-area Huey Lewis and the News), and Belichick's task would be to ensure a similar outcome in the Super Bowl. The next day, his conclusion from all-night study of the Bills' offense shocked his proud linebackers: "If Thomas runs for a hundred yards, we win this game" (in Halberstam, p. 173). As far as the Giants' defense was concerned, that game was won when their starting lineup included only two down linemen and three linebackers—and *four* cornerbacks and two safeties (Dave Duerson was available if they went with a three-safety look). Their job was to shut down Buffalo's downfield threats, receivers James Lofton and Andre Reed, and confuse quarterback Jim Kelly as he read their coverage schemes. Let Thurman Thomas get his yards on the ground. That was their plan, and how it came to pass in the Giants' victory is one way to tell that story.

Here's a very simple story that also accounts for what happened: a 47-yard field goal under pressure at the end of the climactic game of the long NFL season makes for a tough kick (the best kickers in the league typically make that one only 8 times out of 10 tries), and the Bills could have done a better job of getting Norwood into position for the attempted field goal.

Here's another story, this one probably resulting from decayed memories of what really happened and the subtle (and not-so-subtle) insinuation of narratives from other sources: The Super Bowl in January 1991 was this great moment of American unity and patriotism, with Whitney Houston belting out a national anthem so heartfelt and patriotic and powerful that it officially kicked off the war in Iraq, which the heroic coalition forces maneuvering across the desert under American leadership then wrapped up with a decisive victory against the evil dictator Saddam Hussein before Norwood's kick sailed wide right. No more Vietnams, no more light at the end of a long tunnel for America, we want our victory and we want it right away.

Now, a little clarification from the objective side: the timing of the Persian Gulf War was actually more dispersed, with the air war starting on January 17, ten days before the Super Bowl, and the ground war "kicking off" on February 24, four weeks after the big game, and ending about one hundred hours later. Subjectively, I wasn't feeling so patriotic, or at least not so bellicose. I watched the Super Bowl with my fellow graduate students Jon and Lara, a married couple, salt-of-the-earth folks from Pennsylvania who rapidly became like family to me, willing to put up with my aggravation. I'm sure they got fed up hearing me crow about how I'd seen the Giants play in that same Tampa Stadium long ago—back when the Giants sucked, in that same stadium where Led Zeppelin toppled The Beatles' attendance record! They had a big color TV, a "console" if I remember correctly, much better than trying to encompass the Super Bowl on that tiny B&W portable set I had in my cramped apartment. I used to sing Beatles songs with Lara, and Jon and I learned the whole Tom Petty *Full Moon Fever* album, the one with all the hits like "I Won't Back Down" and "Free Fallin'," song by song (those tunes are easy to learn and fun to play on acoustic guitar, but the album isn't really something you would sit down and listen to decades later). With them, and some other students in the graduate program in literature at Binghamton University, I'd taken part in a few protests against what I considered a rush into a war that wasn't clearly necessary. With time I would come to understand how that war was not all that it appeared, either, and that what didn't appear probably deserved more of our attention.

My contract with the Army was concluded, I'd "served my country" in the infantry and in the special forces, "defended freedom" at American outposts in Asia and Europe, and had almost certainly gotten more out of the deal in good times and personal growth than I'd put in to it. I held no grudge and was not particularly anti-military. I was just moving on, taking an apprenticeship in teaching at Binghamton High School—alma mater of Rod Serling of *Twilight Zone* fame—and earning a quick Master of Arts in Teaching (MAT) degree at the university. Like a Rod Serling character, maybe that ad-man on the commuter train to Willoughby who starts to realize the toll his job as an image-manipulator is taking on his soul, I was a thinking man free to enact his conscience, however hazy its contents might be, an undisciplined and half-baked humanist mess of vaguely Christian morality and dimly-grasped ethical philosophy. Still, it added up to getting off that train headed for war, even a war that seemed to be part and parcel of the Super Bowl in a banner year for my team—the New York Giants.

For the life-long fan like me, the 1990 team that won it all stood as the full manifestation of the change in identity head coach Bill Parcells had wrought upon the G-men. Led by their defense, especially their fierce Pro-Bowl outside linebacker Lawrence Taylor, the Giants were tough, fundamentally sound, and not terribly exciting to watch, legendary for what they stopped from happening more than the action they sponsored on the field. On offense, in 1990 two running backs and the tight end all had more pass receptions (Dave Meggett with 39; Rodney Hampton 32; Mark Bavaro 33) than the top two wide receivers (Stephen Baker and Mark Ingram, 26 each). Under coordinator Bill Belichick, the defense ranked 1st in the league in scoring defense and 2nd in total defense by yards, while Ron Erhardt's conservative offense rated only 15th and 17th respectively by those measures. Fundamentally sound: the offense was best in the league with only 14 turnovers, and only 5 of those came off interceptions. Not terribly exciting: the offense ran the ball the second-most times of any team in the league, but only ranked 24th in yards per carry. The game plan for the Super Bowl was famous—Parcells told Erhardt, "shorten the game," with long time-consuming drives. The Giants ended up dominating time of possession in the Super Bowl, 40:33 to 19:27—to put that in perspective, the following year Washington beat Buffalo in the Super Bowl, 37-24, but only held a 36-24 edge in time of possession. Parcells' Giants *owned* the ball in that Super Bowl.

For the Giants fan, Bill Parcells was The Man. Intelligent, sarcastic, and rough on reporters, Jersey-born Duane Charles Parcells got results. After he took over as head coach in 1983, the team only suffered two losing seasons, and at the end of the 1986 season, they won it all. Super Bowl XXI, in January 1987, marked the return to greatness for the Giants, who hadn't won the league title since 1956, when Frank Gifford led the team in both rushing and receiving yards. In their first Super Bowl, Parcells' Giants came back from an early 10-7 deficit on the accurate passing of Phil Simms (22-25, 268, 3TD) to bury the Denver Broncos, 39-20. I had watched that game with my A-team in a bar in Burlington, Vermont, as we were in residence at Camp Ethan Allen Training Site at the time, deployed for winter warfare, learning to ski on the government's dime on the slopes at Stowe. A little later that winter we took a "field trip" to town to check out the big buzz about Oliver Stone's *Platoon*, after viewing which the sergeants debated its realism while I wondered what was its message. Stone had studied at Yale for a while around the time when George W. Bush was leading football cheers from the sidelines there. Stone dropped out, joining the Army and going to Vietnam as an enlisted soldier. In *Platoon*, he seemed to be working out some sort of allegory about sacrifice and the dualism of the human soul, depicting his surrogate, Chris Taylor, in vaguely Greek-mythological terms as the son of two warring fathers, the sergeants Elias and Barnes. My sergeants were a lot more interested in how sloppy the noise and light discipline was on the patrols the movie depicted. The Super Bowl was an easier consensus to reach: Giants win, Parcells The Man. There's your story.

In 1990, it had all come together again, the toughest, most fundamentally sound of the Parcells teams, winning even when Phil Simms went down with an injury, winning it all in a game made especially dramatic by the context of the war. And then, for Giants fans, just that quickly the dream was over. Parcells retired after the season for health reasons, and Ray Handley took the 1991 team to an 8-8 exercise in mediocrity, which would prove to be his ceiling as a head coach. In 1991, Parcells' most indispensable assistant, Bill Belichick, was gone, too, starting his career as a head coach at Cleveland. It wasn't the end of anything, really, and Parcells and Belichick would extend the story of their collaborations with later stints coaching the New England Patriots and New York Jets, all the endings a bit ragged. And that war in Iraq that got off to such a musical start with Whitney Houston's national anthem, well, that ending turned out a bit ragged, too.

• • •

"Runnin' Down a Dream"

That fall semester of 1990 proved to be a triumph for the monastic lifestyle, a logical extension to my military mini-career. I was living in a cramped apartment in Binghamton, surrounded by books, studying my butt off, working all the time, committed to what I was doing. As my MAT advisor had predicted, the semester was action-packed, and focused on a singular purpose: to become the most effective high-school English teacher possible. Like the song says, I was running down a dream, going wherever it leads—part of the adventure was not knowing where it would lead, part of the mystery not knowing what dream I was running down, part of the predicament not knowing who I was. I had taken some risks to get into graduate school after the first moves of my post-Army life proved unsound, when I took a job and was laid off only months thereafter. The shock of that bump in the road helped reveal what I really wanted, mainly scholarship and teaching.

If teaching is preaching, then literary studies, criticism and especially theory, are theology, the systematic practice of purposeful and meaningful personal encounter with the sacred Word. It was the theology that brought me back to the university. Later, with Episcopal pragmatism, I would realize I had to work, and teaching was a noble profession, and I knew where I could probably find a job.

Before I left the Army in 1988, I had tried to get into the highest-church seminary of them all, applying to a doctoral program in literature at Yale. *Rejected.* Turning from the Word to the world, I'd gone the conventional route with a "headhunter" firm and scored an entry-level production-management position at a manufacturing plant in York, PA.

Divinely ignorant of even the basics of economics, I didn't realize until too late that the company was undergoing the scourge of late '80's American business, the leveraged-buyout. I'd been hired in September, and when I came back from the Thanksgiving holiday, I got the news: *Laid Off.* Something seemed afoot here, some lesson masquerading as circumstance.

I retreated to Norwich, and quickly enough found my way into an intriguing, if frustrating, opportunity. I applied for work as a substitute teacher, and someone noticed my military experience. I was called into an administrator's office and offered a mission, a real choice mission: would I like to try teaching "incarcerated youth"? Why not? The job entailed being escorted by an armed deputy into the library in the basement of the county sheriff's office, whither the young prisoner would be brought (I guess they figured a military guy would be less likely to freak out under those conditions). I could work with him on anything we wanted within the general framework of the high-school curriculum and the limitations of the few books available in the library. I got the impression that I was supposed to "relate to him" and help him see the benefits of education. I quickly realized the frustrating part: he could choose not to participate whenever he wanted, like staying home sick from school, and this meant that an incarcerated teenager was determining whether I worked—and got paid (it was an hourly position). Still, this was a stimulating initiation into the most basic dynamic of teaching, individual tutoring as old as the School of Athens.

The job also brought me into contact with a mentor with whom I would work closely for the next six years, Dave Paul, the English department chair at Norwich High School. The district administrator who hired me had suggested I get in touch with him, as he was considered the "go-to guy" for high school teaching, a guru, one of the principal instructors for the pre-service training for newly-hired teachers. He turned out to look like a guru, short, heavy, and bearded, and more to the point proved to be a very bright, humorous, committed, and reflective educator, and he initiated me into a teaching practice that I have built upon ever since. Practice informed by theory (his first precept of composition theory: "fluency precedes control"). Dave was teaching the "dual-placement" college-credit senior English class in conjunction with Syracuse University, and that curriculum included an introduction to the major contemporary schools of critical theory—this was news to me (my undergraduate program, like most, concentrated almost exclusively on the canonical literature itself), the dawn of theological consciousness and a multiplication of interpretive possibilities. We ended up having some of the most stimulating conversations either of us could recall, as I drew upon my background in literature and philosophy, along with the weird sense of humor I had evolved in the strangely ironic and often cynical atmosphere of military service, and he brought to bear the experience of decades of teaching, all these riches of literary theory, and the added dimension of his Catholic faith. Dave and his wife conducted the pre-marital instruction for Catholic couples in their parish, and his ability to discourse back and forth between world and Word struck a chord in me. He was teaching Walker Percy, one of the essays from *The Message in the Bottle,* and I ended up providing a few guest-lectures on my favorite writer for his college-credit class.

Dave helped me secure a long-term substitute position at the high school, the best trial-run anyone could make prior to seeking certification as a teacher: I would stand in for an experienced English teacher while she took 10 weeks maternity leave. All the responsibilities: home room, advisor to the school newspaper, committees, as well as five teaching periods of 10th grade English, write the lessons, run the classes, grade the papers. Sink or swim. While I had my share of days when I swore sinking would have been an improvement on how bad I was in the classroom, and I couldn't fathom how different classroom discipline could be from military discipline, and how far from my grasp, I survived, and even more so felt like this was the challenge for me, a vocation, the work that I should pursue. I could contribute to the good of society or some such humanist nonsense. So now my mission converted to getting back into one of the Houses of the Holy, in this case, the university, my alma mater.

Steven Liparulo

I had included a Master's program at Binghamton as a fallback position at the same time I applied to Yale, so I was already in on admissions. Financial aid was a different story. I had missed all the deadlines, and had to resort to the desperate histrionics I'd learned growing up in my disordered family. Instead of taking the patient route, continuing to work any jobs I could land and straighten out my finances and enter the graduate program the following fall, I was bound and determined to get what I wanted when I wanted it. I sold off guitars and hi-fi gear at fire-sale prices and challenged this guy in financial aid to let me put up a couple of hundred, and he could toss me out if I didn't have the next installment in a month. Who knows, maybe *this* administrator noticed my military background, too, and thought it best to accommodate this passionate trained killer? Stupid heroics.

I got in for the spring semester in 1990, and set right to work indulging in a heavy diet of theology: Renaissance Literature, Romanticism, Practical Criticism, and Milton. It was like eating four desserts for dinner. More than anything, I wanted to get back to the poetry of John Donne, which I found compelling in its mix of mysticism and violence ("Batter my heart, three-person'd God"), the wildness of the "metaphysical conceits" yoking together disparate elements, talking about Christ like a lover. In that Renaissance Literature seminar, led by an old friend from undergraduate days, Professor Al Vos, I engaged with the theory that more than any other would render the world more coherent for me and anchor my teaching practice going forward. Stephen Greenblatt's *Renaissance Self-Fashioning* encoded the critical school of New Historicism, an interdisciplinary approach drawing upon the social sciences as well as literary history, a "cultural poetics" that read texts with regard to poststructuralist concerns such as power, representation, and circulation. While I initially found that New Historicism could help me delve deeper into the "desperate contingency" of John Donne's poetry, translating Greenblatt's concept of "absolute play" (itself an intensification of Clifford Geertz's notion of "deep play" or irrationally high-stakes symbolizing) from the drama of Christopher Marlowe to Donne's verse, it was Greenblatt's interpretation of Shakespeare's Iago that provided a sustaining vision for the critical enterprise.

Shakespeare's greatest villain, Iago is a bitter lieutenant who torments his commanding officer Othello with lurid insinuations of his wife's infidelity. Paradoxically, the villain Iago represents the quintessential Renaissance Man: exploiting free choice, a self-made man. As Greenblatt understands him, Iago prefigures all the great manipulative climbing politicians of the post-monarchist era, mastering improvisations of power, "the ability both to capitalize on the unforeseen and to transform given materials into one's own scenario" (p. 227). Always rushing forward to disguise his utter lack of proof for his accusations, Iago manipulates language to create the appearance of established facts, which he then seems to build upon in a rational manner. At his baldest, the ensign provides this lawyerly improvisation to excuse himself from having to present direct evidence:

If imputation and strong circumstances
Which lead directly to the door of truth
Will give you satisfaction, you might have 't. (3.3.463-465)

Having thus insidiously prevaricated over what will provide "satisfaction," Iago then alludes twice in the same conversation to "other proof," as if building on an already-established substantial dossier of evidence (488, 501). I've recently begun to wonder how much influence the speeches of Iago had upon Milton's representation of Satan in *Paradise Lost*, whose temptation speech to Eve includes a similar revved-up, no-time-to-reflect urgency and false-evidentiary structure. For example, Satan poses no fewer than four urgent questions to Eve in the space of thirteen lines, and then improvises this stuttering conclusion to impose on Eve:

God therefore cannot hurt ye, and be just;
Not just, not God; not feared then, nor obeyed:
Your fear itself of death removes the fear. (IX, 700-703)

Of course, Shakespeare and Milton both had direct access to the source of all lies—as do all of us with souls alive in this fallen world, wherein the Father of Lies is free to bustle and appeal to the disordered passions of our human souls.

Turning from the Word to the world, I found out through a classmate about the MAT program, which in one "action-packed" fall semester, plus a mini-course the preceding summer, took care of all of the educational coursework required for permanent teacher certification in New York State, provided one completed the attached master's degree requirements in literature. At the headlong rate I was going, I would complete the degree in 17 months. I took the MAT mini-course in the summer, along with a literature class in American short fiction, and I was set up for the internship semester in the fall.

Toward the end of the summer of 1990, Saddam Hussein's Iraqi forces invaded their neighbor, the small oil emirate Kuwait, and the United States began the buildup to an intervention that could eventuate in war. From 1981 to 1988 I had been an officer in a military in transition from the debased self-image of losers in Vietnam to a fighting force marked by increased professionalism as defense budgets swelled under President Ronald Reagan, and I was curious about how this whole thing might play out. I had friends whose lives might be at stake in the upcoming conflict, too. It was idle curiosity at best, though—the page had turned, I hadn't really stayed in touch with those military friends, I was a civilian, I had my hands full with the MAT semester, and more than anything, I was looking forward to a great year from the New York Giants.

My days were squeezed pretty tight. I was in Binghamton High School all morning, responsible for teaching one class (an elective in poetry) and observing and team-teaching another with my faculty supervisor, an experienced teacher who gave me plenty of room to work and grow. As part of the MAT program, we were also tasked to conduct action-research and to work up a case-study of a student. The rest of the day included classes at the university twice a week, reading and assignments for MAT "Foundations of Secondary Education" course-work, and planning and grading from the high school classes. My day off for the week was Sunday, when I would play touch football in the park with classmates and then rush home in time for the kickoff of the Giants games like a modern-day Fred Exley. That was about the only TV I watched, on a little black-and-white portable set a poet had given me when I helped him move.

The big exception to that TV rule came in late September, when for five consecutive nights PBS broadcast the Ken Burns *Civil War* series. It was essentially a combination of a narrated film-strip, like you used to watch in social-studies class in fifth grade, and a talking-heads documentary. Beyond the heavy use of powerful period photos from Matthew Brady and an emotionally resonant musical score, what made it work was the talent. Off-screen voices like Jason Robards, Morgan Freeman, and Julie Harris read from primary sources in riveting vocal performances, and the narrator, American historian David McCullough, provided a supple and mellifluous through-line to the account of a war that was fought in over 10,000 places by more than three million Americans, according to the program's opening lines. On-screen, the show was stolen by historian-novelist Shelby Foote, a close friend of Walker Percy since adolescence (*Love in the Ruins* is dedicated to Foote), whose facility with historical anecdote combined with his mint-julep Mississippi drawl to enchant viewers with stories about our shared national cataclysm.

By the time the Civil War was over, the New York Giants were 4-0 on the season, and would run it up to 10-0 before losing to Philadelphia on November 25. I felt like I had a winning streak going at Rod Serling's alma mater, too.

• • •

"I Won't Back Down"

The characterization of General Ulysses Grant in the PBS *Civil War* series benefited not only from the hard-ridden yet commanding voice of Jason Robards, but also from the clarity and conciseness of the source material, mostly Grant's memoir. Grant presents a complex figure in

American history, his story often reduced to a caricature of drunken corruption in the White House, but several of his gifts are undisputed. From his days as a cadet at West Point, he was a master equestrian, some say the best horseman of his age. He seemed to have a natural facility for mathematics—in his memoirs he relates that his ambition early in his military career was to teach math at West Point—and this likely helped him to envision the battlefield and manage the movements of massive formations in fluid combat situations (Perry, pp. 12-14). His other clear gift as a military leader was his simple and direct writing style (p. 75). His written orders rarely left room for question or confusion, and he could produce under pressure. His capability as a writer would save his family at the end of his life.

On the negative side of the ledger, there's little question that Grant had some trouble with alcohol and that he was a poor hand at managing money. By the time he was dying of throat cancer, probably the result of a lifetime of smoking cigars, his family was in deep financial trouble. Mark Twain entered the situation and helped Grant negotiate a publishing deal for his memoirs that included a gargantuan first royalty payment to Grant's widow of $200,000—in 1886 dollars, a fortune, with subsequent payments to quickly more than double that amount (Perry, p. 233). Twain understood a simple fact that may not be so clear to us today: Grant was by far the most well-known and admired American of the 19th century, the general whose 4th of July victory at Vicksburg in 1863 added an exclamation point to the Union repulse of Pickett's charge and Confederate surge at Gettysburg, and his story as the Everyman who rose to the top when more glamorous contemporaries couldn't handle the strain would appeal to a broad audience. During the Civil War, the simple and intent fighting man Grant had been far more popular than the controversial President, Abraham Lincoln. Lincoln might have set the goal, but Grant was The Man Who Saved the Union. So in 1886, with one last opportunity to win a victory for his family, Grant raced against death to produce what many consider the finest military memoir written in English—certainly the best by an American general. More recent American military heroes such as Dwight Eisenhower (who, like Grant, may have made his way to the very top of the World-War-II chain of command in part because of his ability to organize and produce clear and forceful writing), Norman Schwarzkopf, and Colin Powell have all pointed to Grant's memoir as their exemplar.

The military memoir is the kind of "cultural text" that can benefit from New Historical study, a genre engaged in constructing images and circulating representations, setting personal narratives against the backdrop of highly-charged political circumstances (since all important military memoirs are war stories, and all modern wars are at root political projects). Schwarzkopf and Powell, authors of the military strategy for the first Gulf War, were both Vietnam veterans (Powell also commanded an infantry battalion in the Second Infantry Division in Korea about a decade before I served there). In their memoirs, both are fairly explicit about understanding the damage that war and its political mismanagement did to the public image of the military—and the opportunity for rehabilitation that they were granted as the Gulf War came to pass. Schwarzkopf writes that in 1972, reeling from the impact of the failures in Vietnam, "the Army was lost and groping to find its way" (p. 189). This sense of restoring something lost factored into the big charismatic general's positive-self-talk inner monologue prior to a press conference in the fall of 1990, related in his memoir: "Think back," he tells himself, "to what caused the disenchantment of the American public with Vietnam: they felt that they were constantly being misled with false body counts and optimistic talk about the light at the end of the tunnel" (p. 334).

Instead, Schwarzkopf and Powell leveraged the massive media coverage of the coming war to present their game plan directly to the public— *we've got this*, they wanted to assure the American public, we're going to win this game before it's ever even played because we have a plan to use America's beautiful lethal technology with massive industrial impact. Schwarzkopf identified four progressive battlefield goals: attack leadership and command and control; gain and maintain air superiority; cut enemy supply lines; and destroy the Republican Guard, Iraq's nominally "elite" armored fighting force (p. 381). In a widely broadcast briefing, the Washington-insider Powell summarized the plan even more succinctly, famously claiming that we are going to cut it off and then kill it (p. 509). This was a lot more like Belichick and Parcells coming out of film study with simple and coherent objectives—*let them run, stop the pass; shorten the game*—and a lot less like the daily press briefings in Saigon that eventually became ridiculed as "the five o'clock follies." Reading Grant probably helped them gain that sense of focus, or at least to represent themselves as such when it was their turn to write the story of what happened.

In his memoir, Colin Powell mentions that he and others in the George H. W. Bush administration got preview copies of the *Civil War* episodes as they were planning the Persian Gulf War. He reports this conversation with Schwarzkopf after the series aired: "At least now people know what war is about," Powell reports saying, with Schwarzkopf replying that "it's damn good they do" (p. 492). In this telling, they make it sound like Ken Burns had provided America with its Nick Adams moment for the Gulf War—no more innocence after hearing about how Burnside screwed up at Fredericksburg! In this exchange these two four-star generals demonstrate the political understanding that got them those stars (the US Senate has to confirm the appointments and promotions of general officers), reflecting the importance of managing images and expectations. Schwarzkopf writes that watching the tapes of *The Civil War* provided by Secretary of Defense Dick Cheney "renewed my conviction that if I had to send my troops into battle, I would find a way to minimize the loss of life" (p. 395).

Ultimately the Bush administration's larger campaign to sell that war to the American public presents what I consider to be a case study in improvisations of power. Powell worried about how "President Bush had taken to demonizing Saddam Hussein in public just as he had Manuel Noriega [leading up to the 1989 invasion of Panama]. 'We are dealing with Hitler revisited,' he [Bush] said on one occasion, and described

Saddam as 'a tyrant unmoved by human decency'" (p. 491). As T. R. Fehrenbach had observed in the context of the Korean War, his degree of irony hard to determine, for Americans "war must always be for a cause, a transcendental purpose: … it must not be to rescue allies, but to destroy evil" (p. 181). It's easy to imagine Bush, a sinner like me, ambitious like Iago, playing to his audience with these manipulative allusions to the most recognizably evil figure in the 20th century (Saddam helped by sporting that villain's moustache). Powell's concerns were mostly pragmatic, however, wary of the eventual let-down in initially representing Saddam as an evil to be destroyed only later to leave him in power—as we did—since the United Nations resolution under which the war was prosecuted only covered forcing Iraqi troops out of Kuwait. Saddam would continue to present problems for more than a decade, a problem only "solved" after further improvisations of power and evidentiary legerdemain that put Colin Powell in an awkward position at the UN early in the 21st century.

It took investigative journalists at *Washington Monthly* about a year to dig into the depths of the image-fashioning involved in selling the American people their first Gulf War. In one highly-publicized episode, a Kuwaiti "hospital volunteer" testified to a Congressional committee about Iraqi forces dumping sick babies out of their incubators as they occupied a Kuwaiti hospital. Later research determined that the fifteen-year-old Kuwaiti girl had never volunteered at that hospital, but was in fact the daughter of the Kuwaiti ambassador to the United States, and the whole story was the product of collaboration between "friends of Kuwait" and a public relations firm, Hill and Knowlton, that had represented Big Tobacco in the recent past and would help the Church of Scientology try to improve its image in the not-too-distant future (Wright, p. 217).

As the war got under way, the mainstream media seemed to understand the opportunities for big business in war stories, and started to fall in line with the favorable war-coverage that would intensify to the point of fawning obeisance bordering on idolatry in the coming decades. In his memoir Powell describes an aviator interviewed by a TV reporter immediately upon his return from a combat mission over Iraq, who replies, in part, "I thank God I'm an American fighter pilot." Powell writes: "I sat there, melting. This was the military I wanted the country to see, not the old stereotyped dropout from nowheresville, but smart, motivated, patriotic young Americans, the best and the brightest" (p. 508).

I had seen this contrast in the characteristic images of our fighting men up-close and personal when I matriculated from service in an infantry battalion to a special forces group. In the infantry, nearly all the men under my leadership were younger than me and almost certainly less well-educated (some were no doubt "dropouts from nowheresville" and headed for nothing but trouble). In the 10th Special Forces (SF) Group, on the A-team I commanded most of the NCO's were older and more experienced in the military than me. In the group as a whole there were plenty of sergeants with college degrees, not to mention all the high-flown qualifications from military schools all over the world. Officially a *Special Forces Operational Detachment-A* (ODA), a "Green Beret" A-team is a unique military unit, comprising one commissioned officer, one warrant officer, and ten non-commissioned officers (NCO's). Commanding an ODA is like a young, smart, but inexperienced coach taking over as offensive coordinator for an NFL team with a seasoned Pro-Bowl quarterback and lots of veterans at the skill positions (in both cases, the numbers add up to 12). Young Coach has to recognize that they expect him to be a good organizer and planner to help them sort through myriad details by providing detached analysis and clear priorities, and Young Coach has to let them take care of their own areas of expertise. I don't fool myself into thinking I was a particularly good SF officer, but instead am grateful for the chance to learn what it's like to work with the best and brightest, people far more skilled than me, and to provide them something valuable that I could contribute—an analytical process that could provide a clear vision for how to get things done. At the very least, I could provide a healthy dose of Socratic skepticism that might help us avoid obvious mistakes.

Farewell to Football?

The Five Paragraph Operations Order continued to supply the "cultural codes" for organizing our narrative as an A-team, just as it had on the Korean DMZ, as we lived out missions from planning through execution, however different the details of those missions were from infantry to special forces. It also organized our cast of characters. The Situation paragraph is largely an intelligence function, and the A-team includes an intelligence sergeant. My job was to review his work and make sure that any implications of the enemy situation (which to the military way of thinking includes the weather) on our plans for executing the mission made sense. The Mission paragraph itself is directly dictated by higher headquarters (we used to get it on a little slip of paper when I was running patrols on the DMZ), and it was my job, in conjunction with the team sergeant (technically the operations sergeant, and effectively the quarterback), to analyze the mission in order to generate a concept of the operation. This is basically how the Execution paragraph, the heart of the matter and the game plan, gets developed—how are we going to organize, move, and act to accomplish the mission? Run the ball to set up the pass? Come out passing to open up the defense? Line up with three wides? The most important decision I would often make was whether we would operate as a single team or split into two smaller units—if so, how would the team subdivide? Depending on the type of mission, the team sergeant would be assisted by the weapons sergeant and engineer in developing detailed plans for execution. The warrant officer, technically the assistant detachment commander, was typically responsible for the Logistics (or Service and Support) paragraph, assisted by the engineer and medical sergeant. The Communications (or Command and Signal) paragraph was the responsibility of the communication sergeant to plan, although as the commander it was where I had the most specific and direct responsibility. In the field, I was personally accountable for communication with higher headquarters, typically using low-power high-efficiency radio transmissions that bounced signals off a layer of the ionosphere and could provide secure communications over hundreds or even thousands of miles using compact field radios and precision cut antennae. Even though I was technically responsible, as every commander is, for "everything that happens or fails to happen" in my command, exerting that responsibility in concert with eleven other highly-trained and motivated professionals was an ongoing and fluid learning process for me.

In the late 1980's, before the situation in the Middle East started absorbing most of our military resources, 10th SF Group focused on the European theater and the deeply-troubling *Dr. Strangelove* logic of the Cold War (Mutually Assured Destruction—MAD), and we were the Army's experts in winter warfare. One training mission of ours in particular stands out as a representative "day at the office" for me back then. As part of a group-wide exercise, my team was given the mission to infiltrate a site on the Fort Drum, New York, military reservation to conduct a raid on an enemy installation. In practical terms, this meant that the team went into "isolation" barracks at Fort Devens for a couple of days to work up detailed plans for making a parachute drop at Fort Drum and skiing for several days through the woods to reach the target, which we would assault with live fire and explosives.

The planning ranged from studying the terrain and identifying a route for skiing—with heavy rucksacks, at night—to developing procedures for safely handling live ammunition and C-4 explosives and their detonators during a winter airborne drop, to deciding which rations to take and how many. The medic had to conduct refresher training on cold-weather injuries, the engineer similarly got us back up to speed on rigging C-4 with time-delay fuses, the intelligence sergeant and I subjected the weather reports to intense study, and the communication sergeant worked closely with me to make sure we would be able to maintain our wireless connection. We would be operating independently a long way from help in the frozen wilds of far northern New York, so if anything went wrong, we would need to be 100% sure about our radios. It took all the experience and ingenuity of the warrant officer and team sergeant to work out the plans for loading all the necessary gear into our rucksacks, which would be rigged to our bodies for the jump, and packing our skis into sleds called Akhios which would be airdropped along with the team. The level of collaboration and expertise was phenomenal, the excitement mounting like a team getting ready for a playoff game.

Kick-off: on a cold, sunny afternoon, the ramp dropped at the back of a C-130 transport plane, and my team groaned to stand up, loaded down with our field gear, rucksacks, parachutes, and weapons. We were wearing "Mickey Mouse" boots, oversized rubber boots filled with felt insulation in valved air chambers between heavy rubber outer layer and lighter inner rubber "skin," and while these were the choice footwear to avoid cold-weather injuries on the ground, they made the shuffle down the ramp even more awkward. We hooked up, and on the green light stepped off the ramp into the cold air a thousand feet or so above Fort Drum. Not quite as smooth as the barrage-balloon jump in Belgium, this ramp-exit was still a lot easier than coming out the door on the side of the aircraft, which creates an exit shock like getting sucked up a vacuum-cleaner hose. Just trudge down the ramp until you step out onto air—for a few sublime moments, *free fallin'*. Wait for that opening shock. Look up, check for deployment of the "silk," look down to make sure you weren't stepping on someone else's canopy, look all around to orient yourself to the drop zone. Landing in the heavy snow on the drop zone was an unnaturally gentle stop, almost arresting in its silence, a dramatic contrast to the usual car-wreck collision of the "parachute landing fall" they teach you in jump school. You just stuck there in the snow, a raisin in the pudding—and then realized that you weren't going anywhere until the guy closest to the sled worked his way free and got his skis off the Akhio. Just like you planned it, he came gliding down the line, handing out skis from the sled dragging behind him. It took forever, though, and just to drive the point home, the Air Force overflew the drop zone with A-10 Wart Hog attack planes, which in "real life" would have been chewing us up with 30mm rotary cannons. (Or maybe they were demonstrating their capability to protect us as we got off the drop-zone—in the "simulated intensity" of these training exercises, it was hard to know who was friend and foe sometimes.)

We cleared the drop zone, skied for a couple of hours until the light started to fade, and then occupied a patrol base. We had planned and rehearsed it, all part of the Execution paragraph, everyone had their part to play, and it mostly went off without a hitch. Then, in accordance with Paragraph Four, we set up North Face tents and broke out MSR camp stoves for hot drinks and food. My job was to carry out Paragraph Five, help the commo sergeant cut the antenna and to write up, encode, and transmit the message: "we're good to go."

After a leisurely morning spent drinking coffee and checking out all our equipment, we skied all day, approaching the target site around dusk. We stepped out of character briefly to coordinate with a range-control officer who supervised the live-fire exercise, but soon were back in our tactical mode, approaching the target using patrolling techniques to observe the target, finalize the plan for actions at the objective, and make the last cross-loads of equipment, getting all the explosives in the hands of the engineers and all the controlling pyrotechnics with the team sergeant and me. The medics, whose SF training qualified them somewhere near the level of a physician's assistant, were standing by in an "administrative" mode, since this was a real live-fire exercise at night, and potentially dangerous. The target was an ice-fishing hut, and at my signal (doctrine says "initiate an attack with your most lethal weapon," so I imagine we opened up with a high-explosive round from a 40 mm grenade launcher, the M-203 which I tended to favor as my field weapon), we commenced to fire according to the plan devised by the weapons sergeant to distribute fire in support of the concept of the operation. Once all our ammo had been fired—it was easier to shoot it all on the range than to account for any live ammunition on our exit—we moved onto the target and the engineers rigged the hut for demolition. We moved back to our assault position, taking cover as the engineers called out "FIRE IN THE HOLE." With a low thumping roar, the ice-fishing hut disappeared into a cloud of splinters. Once I got a head count that confirmed we were all safe and sound, I called off the play of the problem and asked the engineers and weapons sergeants to take a bow for

Farewell to Football?

a mission well-planned and executed. Our cheers echoed through the cold dark woods surrounding the range.

And then the fatigue set in, hard and cold, as we lost the blood-pumping heat from the live-fire exercise and realized that we had at least an hour of clearing the range and re-packing our gear ahead of us, along with another hour or so of skiing to our next patrol base. We made it through the routine of setting up our camp, but with noticeably less clockwork zest than on the first night. I'm sure that every one of us, when our turn came to sleep, spent a moment in prayer thanking God that we had come through the mission thus far safe and successful, and maybe thanking God that we were American special forces soldiers. Sleep came quickly that night, and when the hour came to stand security in the cold dark, was pretty hard to fight off.

The next day we skied an hour or so to a pickup zone, where SF helicopters "exfiltrated" us all the way back to Fort Devens, showing off the "nap-of-the-earth" capabilities of their Black Hawks—that plus the forced-air heat blasting away at us still bundled in our winter field-gear gave us all that back-of-the-station-wagon car-sick feeling for a while. They eventually cut it out and flew nice and level for the last hour or so. The battalion commander had beer waiting when we got back to the "isolation" barracks and completed our after-action review. That settled our stomachs.

And so at their best were the days of my life, my days at the office commanding the best and the brightest, from 1986 to 1988. After that peak experience, I had fulfilled my contract with a year of reserve service, and found the slack pace and lowered standards of the part-time Army a little too close to "nowheresville," so I cut the cord entirely by resigning my commission. By the time of the great war to destroy evil in Iraq, like that long-winded Captain Willard in *Apocalypse Now* said, I wasn't even in their Army anymore, benefiting from some detached, analytical, and perhaps skeptical perspective on the whole affair. I couldn't say for sure, but it looked like a lot of *representation* going on.

In 1990, the mainstream media seemed like maybe it fell in love with "the best and the brightest" and lost track of the larger narrative.

If the war wasn't a football game and therefore a chance for stars to shine, what was it? One way to tell the story is as this amiable narrative about relationships: we were getting into this fight because Iraq had attacked our ally … Kuwait? The tumble of questions we should have been asking was worthy of Iago. Where is Kuwait? When and how had Kuwait become our friend? How many Americans knew who our friends and enemies were in 1990? Were we allied with Syria and the Soviet Union—wasn't there a Syrian general on Schwarzkopf's combined command staff, and hadn't the USSR chosen not to veto the UN resolutions authorizing this war? Hadn't we previously been allied with Iraq, providing them weapons, including chemical weapons, when they were fighting against Iran? Was Iran going to be allied with us in this war against Iraq? Why did General Schwarzkopf in his memoir describe Iran as an "Aryan" country while Iraq was "Arab"? How do those contrasting words relate to "Shia" and "Sunni"? Why did General Powell in his memoir describe the Saudi objections to American Bibles and female soldiers and Jewish worship services as "Arab" issues and not "Muslim" issues? Would Fehrenbach call this a war to rescue an ally or to destroy evil? Apparently our relationships in this bustling world were complicated, and would only grow more and more complicated as we moved more than half a million of our soldiers (with or without all their booze and prostitution and pornography) into the Islamic holy land and made war against a largely secular Arab state.

Apparently, there was no time to sort out these questions—the whole *point* of improvisation was breathless headlong urgency, Iago never granting Othello the chance to regroup—when the best and brightest were putting on a video-game show of air-power and smart-bombs, wowing all those fawning reporters with bombsight video of the Highway of Death. Of course, like the NFL, the broadcast news networks really are in the entertainment business. A few months before the war broke out in all its Super Bowl glory, President Bush had given the newsmen their kind of story, a defiant-hero sort of narrative: George Herbert Walker Bush, of all people, a sinner just like me, Episcopal son of patrician

Farewell to Football?

Senator Prescott Bush, like his father a Yale Skull and Bones man, had found his media bravado, started sounding like a Tom Petty song. "This will not stand," he had proclaimed to the knot of reporters greeting him while Marine One, his presidential helicopter, roared like a rock concert behind him as he approached their microphones, perhaps fighting back his Phillips-Academy-in-Andover instincts to make the auxiliary verb "shall not." *You can stand me up at the gates of Hell, but I won't back down.* This. Will. Not. Stand.

In the *Civil War* episode concerning the pivotal battle at Gettysburg, the high water mark of the Confederacy, Shelby Foote takes a page out of Faulkner, relating how every southern boy can imagine the scene just before Pickett's Charge, that sense that it hadn't happened yet—the counterfactual narrative. I imagine that every New York Giants fan, and probably every Buffalo Bills fan, though for different reasons, imagines a similar infinite present during the fourth quarter of that Super Bowl game in Tampa. Night has fallen and the day's battle is about to be decided, but no one has won or lost anything yet.

There we are, ever and always, wondering.

What if Pickett had made it to the top of Cemetery Ridge? What if Truman hadn't canned MacArthur in Korea? And what if that war in Iraq hadn't come to pass? What if the presence of all those American troops in Saudi Arabia hadn't radicalized Osama bin Laden? What if Prescott Bush's son *had* backed down and let Saddam Hussein's aggression stand? What if ….

What if Norwood makes the kick?

CHAPTER 7

• • •

Perfect Starts (1992)

MANDRAKE
When did you first... become... well, develop this theory?

RIPPER
Well, I first became aware of it, Mandrake, during the
physical act of love.

MANDRAKE
Hmm.

RIPPER
Yes, a profound sense of fatigue, a feeling of emptiness
followed. Luckily I was able to interpret these feelings
correctly. Loss of essence.

MANDRAKE
Hmm.

RIPPER
I can assure you it has not recurred, Mandrake. Women
sense my power and they seek the life essence. I do not
avoid women, Mandrake.

MANDRAKE
No.

Farewell to Football?

RIPPER
But I do deny them my essence.

(FROM STANLEY KUBRICK'S *DR. STRANGELOVE, OR HOW I
LEARNED TO STOP WORRYING AND LOVE THE BOMB*)

• • •

This is how we got to be champions.

NOVEMBER 14, 1992: Section IV Championship. Norwich 26, Johnson City 0, Schoellkopf Field, Ithaca, New York.

"This kid, Bear, was on the streets since he was in diapers. His older brother fell out of a chair in my class, dead drunk. Bear was a *tremendous* athlete. Bear had an imaginary friend, Martin, and he would talk to the opposing guys, talk to them about Martin. Bear was a street kid, he wasn't a *name* kid, but man, was he a competitor. I think about the Section IV Championship game at Cornell against Johnson City. He's covering the wide-out from Johnson City, and they throw a ball, and Bear looks like he's beat, but the ball's overthrown. The kid comes back and starts up, 'I had you beat, it's going to be a long day for you.' Bear answered him, 'no, you didn't. Martin had you deep, I had the under coverage.' That kid was *done*—beat by double coverage from an imaginary friend. Bear ran in a blocked punt for a touchdown. Caught a great pass. Had an interception, *turned the game around*, and was the MVP of that game! He's always going to have that."

Coach John Pluta is talking about a game played more than 20 years earlier, but it's as if he's watching the game live and calling it for a radio broadcast. Maybe that's because he's not really talking about football, he's talking about people, young men who really *needed* football, who benefited from the presence of a strong, demanding, caring male in their lives. A coach.

In particular, he's talking about a young man I knew pretty well, too. Bear was in my English class at Norwich High School in the early

90's, and so was his sister—but she had a different last name from him. I knew their mom, who is a waitress, and in fact the day before I met John Pluta for our interview in 2013, she served me lunch at a restaurant in town. Before I left, we had a brief chat, because my mother had coached Bear's mother long, long ago, when I was just in grade school, but Bear's mom still remembered what my mom taught her about waiting tables—if you learn how to use your head a little more, you can save your legs a whole lot of work. A little lesson in "theory and practice" there.

When John talked about how Bear wasn't a *name* kid, he was referring to the small-town code for *status*. When I was growing up in Norwich and my mother was working as a waitress I wasn't a name kid, either, and by the time I was in fourth grade, my mother's last name was different from mine. She married an alcoholic who would be dead before I graduated high school. When you teach and coach in public schools, you work with all kinds of kids from all kinds of homes with all kinds of names.

John is talking about a game played on the Astroturf at Schoellkopf Field, an unnaturally green pitch only a stone's throw from the World-War-I-era building with the battlements where my mother pinned on the gold bars when I was commissioned as an Army officer on the campus of Cornell University. Throwing the football was the key feature of the Norwich game plan that day, as Pluta explained to Tom Rowe of the Norwich *Evening Sun* at the time:

"They were almost always putting nine guys on the line, so we wanted to loosen them up a bit with the pass. We can throw the ball with the best of them and we did."

Not long after Bear started the scoring for the Purple Tornado with the return of that blocked punt for Norwich's first touchdown, quarterback Chris Maynard connected with the tight end for the second, followed not much later by another touchdown pass, this one to Bear, to take an 18-0 lead at half-time. The Norwich defense never let up, holding Johnson City to a meager 72 yards of total offense for the game, while the Purple Tornado "O" turned to the running game after the intermission, gaining 158 yards in the second half as they salted away the shutout.

That 1992 sectional championship was one of the crests of the wave John Pluta rode as head coach at Norwich. Descended from Slovakian immigrants who settled in the Binghamton area, he had come to Norwich as an assistant in 1986 and had taken over as head man three years later. In only his second year, he'd taken the team to a divisional championship, the first in twenty years. It was such a big deal that Pluta's wife, Ginny, collaborated with coaches and players to put together a scrapbook as a 1991 Christmas present for the head coach, presented to him at a banquet.

Chris Maynard's contribution to the scrapbook tells the whole story of coaching to me, and also says a lot about quarterbacks. The young man whose passing loosened up the Johnson City defense in 1992 was a keen-eyed observer in 1991.

It all started on August 19th. The coaching staff spelled it out during the first practice of the year. Mr. Pluta stood in front of us as he confidently told us we had an excellent chance at becoming Division III champions. As he said this, I looked in the eyes of the coaching staff and players in that room and I could tell that there were no doubters. This is how we got to be champions.

This is a scrawny sophomore quarterback (listed in the program at 6 feet, 135 pounds, he almost always wore black tights and close-fitting black long-sleeved undershirts beneath his purple and white football uniform, long, lean, and angular at the center of the storm), but here he is looking coaches and players alike in the eye and taking their measure. No doubters. And here is the quarterback making the call with a simple declarative sentence worthy of Hemingway. *This is how we got to be champions.*

While Chris Maynard would end up in my English class a year later, I can't take any credit for his lucid prose style. In fact, in August of 1991, while he was looking everyone in the eye, I was just getting ready to start my pre-service workshop as a newly-hired teacher at Norwich High School, thanks to a mentor who went out on a limb for me. In the world of college coaching, they have a phrase for the critical moment in the recruiting process when a position coach makes an impassioned pitch for a player he wants the head coach to close on for the team: it's called "standing on the table" for the player. Department Chair Dave Paul had gone to the high school principal to stand on the table to get me an interview, and I had done the rest, thanks to Dave's previous mentorship and all I had learned in the MAT program under Dr. Deborah Britzman in Binghamton. 1991 would be the start of my full-time tenure-track career as a high school English teacher.

The thing I notice more than 20 years later looking at Maynard's contribution to the scrapbook is the way he prepared the Norwich Football stationery, drawing parallel lines on the blank letterhead paper like a composer laying out staves prior to writing out a score. This is how quarterbacks tend to do things, very neat and orderly and with an overwhelming sense of control, black sleeves under crisp white jerseys. NFL TV analyst Phil Simms, who in his playing days led the New York Giants to the Super Bowl victory against Denver after the 1986 season, used to give out post-season awards for the "All-Iron Team," an allusion not to the metal but to Simms' obsession with well-pressed uniforms. First the quarterback draws out the lines, neat and even, and then he writes the clear and concise prose. There's an excellent chance, too, that this was also the result of good coaching. Pluta used to send his team onto the field with a concise prayer: "Play to the best of your ability and may no players be injured; play hard, play like men, play like champions, play Norwich football."

Pluta tells me that the first practice of the year would always follow the same script. While the dew was burning off in the morning they would run conditioning exercises and individual drills, get players organized into position groups based on their preferences (later on, they might get moved to where they could best help the team, but to start with they chose their positions). First day, afternoon session, as the heat rose up in shimmering waves on that practice field just a few hundred yards from the Chenango River and thunderheads gathered overhead, they would teach the "22 right" play, the first in a series of running plays. "22 right" denotes a run in the 2-hole between guard and tackle on the right side. Returning players who knew it would line up and run the play, and the whole discipline of coaching a football team would start from there. As Pluta explains it to me, coaching is teaching and there is a *whole-part-whole* logic to the process: experience and learn what the play looks like as a finished product, in 3-D; study and learn your part in it as an individual, get coached up on all the techniques necessary to make the play succeed; then come back together as a team to run it "live" against air. Repeat toward perfection. Eventually, you'd run it live against your own defense, and then run it for real against opponents in games. This is how you become a team.

At the time, I shared the skepticism of many teachers about the value of high school football, about whether the sport demanded too much from the athletes and distracted them from academics (Dave Paul once questioned the celebration of violence encoded in the weekly Purple Hammer award for hardest defensive hit in an NHS game). I'm still ambivalent, and in fact have recently talked to some scholarship college football players who concluded that the sport took too much time away from their academic endeavors. But in talking to Coach Pluta 20-years-plus later, I also understand much more fully how there was and is something meaningful if not profound going on after school, in the locker room and on the practice field. With the right coaching, what Joe Ehrmann calls "transformational" in his book *InSide Out Coaching*, student athletes are learning how to practice individual problem-solving in pursuit of a group goal, under the pressure of determined opposition and adverse conditions. Given my background in the infantry and special forces, I guess I can see why so many people want to emphasize the parallels between the military and football, even though I also see that in those football-is-war analogies lies a dangerous temptation to excess and illusion, a misunderstanding of the military and an inflation of how important the game of football ought to be. I think the danger increases as players progress from high school to college to the pros. Another big danger lies in what Ehrmann calls "transactional" coaching, certainly familiar to fans of big-time college football, where scholarship players serve at the pleasure of the coach and can get exploited like coins transacted in the coach's pursuit of his own success.

Pluta's high school football was very specific in its pedagogy, which was organized into a "football system" by Coach Dick Hoover in Vestal, New York. From the perspective of an offensive player, the system is "designed to give you an opportunity on every play to create some sort of advantage based on where the defense lines up." The advantage could come from better individual technique, understanding how to line up and move to neutralize what the defender was doing (a lot of choreography of "inside shoulders" and "outside hips"), or it could be a call with another player working out who would take whom where (over, under, even, odd)—blockers working out who on the opposing team would be most dangerous to the play and how they would work together to keep that player from making the stop. "That way," Pluta explains, "you're giving kids ownership, and they're not afraid of making mistakes." They are working, on their own and in partnership, to figure out how to make plays. On the sideline, Pluta wouldn't spend much time with players considering "why." Instead, the typical exchange would be: "What did you do? How did that work out for you?" Let the players work it out for themselves to a certain extent.

Pluta reveals to me something else he used to do as head coach that gave his team considerable confidence going into games, something that reminded me of patrol planning and the rehearsal of actions at the objective (theory: rehearse as much as possible, but at a minimum rehearse what is most important). The last ten minutes of the offensive period of practice was devoted to Perfect Starts, a process in which they would run through as many of their basic series of plays as they could without error in that ten-minute stretch. If there was a mistake, the unit would go back to the beginning. After a couple of weeks of practice,

Farewell to Football?

Pluta points out, "we could go through all of our base plays in ten minutes. We were a high school team that could drive the length of the field without a mistake."

They would need that assurance at the end of the 1993 season, when the Purple Tornado again made it deep into the playoffs. That year they traveled to Rome, New York, to play Chittenango, and in addition to the local "media" (Norwich's single newspaper and radio station), the game was being covered by Steve Wulf of *Sports Illustrated*, who was working on a nostalgia-trip "Bedford Falls" sort of piece about the town where he started his sports-writing career. Norwich was drawing some additional national media attention due to the success of its basketball team and the commitment by 6'-9" power-forward Bobby Lazor to Jim Boeheim's Syracuse program the week before the football playoff game. (Lazor was in my AP English class and told us that the stupidest question asked at the press conference was "other than basketball, what do you plan on doing at SU?" "Going to classes," Lazor replied. He would later transfer to Arizona State, where he was named *Playboy* Anson Mount Scholar-Athlete of the Year in 1998.)

Behind 6-7 at half-time, Norwich needed a Perfect Start in the third quarter, and they got it—two, in fact. On successive drives, the Tornado offense stuck to their running plays inside, just like they learned them starting the first hot muggy day of practice in the shaggy grass of their practice field, now running them on the perfect plain of artificial turf under the lights in a pressure-packed playoff game as winter was coming on, "22 right," "22 left," the whole 20-series, linemen calling out their blocks in breath pluming out like locomotive steam, perfectly in synch, the running back patient as the holes open up, keep running the base-series plays until the opponent figures out how to stop them, a high-school football team driving the length of the field without mistakes. Halfback Jason James scored two touchdowns along with a two-point conversion as Norwich surged to a 20-7 lead. It wasn't enough for a perfect finish, though, as Chittenango came back in the third act of this football drama to eke out a 21-20 win, ending Norwich's season. Maybe they didn't lose, but the clock did run out on them. This time, Coach Pluta's post-game comments went out to a national audience via a feature story for *Sports Illustrated* two days after Christmas, 1993:

"They were crying at first," he reports concerning the bus ride home, "but they kept their heads up the whole way, and they began talking about all the good things that had happened to them. To tell you the truth, I was never prouder of them than I was that night" (p. 109).

Jeremy Frink (61) and Coach John Pluta
embrace at the conclusion of a Norwich Purple
Tornado football playoff game, December
1993. Photo Courtesy of Frank Speziale.

So it wasn't George Bailey in *It's a Wonderful Life*. But maybe it was a perfect finish to a season of football, a sport in which according to Pluta everyone gets knocked down and you only fail when you stop getting up. The temptation to quit is always there, in anything hard we try to do. Whether it's completing Army Ranger School or getting married and raising kids or playing high school football, that temptation is always coiled and lurking in the weeds, ready to whisper discouraging words into our ears. Overcoming that temptation to quit is surely one of the enduring victories for a championship football team, and one of the coaches from Pluta's staff captured that thought for the scrapbook back in 1991. Corey Wolford, who coached the junior-high "modified" team, spelled it out in the neat steady hand of the high-school math teacher— no staff lines required:

> *It was a long, hot preseason, and the players and coaches never let down or took a break. I was fearful that you were pushing too hard and might get a lot of injuries or have a lot of players quit. However, this didn't happen, but instead I think that the team became closer and gained confidence that they had paid the price to win a championship.*

• • •

Awards Night

What was wrong with me?

They had a nice *corsage* to pin on my lapel and I didn't even have a lapel. I'd chosen to wear a short-sleeve polo shirt in school color purple. What kind of stupid stunt was this? It wasn't like I was coming right off the golf course or anything.

Well, it had been a rough day, that June 24, 1994. I'd spent most of the day crying.

My high-school classmate John had died on Tuesday, and they held the memorial service on Friday. That was my warm-up to the awards-night ceremony at Norwich High School, where I was representing the English department, which I would be leading as chair the following year. And I couldn't even manage a stupid sport coat.

Good old John, that kid with the crooked grin, howling with laughter in the driver's seat beside me as his parents' Opel station-wagon pitched up so that we were gazing at the stars through the windshield like a couple of stoned astronauts, having misjudged the distance to the ditch in backing out of a parking spot at a weekend party somewhere in the environs of New Berlin. If it hadn't been for John and his crooked grin and funny stories and color slides coming back from his Army tour in Germany, I never would have considered joining the military. Now John had lost the battle with brain cancer that started back when I first got out of the Army and initiated my teaching career as a substitute at Norwich High. At first he had surged ahead and the cancer—a baseball-sized tumor on his brain— had gone into remission, but now, five years later, cancer won.

I hadn't been in close touch for a while, but boy did I get caught up in hurry at the memorial service. A woman who had been responsible for John's terminal care got up to speak, and she didn't hold back. Every description of his loss of speech and soiled diapers landed like a punch to the body or a solid head-shot. And the tears came in buckets and I remember thinking—*what on earth is this? What is wrong with this person? Why is she going on and on with this crap?*

Somewhere in there it came to me as an epiphany, as if written in the stars we gazed upon through that Opel windshield: there are worse things than dying. We all loved John and were going to sorely miss his gentle soul in our crappy earthly lives, and I'm sure we all would have been sorely tempted to hold on to him. Therein lay the trap of attachment: for our own selfish reasons, we didn't want to let go of John and let him get on with the journey God had called him to. This woman was here, like a cranky Old Testament prophet, to lash us back to reality with a few unpleasant facts. Dying from brain cancer is one of those Old Testament ordeals that happens to people from time to time even in our modern/scientific/medical age, who knows why, God's will entirely beyond our knowing, and it would be the worst misuse of our capabilities to prolong it a moment more than it needed to take. There are worse things than dying. The worst thing we can try to do is to defy God's will.

Farewell to Football?

1994 had been a year for crying, or at least a very sad spring. My father died in May, a year of grace for a dying alcoholic had come to an end for the old man, and without any chance of knowing it, my old friend John had been my mentor in how to go through that process. My sisters had gone down to Florida the previous summer and found our father living in the worst kind of alcoholic squalor, living like trash in a trailer, drinking a gallon jug of cheap wine every day, suffering from what is called "wet brain syndrome," a horrid staggering, demented, confabulating end to the career of a heavy drinker. Because my father had enlisted in the Army in New York state (joining up as a volunteer right after Pearl Harbor), he was eligible for a spot in the state veterans home just south of Norwich. My sisters took care of the details and I kept my distance. Let them get their hearts broken—I knew better.

Gus dried out and got to eating regular meals and turned out to be a right decent old gentleman, or at least knew how to play one in a late feat of a salesman's self-fashioning. I started visiting him about once a month, and we made a kind of peace. We could talk as old veterans do, telling BS stories about the Army days. He had served in an artificial moonlight unit on the Sicilian-Italian front, battlefield illumination only used in World War II. Before then, the technology for coordinating massive air-defense searchlights didn't exist, and afterwards the military turned to individual night-vision devices, like the kind I used on patrol in the Korean DMZ. What did you do in the war, Daddy? I lit up the battlefield by bouncing searchlight beams off the bellies of clouds. Unique, I'll give him that. (He was far from unique in screwing up, getting drunk and fighting and losing rank as soon as he'd earned it, like one of those scandalous enlisted men in *From Here to Eternity*.)

It turned out that Gus had bladder cancer, and by spring it was terminal. I had learned from John what to do in this eventuality. When I first got out of the Army and was taking John up to the medical center in Syracuse for the radiation therapy that temporarily put the halt to his brain cancer, we had talked about what it was like when his father died. Ward was an old guy to have a kid John's age—there were a lot of offspring in that family, with a long gap between John and his next-youngest sibling—and he was an eccentric character. An old man who looked more than a little like the science-fiction writer Arthur C. Clarke, Ward suffered from a condition that made his eyes bulge, all in all fitting to his affable and slightly comical character. He was an amateur photographer of some talent, and it was fun to watch him work in the dark room and especially at the printing stand, puffing away at his pipe, muttering, explaining, patient, accepting. It must be great to have a Dad like that, I remember thinking when we were in high school. John loved him dearly, and when it was Ward's time to go, John told me, he was with him the whole way. John was sleeping in the same hospital room when his father died. You just had to be there for him, I remember as the lesson, keep him company and let him know that when it's time to go, he has your blessing.

Enriched with that initiatory wisdom, I tried my best to be there for Gus as he drifted in and out of consciousness in his last days, trying to overcome the petty resentment about how seldom he had been there for me (the one time when he hovered like Banquo's ghost at my Ranger School graduation seemed like the exception that proved the rule). I held his hand and told him it was OK. It's OK to go. Don't hang on when it's time to go. I recall that once during that last week, he bolted upright and sat staring straight ahead, a look of abject terror in his eyes. I remembered my grandmother telling me that when her grandfather died, he sat upright and looked at the wall, though he had been blind for years, and told her, "it's a beautiful world to live in, and it's a beautiful world to die in." I don't think that my father was looking through the windshield and seeing the stars of a beautiful universe. I don't know what he was seeing, but it terrified him.

Gus's funeral was a muted affair, but under the surface I knew things were working, tectonic plates slowly shifting. For men in American culture, I believe, when your father dies it rearranges your attachment to work, deepens the quest for significance through work. My work was now teaching, and I wasn't the kind to bag on a responsibility just because

Farewell to Football?

I'd had a sad day. I was in the classroom the day after my father died, and my team-teaching colleague, the estimable Dan Callahan, wryly observed: "So, your father died? You kind of slipped that in there, like Camus in *The Stranger*." So I spent the afternoon blubbering at John's memorial service and showed up for the awards-night program in a purple polo shirt.

Nothing could have been more life-affirming or soul-expanding than recognizing excellence in young people and knowing in all humility that you had played some part in their development. When I gave out the departmental award for best senior writer, I felt it in my heart, a rare moment of generosity. This was a student who had been in my class as a junior, and one of my assignments had set off a reaction in her, recruited some of her best and brightest stuff, and the paper she worked on, drafting and revising over and over again, became a bit of a legend in the English department, and may well have been the reason she won the award. It was the kind of assignment I never would have devised had it not been for the semiotic mentoring of Dave Paul and Rich Bernstein in Norwich and the poststructuralist and feminist initiation of Deborah Britzman in Binghamton: "discuss the codes you see at work in Disney's *Little Mermaid*." It sounds deceptively simple, until you start to reflect on the codes of gender and cultural identity at work in a big-budget commercial cartoon rendering of a surprisingly brutal Hans Christian Anderson fairy tale (walking on land will feel, to the converted mermaid, like the constant stabbing of knives, and she has the option to stab the prince who snubs her). Then put emphasis on "the codes *you see* at work," an invitation to reflect on what Rich Bernstein would call "the subject position." Think about your thinking; theorize your theory. We were running that kind of English department, a "theory and practice" shop, and for some of our students, this young woman in particular, it gave them what they needed to move on in their intellectual journey, occasionally in a pretty big way. Maybe, if they're good at their jobs and dedicated to student learning, teachers can be just as transformational as football coaches. Well, maybe, if the kids will just buy into it.

Steven Liparulo

My own teaching reflected a combination of the theoretical preferences of my graduate education and my departmental colleagues with the emphasis on American literature in the 11th grade English curriculum. I called my course The Text of American Identity, signaling explicitly that I would be taking a cultural-studies approach to identity politics as revealed through close textual analysis. Mostly I stayed in the canon, teaching Hawthorne's *The Scarlet Letter* and short stories by Hemingway, but I also introduced a work from the emerging "multicultural" repertoire (with a tip of the hat to Professor Constance Coiner at Binghamton, who died in the 1996 explosion of TWA flight 800), Zora Neale Hurston's *Their Eyes Were Watching God*. There were a couple of "texts," however, that reveal a bit of the personal semiotics I was working out, however subconsciously—trying dimly and with uncertain focus to decipher a text of my own identity.

I taught two films that could easily be dismissed under the heading of "what was I thinking?" Billy Wilder's 1950 *Sunset Blvd.* and Stanley Kubrick's 1964 *Dr. Strangelove*. It was common practice in those days to "teach" the film version of a novel or play the class was supposed to read, and I tended to think that a bad idea. Why encourage students not to read? Instead, I taught films that were "texts" in their own right—no book to read. To write the assignment, you had to "read" the films, including at least the rudiments of film style. So while both of these movies are kind of depressing, they are also so overloaded with interpretive possibilities that they serve as great writing prompts, *Sunset Blvd.* especially (that monkey! that wheezing pipe-organ! all that leopard-skin!). *Dr. Strangelove* is also at least putatively funny and on the level of identity politics works the gender concept pretty thoroughly, loaded as it is with phallic images and allusions (it starts with the mile-high penetration of aerial refueling and ends with Slim Pickens astraddle an atomic bomb). The films offered plenty to read, and given how politicized public education is now, I don't think I could currently get away with reading films about older women exploiting younger writers and the origins of conflict and war in sexual dysfunction. I guess that maybe because they were both black and white films, they just got dismissed as corny old movies. Fair enough, but beware what lurks beneath the surface.

For me, on a level I wasn't ready to acknowledge consciously, I think they were allegories for my failure to love. *Dr. Strangelove* in particular lined up with my experience in some pretty strange and telling ways. The title character, a brilliant physicist brought over to the American side at the end of the war against Germany (like a few of the more prominent rocket scientists who got us to the moon when I was a kid), tools around in a wheelchair and fights a farcical battle against his disordered passions erupting in uncontrollable Nazi-salutes and self-strangulation attempts from a gloved hand (example of how students could read "film style" thematically: in a typically esoteric Kubrick switcheroo, the *right* hand wears the Satanic black glove and rises up in beguiling rebellion against humanity). Wounded, impotent, and fully capable of destroying all life on the planet, Dr. Strangelove is played so broadly by the manic Peter Sellers that it's a little hard to take the points inherent in his character too seriously. General Ripper, acted with ferocious intensity by Sterling Hayden and shot by Kubrick in a devastating film-noir style (low-angle and low-key), is a little easier for me to connect to. Sharpened to a razor's edge by a military formation that renders all life adversarial, Ripper talks about the physical act of "love" as if he really means war—since his post-coital vulnerability terrifies him into hoarding his "essence" or manhood. No, the enemy "women" will not invade his manly stash of "essence," not without a good fight, at least. This way madness lies, of course, and the film represents the logical destination to this path, the general's suicide, a precursor to the planetary suicide the film will ironically score with Vera Lynn's quavering hope in the ending sing-along. *We'll meet again, don't know where, don't know when.* While Mandrake's war wounds are quickly disclosed—his gammy leg, all shot up, his torture at the hands of Japanese captors—we can only wonder about the trauma at the root of Ripper's disorder. What could harden a man's heart so severely?

Of course, as the kids tend to say when presented with a complex problem they'd rather not have to write about, it's just a movie. It' not like it happens in real life.

• • •

Super Bowl XXIX: Man of the Year

Another Super Bowl, the first one in several years that I would be watching alone. The kickoffs were getting later and later as the lust for excess seemingly inherent in American culture hyped up the game into some sort of combined holy ritual and miracle cure—the Super Bowl starts wars and cures cancer. 6:00 Eastern now, two hours later than nine years ago when the Giants beat the Broncos and I watched in the boozy fellowship of my Special Forces A-team at a bar in Vermont.

This one might as well have come on in the dead of night. I was alone because something had ended. It gets so dark so early in those days of the bleak mid-winter, the end of January, 1995. Something had ended but something still remained, the ghost of the thing that was lost. I was good and depressed, alone as the rest of the world indulged the illusion of community in the feast of the Super Bowl, celebrating the NFL Man of the Year, San Diego's Tasmanian Devil of a linebacker, Junior Seau, honored for his philanthropy in a variety of community outreach programs. The pre-game shows careened from endless variations on a few basic game-plan insights from dozens of former-player *analysts* ("look for Young to come out throwing," duh) to celebrity pufferation and least-common-denominator pop music. If I heard that sappy Hootie and the Blowfish song one more time, the one about letting her cry, I was likely to put my hand through a wall.

I was the one crying. I had embarked upon a romance—what my family would call a "relationship," using the transactional discourse that meant that the thing was doomed before it was even started—before I left Binghamton to come back to Norwich to start my teaching career proper, and we had moved in together and started the adventure, full of hope for love and success. We had celebrated the election of Bill Clinton and some awesome climactic World Series games. On the other hand, the New York football Giants were ominously horrible throughout the span of our affair, the Ray Handley years.

In football, some games are over almost from the start—newly-retired coaching genius Bill Walsh saw that when he watched his first Super Bowl as an observer. His 49ers, now led by head coach George Seifert, took on the Denver Broncos in the New Orleans Superdome after the 1989 season, and he could see, almost despairingly, that everyone was open, right from the start. That game was over before it began. San Francisco won a blow-out, 55-10.

We had taken a trip, my lover and I, in the bleak mid-winter of our first year together, a trip indeed intended as a remedy to the depths of winter, a visit to the artists' colony at Woodstock. A weekend away from the droning grind of a school year. And almost from the moment we checked into the hotel room, I knew that something was already dead and just hadn't fallen over yet.

I recall it with the nightmare logic and low-key lighting of that scene from *Dr. Strangelove* when Peter Sellers' Group Captain character tells the mad general that he can't come over and help him right now, the string's gone in his leg, implying that an old war wound sometimes rendered his leg paralyzed and useless. In my mind's eye that hotel room in Woodstock was lighted the same way, somehow drained of color and hermetically sealed, all bleak contrast, and I was acutely aware of my own paralysis, that white noise jamming the circuits like on my trip to Seoul with the fine-figured Jina. I could not open my heart to love. I still could not identify the wound, but I knew that the string was gone. "I do not avoid women, Mandrake. But I do deny them my essence."

And that was it, the affair was over but took a couple of years for its ending to unfold in time. Not long before the Super Bowl, we'd had our melodramatic soap-opera scene to put an end to the game with a proper pistol shot. I'd discovered, like some sorry film-noir detective, that my love had taken another lover, and I had worked up a breathless end-of-the-movie speech like when Barbara Stanwyck jams one hand into her hip and tells everyone off, only I had written it down in the form of a letter, which she had found and read after returning from an overnight away (with *him*, no doubt). I was at the school playing basketball, and when I got home it all broke loose on a cold dreary Sunday morning. Foolish people making themselves miserable together, lashing at each other with words, words, words.

In anything hard we try to do, love, sports, war, we are tempted to quit. In a sense, all temptation is to the same sin, what Augustine called *concupiscence*, the temptation to choose the lesser, to give up rather than fighting for what's right. In my family, the lesser was frequently chosen in marriage, compromise going in and resignation coming out, choosing poorly or rashly and then failing to sustain a commitment and bailing out. Between my mother and three sisters, they had been married *fourteen* times. Keeping my distance, I had tried to avoid the problem altogether, which really meant it would just retreat into the shadows only to show up again unexpectedly, a demon allied with the whole legion of the repressed. Some of the better football coaches had evolved a transformational pedagogy for perfect starts and a theology for not quitting; I felt sometimes, giving up and indulging in self-pity, that my family had provided me a transactional formula for disaster predicated on choosing the lesser, living together instead of getting married, "in a relationship" instead of in love.

By the time of the Super Bowl, that volatile part with the big Barbara Stanwyck hand-on-hip tell-off speeches was over, too. My lover had found somewhere else to live and I was into the dark alone part. It briefly occurred to me how pathetic I was, looking forward to a stupid football game like it was going to save my life, start a war, cure cancer.

At first, I thought it really couldn't get any worse, because this game was over before it started, too. San Francisco scored on their third play from scrimmage. Then something peculiar began to happen, as they replayed the touchdown over and over again, Al Michaels making the play-call and former-player analysts Dan Dierdorf and Frank Gifford providing the commentary. Jerry Rice scored on a seam route down the middle of the field, 44 yards, easy pitch and catch from Steve Young to the greatest receiver of all time, and the rout was on. That isn't what the replay really showed, though. San Diego had the right coverage on, and two defensive backs converged on Rice just after he caught the ball. They should have knocked him down for a short gain, could possibly have even forced a fumble, but they didn't. It was as if they ran right through him—was he but a specter?—and Rice made the play, the first of 6 touchdown passes for Young, a record that still stands. How could that be?

Here's the peculiar thing: it occurred to me that I could explain this phenomenon to my mentor, Dave Paul. I was taping the game and I could show him the play and then present my theory: those two defensive backs know who Jerry Rice is—the greatest wide receiver to play the game—and they are trying to tackle the Myth of Jerry Rice, and of course they can't do it. That play was over before the ball was even snapped because the play has to happen in the minds of the players before it ever happens on the field, and in the minds of the defensive backs, it couldn't happen. Sure, they'd made that play a hundred times before, drawn it up on the chalkboard, run it against air, against their own teammates, and even in games, whole-part-whole, but they'd never made that play against an imaginary man, the Greatest Of All Time, and they never would.

Is this the working of the Holy Spirit, this deeper insight into the game, or is that just human learning, the theory and practice of football semiotics? Was the work of the Holy Spirit the evocation of an audience? I can tell someone about this, I can *witness* to this play! I can give this play and its semiotic as a gift to someone I love. I can give this gift to the mentor who stood up on the table for me and who gave me the gift that allowed me to see this way, to *discern* the play. I could show him that I wasn't dead yet, that I was indeed resurrected from the little human soap-opera near-death experience that had recently gotten me down. You only fail when you stop getting up.

CHAPTER 8

———————— • • • ————————

The Last Season in the Astrodome (1996)

"These owners fashion themselves as the jungle animals
of the free enterprise system. In reality, they're the
pussy cats of a monopoly world, and the characteristics
of a monopoly are high prices and low service. If they
had to do business in the real world with their methods,
they would all go broke. If they couldn't look to the taxpayers to bail 'em out, they'd run their businesses and
quit doing stupid labor contracts."

–HOUSTON MAYOR BOB LANIER, 1997. (IN ED FOWLER, *LOSER
TAKES ALL*, P. 175)

• • •

OCTOBER 27, 1996: San Francisco 49ers 10, Houston Oilers 9, Houston
Astrodome. A typical Jeff Fisher score and outcome: the head
coach's Oilers held the high-flying 49ers to a mere 10 points—a lone
touchdown—but still managed to lose by a single point. Fisher had
played defensive back for the Bears and was on the Chicago team that
won the Super Bowl after the 1985 season by completely stifling the New
England Patriots, though he was on injured reserve and was essentially
making the transition from playing to coaching. The Oilers team that
Fisher took over as head coach in the middle of the 1994 season reflected the influence of coach Buddy Ryan, the architect of that 1985 Bears
defense who had served as defensive coordinator of the Oilers before

leaving to take the head coaching position with the Arizona Cardinals. Fisher had followed Ryan to several assignments and was steeped in the Ryan defensive ethos of tough unyielding football, with lots of pressure on the quarterback. His teams were undeniably boring, too, and the 10-9 loss to San Francisco was a pretty good snapshot of Fisher football. The Oilers held the 49ers to 238 yards of total offense, well under their average, and still lost, and lost by one point.

The game had started out looking pretty good for the home team when the Oilers knocked out Pro-Bowl quarterback Steve Young on the 49ers' first offensive series. Young was always a phenomenally dangerous quarterback on the move, but over the years he paid a price for that mobility with a series of concussions that eventually cut short his stellar career. In the game at Houston, Young rolled out into territory where no quarterback really belongs, alone in the flats with a charging big man setting his sights on him. Micheal Barrow, outside linebacker for the Oilers, made his living as a hard hitter with above-average speed, and he took Young violently down to the notoriously hard Astroturf surface. Young didn't get up, exiting the Astrodome in an ambulance with a concussion. He was replaced by the 49ers third-string quarterback and still the Oilers lost by a single point. Even though Fisher's defense held All-Pro Jerry Rice largely in check, rookie wide-out Terrell Owens scored the fourth-quarter touchdown on a 20 yard reception, after the big play of the game, a 49 yard completion to fullback Terry Kirby. The Oilers defense was pretty great for three quarters but it wasn't quite good enough for the win.

It almost seemed as if Coach Fisher and the Oilers' owner, Bud Adams, had done everything they could to suck the life out of the game. The Oilers played in the dying Astrodome, on artificial turf under artificial lighting, and Fisher's game plans were boring and conservative—he always struck me as the kind of coach who would probably field a team of all linebackers if he could figure out how to get away with it (and Adams would surely have gone along with the scheme if it meant paying typically-low linebacker salaries). Years later, as the head coach of the then-rechristened Tennessee Titans in 2005, Fisher would take a defensive back, the diminutive Adam "Pac-Man" Jones, as his first-round draft choice—when future offensive stars like Aaron Rodgers, Roddy White, Vincent Jackson, and Frank Gore were still available. For his part, by 1996 Adams had managed to antagonize entirely the Houston fan-base with his endless griping about how he couldn't make a dollar in the outdated Astrodome and paying the heavy salaries he would have to pay to stay competitive in the League. In his day Adams had been the co-founder of the upstart American Football League at the end of the 1950's, throwing in with Lamar Hunt of Dallas, who moved his Texans team to Kansas City after a couple of years competing with the Cowboys, but in Houston Adams had long since worn out his welcome for a lot of fans. By 1996, when I had my choice of great seats for that game against the 49ers, it was settled fact that the Oilers would be leaving Houston for Tennessee, but the pressing question was whether they would make their exodus next year or if they would stick around for one more season in the Astrodome. How much worse could things get?

Well, they went 8-8 for the 1996 season, which is pretty much a perfect record for a Jeff Fisher team.

I was really into football in those days. 1996 was my first year in Houston, as I'd been accepted into the nationally-ranked Ph. D. program in Creative Writing at the University of Houston. I went to the Oilers game with one of my colleagues from "The Program," a guy from California who rooted for the 49ers, and in terms of pro football, I felt privileged to have walked in on the last act of a pretty dramatic spectacle of disordered attachments, an epic of ambivalence, and the finale to what we now call franchise free-agency—the tendency of owners to move their teams to the city that offers them the best deal. The history of the Houston Oilers was like a panorama of American history, a saga of the greatest game in a sports-mad country and a soap opera of the love-hate relationship between a city's fans and its team, and especially in this case, the team's owner.

Farewell to Football?

The lore of sports in America is full of half-truths about the mutual loyalty between a city and its sports team and the tremendous economic benefits that accrue from having a pro sports team in your city and how sports can single-handedly cure communities of racism and discrimination. The historical record tends to tell a less coherent story, and while the credo of the Old West (at least as mythologized by Hollywood) held that "when the legend becomes fact, print the legend," I find the truth, full of conflicting desires and disordered passions, a whole lot more consonant with the collective experience of a fallen human race. So I'm going to follow the history and seek the truth.

The history of the Houston Oilers is really the history of the AFL and Lamar Hunt's challenge to the Roman Empire and the ascendance of pro football to its current stature as America's Game. It all began with the alliance between mild-mannered Hunt and flamboyant Adams, two Texans rich with inherited oil money and willing to invest in an upstart league. It was a funny story of mismatched partners, setting themselves up as Princes of Pro Football and taking off on the adventure of a lifetime in the post-war boom years that could have provided the national anthem for free-market entrepreneurship, a rich-boy's *On the Road*, the AFL's David taking on the Goliath NFL, had not their ballad ultimately followed the seemingly-inevitable declension into the dirty little tale of just more decadent crony capitalism, just more bilking the taxpayers to support the profits of the super-rich (something similar to what Ike warned the country about concerning the military industrial complex when he left office in 1960—the same year the AFL got under way).

In the early days, the competition from Hunt's new league didn't collapse the NFL's empire, as many of the fearful and monopoly-minded older-generation owners feared, but instead proved massively stimulating to the entire enterprise of professional football. Suitably enough, a championship matchup between Hunt's Dallas Texans (later the Kansas City Chiefs) and Adams's Oilers for the AFL title in December 1962 made it clear that the market for pro football—when it was as exciting and dramatic as a double-overtime playoff game—was far more extensive than most had dreamed, especially with the rapid expansion of television coverage of the games.

Bad weather up and down the east coast meant that a lot of people were indoors and tuned in to football on Sunday, December 23, and had already seen a pretty great contest by the time referee Red Bourne hesitated for a second after Texans captain Abner Haynes replied to the prompt to call the coin toss preparatory to overtime with the curious expression "we'll kick to the clock." What? Had he made a huge mistake, thinking he would get to call the direction of the kickoff (a clock in a tower at one end of Jeppesen Stadium in Houston, a favorable direction given the wind) when his choice of verbs ("we'll kick") meant that he could only claim the kickoff for his team? Would the Texans lose the game without ever even possessing the football? That was great live televised drama—and the AFL had the TV audience to itself, since the NFL took a week off before its title game on December 30. If the NFL came of age in December 1958 when Johnny Unitas led the Baltimore Colts to an overtime win over the New York Giants in the nationally-televised championship game—what Tex Maule called in *Sports Illustrated* "The Best Football Game Ever Played"—then pro football collectively evolved four years later when the junior league met the challenge and upped the ante. Double overtime, sudden death! (By the way, Haynes and the Dallas Texans ended up winning anyway, and Houston lost by three—after winning the first two AFL titles, the Oilers/Titans would never win another championship.)

The history of the Houston Oilers is also the history of the civil rights era. Judge Roy Hofheinz, the master politician and self-described "huckster" who led the massive project to build the paradigm-busting Astrodome, had quietly desegregated Houston's public facilities when he was mayor in 1955, striking an agreement with the press not to publicize the move so as to avoid aggravating segregationists (Gast, p. 39). The city would use a similar tactic when it desegregated lunch counters in 1960, well before the more famous confrontations led by Dr. Martin Luther King in Birmingham in 1963 and Selma in 1965 (p. 56).

Farewell to Football?

The story of desegregation is full of contradictions, of course, and the Houston Independent School District (HISD) only began a twelve-year integration process (one grade at a time) in response to a U. S. District Court order in 1960 (Carroll, p. 76). The Houston Oilers played their games in their early years at Jeppesen Stadium, which while located on the campus of the University of Houston was owned by the HISD (p. 78). Stadium seating was segregated, and on September 25, 1960, the NAACP announced a boycott of the Oilers game against the Oakland Raiders in protest, reducing attendance to 16,451 (p. 101). By 1965, however, Jeppesen Stadium and the City of Houston looked a whole lot more favorable when AFL players moved the January All-Star game to the Oilers' home stadium after they found the open racism in New Orleans intolerable. African-American players couldn't get cabs to serve them, were denied entry into clubs, and were frequently subjected to racist verbal abuse (MacCambridge 2005, p. 249; Lamar Hunt had seen these Jim Crow laws as a "major problem" when considering New Orleans for a franchise in the league he was dreaming up in 1959, 2012, p. 90).

The history of the Houston Oilers is also the history of America's manned space program, the race to the moon, and how Houston became Space City and the salutation in the radio traffic from American astronauts (in 1970, the world was galvanized by Jim Lovell's report from Apollo 13: "Houston, we've had a problem"). President Kennedy had announced the goal of putting a man on the moon within the decade at Houston's Rice Stadium, and NASA had moved the Manned Spacecraft Center to Clear Lake, south of Houston, in 1961. The astronauts showed up in 1962, and Gus Grissom, the second American to fly in space and the commander of the ill-fated Apollo 1 mission (which ended in a fatal fire on the pad during a test in 1967), was on hand for that landmark AFL title game in December. By 1964, Houston's baseball team changed its name from the Colt .45's to the Houston Astros, and the Harris County Domed Stadium became unofficially but permanently the Houston Astrodome, and Grissom was the senior astronaut in the house for the grand opening in April, 1965.

Steven Liparulo

The history of the Houston Oilers is most of all the story—the psycho-drama, really—of owner Bud Adams and his wavering commitment to the city. In their first decade, the Oilers led a nomadic life. For the 1960-64 seasons, the team called Jeppesen Stadium home. Then came a sort of prototypical schizoid episode in which Adams and Hofheinz reached a "gentlemen's agreement" that the Oilers would move into the Astrodome in 1965, only to have Adams re-think the deal and instead move his team into Rice Stadium, but not before he raised prices for season-ticket hold-ers premised on the upgrade to the dome. The owner did not re-think the price-raise (Fowler, p. 30). After two years at Rice, Adams was back to complaining about poor attendance and losing money and threatening to move the team to Seattle. Under these circumstances, a deal was struck to move the Oilers into the Astrodome, leaving Rice with an unfulfilled contract that it chose not to remedy legally (p. 32).

After innovative coaching legend Sid Gillman brought in player talent and radically improved the team in 1973 and 1974, Adams some-what predictably and pathetically griped to a sportswriter that "it em-barrasses me to be the owner of the only club losing money in the NFL. It makes me look like a poor owner, and I don't want to be the laughingstock of the owners around the league. If I spent as Sid wants me to spend, I'd be the winningest owner—but I'd also be the brokest" (Fowler, p. 35). In the following decade, Adams got the taxpayers to spare him the embarrassment of a sub-par building. "In 1987, with Bud Adams and the Oilers complaining about lack of seating, and threat-ening to move to Jacksonville, the [Astrodome] underwent a $50 mil-lion dollar renovation" (Gast, p. 179). In 1997, after three and a half decades of this drama, Adams moved the Oilers to Tennessee, play-ing one year as the Tennessee Oilers in Memphis and then finally set-tling in Nashville at a football-only outdoor stadium as the Tennessee Titans.

It was as the Tennessee Titans, with Jeff Fisher as head coach, that the team would come up one yard short and lose the Super Bowl to the St. Louis Rams at the end of the 1999 season.

Farewell to Football?

The story of Bud Adams and the Houston Oilers is in the main the story of the ownership class in the NFL and the business model that Houston Mayor Bob Lanier called "a monopoly world." Ed Fowler, the *Houston Chronicle* sportswriter who swings a little wildly in his 1997 book about Adams and the Oilers, *Loser Takes All*, asserts that "this is an industry in which the businessman faces no competition and no imperative to create demand for his product"(p. 29). In his astute 2013 work, *The King of Sports*, Gregg Easterbrook essentially agrees, with considerably more command of the facts. In the machinations of owners like Adams, frequently turning to the taxpayers to upgrade or replace their stadia and then personally reaping the considerable profits generated by the luxury boxes in those buildings, Easterbrook finds that "subsidized pro sports are a risk-free mechanism for converting taxpayer's money into private gain" (p. 52). In a simple formulation, the owners of the NFL, with the help of star-struck politicians, have figured out how to socialize risk and privatize profits, and as Easterbrook also notes, "NFL franchises are government-subsidized and protected by government against economic competition—the paradigm of feudalism" (p. 61). While wrapped in the American flag and self-fashioned as the jungle animals of the free enterprise system, in Mayor Lanier's phrase, owners in the contemporary NFL tend to operate according to very different, remarkably un-democratic principles. This current NFL ownership situation has come a long way from the mid-20th-century David v. Goliath scenario of Lamar Hunt and his AFL "foolish club" of sportsman-millionaires taking on the big, bad NFL, but that's pretty much how empires work—if the rebels can't be crushed, they can be coopted. Merged into the NFL in 1966, the AFL owners have quite willingly morphed from foolish rebels into feudal princes.

In 1996, in my academic life I had journeyed to Houston to learn more about telling stories, about characters and plots and points-of-view, to earn a Ph. D. in Creative Writing (Fiction), to become a Doctor of Storytelling. As part of my graduate education, I would soon read a text from the early modern period in Italy (historically, the time of transition from feudalism toward recognizably modern economies) that could tell the story of this evolutionary stage in late-capitalism when the Princes of Pro Football were learning hard lessons that would change how they went about their business: Niccolo Machiavelli wrote in *The Prince* in 1513 that "there is nothing more difficult to execute, nor more dubious of success, nor more dangerous to administer than to introduce a new order of things; for he who introduces it has all those who profit from the old order as his enemies, and he has only lukewarm allies in all those who might profit from the new" (Chapter VI). Lamar Hunt knew that from the start of his introduction of a new football order he would face enemies in the NFL, but he probably didn't expect Bud Adams to turn out so lukewarm in his commitments to anything other than himself. As it turned out, Adams may have just been a few steps ahead of the rest, and another definition for "lukewarm" in this context might as well be "more than willing to socialize risk and privatize reward," more than willing to follow the money and leave behind the city finally fed up with the endless demands for more taxpayer money to convert into the owner's private gain. But the bigger lesson is readily recognized by our contemporary observers Lanier and Fowler and Easterbrook. Hunt needn't have worried about his success, as the market for pro football is so robust that even the worst management, given enough leverage over the local taxpayers and politicians, can hardly fail. Even the foolish fail upward in this racket.

• • •

Tuesday is creative writing day (or: *here I go, griping about everything just like I accused Bud Adams of doing, and not applying the rule of charity*).

As the jocks say, I was in Houston on scholarship. A free choice of the will, franchise free-agency for a franchise of one, in the enterprise of writing. After five years of teaching, I had decided that the profession suited me, but maybe I should try shifting up a level, see how college teaching fit, like an athlete trying out to play "college ball." I wanted to try to take my writing further, too, so I had headed down to the Texas Gulf Coast, to the Ph. D. program in Creative Writing at the University of Houston, reputedly the best in the country.

Coming in as part of "The Program" meant I was coming in on a team (of twenty–some graduate students in English, mostly creative writers), and there was even something of a training camp in the dread high-summer of Gulf-Coast Texas, a pre-service August week of orientation before the fall semester started. The heat seemed far more monstrous than in any of the hot Southern places where I'd lived while serving in the Army, in Kentucky, Georgia, North Carolina, and much hotter than my childhood homes in Gulf-Coast Florida. It felt as if a massive furnace was stuck on high and blasting heat everywhere here. Good thing we weren't running gassers or grass drills in that inferno. The graduate student orientation focused on getting us ready to teach, since we weren't actually on scholarship—the majority of us held teaching *assistantships*, which meant that in addition to taking our graduate degree requirements, we were teaching part-time (two sections of freshman composition per semester). We also were paid a modest stipend, considerably less than half of what I had been making as a full-time high-school teacher. Like athletes on scholarship, we were exchanging our services for less than market value, betting on the future employment that this "apprenticeship" could enable.

Our team featured some substantial diversity, since the UH Creative Writing Program is nationally-competitive and draws graduate students from all across the country, and even some from other countries. The program awards both Masters of Fine Arts (MFA) and doctorate (Ph. D.) degrees, so the students range in age and experience considerably. Some had just finished undergraduate degrees in the spring, not much older nor much worldlier than students I had taught in high school, while others, especially Ph. D. candidates, had completed graduate degrees and pursued careers, and there were a few students older than me. It wasn't diverse like the Army (I never did quite figure out the right answer to African-American Boss Buffalo asking me if his butt was black), but it was diverse, and I was going to have to figure out how to fit in with people whose approaches to life and work were notably foreign to me. Objectively out of place, I faced two distinct temptations, often indulged: to play the condescending if avuncular "senior fellow," superior by training and accomplishment, Old Man Liparulo, or to try to play it cool and fit in—essentially, to play the fool, a very stupid option, and of course, the easiest.

I knew I could handle the academic work, even though it was pretty demanding, a creative-writing program added on top of a doctorate in literature, and it typically took five years or longer to complete. The literature components were traditional, comprising course work in the established canon of Western literature, three written exams (covering either canonical periods or genres), and an oral exam dealing with an in-progress critical work, and when they were finished, I felt like I had mastered a body of work and that I could talk knowingly about literature. The creative writing components, on the other hand, a total of five semester-long workshops and a creative dissertation, did no harm, I suppose, though I felt largely unguided. Unlike any other academic program I had been involved in, the creative writing program pursued a kind of learning I didn't really recognize—there wasn't a clearly defined body of specific content to "cover," and there was a marked skepticism toward method (as I understood it, *method* would somehow threaten or diminish the power of *creative genius*, which seemed to be the reigning spirt of place around here, favoring art over craft).

I may have come in with mistaken expectations. I'm not sure that the exploratory "workshop" method with minimal curricular guidance was the best way for me, personally, to learn how to write fiction. Part of the problem was I hadn't worked with fiction as an undergraduate and had developed critical habits as a scholar that I might have to unlearn in the creative realm (like wanting a reading list and a clearly defined methodology). Looking back on it, for the creative writing part, an old-fashioned apprenticeship with a seasoned writer would have been more productive, had I been able somehow to swing it. I suppose this was available in some cases (the poets seemed to get that kind of attention from mentors), but the fiction faculty changed so often that there wasn't always an opportunity for that kind of mentorship to develop. This was all, in fact, a typical development in American higher education, the migration of career preparation out of "the field" and into the university (for example, the University of Houston includes a college for hotel and restaurant management). I remember realizing at some point during the Clinton presidency that *he really thinks everyone should get a college degree*—and I wasn't at all sure that was wise (but it was good economics and politics if you were in the higher education business, since his administration was doing all it could to make student-loan credit easy to get and hard to discharge; as of this writing, student-loan debt in America tops both credit-card and auto-loan debt).

The typical creative-writing workshop was, to my way of thinking, more hit-or-miss than the teaching I did in high or the military training I received in the Army. I was often tempted to think that mine were the superior experiences—the arrogant Old Man Liparulo persona. For a writer's workshop, the routine was you would distribute copies of a work-in-progress to the dozen or so other members of the class, and then the next week the class would discuss the work (typically, in fiction, three works would be "up" per week, meaning something like a psychiatrist's hour spent on each work, with breaks in between). The faculty writer would pretend to play a fairly detached role, facilitating discussion, but in the end whatever he or she said carried the most weight. For the most part, the value of the workshop came down to who was sitting around that table, and often that meant a parade of personal preferences masquerading as critical comments ("I liked when that guy knocked on the door"). I guess that's a kind of learning—hearing other people respond to your work, celebrating the subjective—but I found it confusing, since it wasn't really clear what lay behind the responses. What were the criteria for critical evaluation? That isn't, apparently, how "creative writers" think about their work.

While "The Program" was nominally skeptical about method and rather sanctimonious about creative freedom (driven, I suspect, by a mythology of the creative genius as social transgressor), there was a kind of a shadow consensus about what constituted "good writing," and it resembled what I like to call "Hollywood Humanism," the story logic of mainstream Hollywood films. This is first and foremost a character-centered aesthetic anchored in emotion, in which action arises out of character motivation. So far, so good, as we're not that far from what Aristotle said about drama and tragedy in Greek antiquity. The "humanism" comes to the fore in terms of character motivation, which leaves out any sense of guiding ideas, politics, faith, family—motivation is really reduced to the raw subjective motor of *desire*: people should get what they desire, that is the definition of "fair," how the world is supposed to work in the Gospel According to Hollywood. In most American movies, and especially so the bigger the budget, the main character is motivated to satisfy his own desires, especially for sex and power, the latter of which generally translates to violence. Hollywood likes to claim it makes a lot of love stories, but what they mean by love is pretty distorted, I think, resulting from a feat of logical legerdemain: love is truth; by love we really mean sex; sexuality is really truth. Characters reveal truth in terms of their sex objects, and characters will do anything to have sex with whom they want to have sex. Ultimately, Hollywood tells us, people will do anything to get the sex they want, and then they'll make up nice things to say about love. To say the least, this is a debased concept of love, worthy of a Hollywood culture that runs deep in alcoholism, promiscuity and divorce, drug addiction, depression, and suicide. But, man, those stars look great on film!

As I saw it, Old Man Liparulo bumming out, Hollywood Humanism in the creative writing workshop lost its grandeur, becoming something fuzzier, not even celebration but indulgence, focused not so much on power and violence as on endlessly detailed individual psychology, deviance, and obsession, stories about creepy people endlessly concerned with themselves. (I remember encountering a writer in the only fiction

Farewell to Football?

workshop I took in Binghamton, to complete my MA in English, who consulted the American Psychological Association's *Diagnostic Statistical Manual of Mental Disorders III* in developing her characters.) Workshop Humanism favors this milder version of the manifesto: anything emotional is true. People should get what they want, should be able to *feel* what they want to feel. They don't, of course, because human life is overwritten by power and ideology, faith, family, society, so then they whine about not getting what they want. I don't know, I'm probably just remembering the crappy stuff. In fact, in looking back on it, I realize that my navigation was still a few degrees off, as if I had missed another insider's orientation like I had way-back-when in Buffalo and thus hadn't gotten in on the declination diagram. Besides, in "creative writing" as in football, not everyone makes the team, not everyone cracks the starting lineup, and very few make it to the top of the pyramid and go pro. The writers I knew from The Program who found substantial success didn't actually fit this pattern of a community of self-centered people anyway. My personal problem, though, really was that I was a selfish outsider.

To put it in technical terms, my professional problem was that I was interested in *thematic* elements of literature, not just the emotional. I didn't get what I wanted and so I'm whining about it. I did complete the program, though. Old Man Liparulo, Doctor Steve. I guess I was hoping that the bigger challenges a writer faces, like project-management and research for book-length works, would be given some attention, but it's much easier to structure workshops around short, self-contained works, much easier for the teacher, and here comes another unique feature about creative writing programs. The expectations and working conditions for creative writing faculty were different from what I was used to, as well, and the prevailing business model in big creative writing programs amounted to bringing in someone with a good reputation and treating them to an easy job. Tuesday was Creative Writing day because faculty writers weren't expected to be on campus more than once a week. Some of our faculty commuted to Houston from other parts of the country. (They weren't riding on the bus like me commuting to Ithaca for ROTC day, either.)

So, I didn't really get what I came for in terms of the creative-writing half of the doctorate. That was the chance I took, and there weren't any guarantees. That risk puts the "free" in free agency, right? I wasn't an NFL owner, so I had to privatize the risk as well as the reward, if there would ever be any reward.

It all comes down to a fundamental difference in goals. As a writer, I was probably skeptical toward sentiment, less interested in what people were feeling and more concerned with how things worked, whether you call that function or power. When I was studying for my master's degree, thinking and working like a critic, I became fascinated by the treatment given to power by the French theorist Michel Foucault. While he was by trade and training a historian of ideas, Foucault ended up also providing tools for theorizing and interpretation, so his work was adopted by scholars in the social sciences as well as in literary studies (one of his major works, *Madness and Civilization*, was translated into English by Richard Howard, the star faculty poet at Houston when I started the creative writing program). His fans generally point favorably to his insight that the operation of power can be detected through studying "discourse," the organization and hierarchy—the "privileging" and devaluation—of knowledge. Some even believe that power can be *resisted* through destabilizing "discursive formations" that "valorize" evils such as racism and sexism. For me, an off-hand remark he made in an interview sums up my attraction to his work: "My point is not that everything is bad, but that everything is dangerous, which is not exactly the same as bad. If everything is dangerous, then we always have something to do. So my position leads not to apathy but to a hyper- and pessimistic activism"(p. 343). Of course, to "problematize" Foucault's work, there's a danger in all this critical power, too—it isn't just an intellectual resource for critical inquiry, it's also power made available for transgressive purposes and tools which activists can use to destabilize authority and tradition in favor of relativism and "decentered" power. Like all power, it presents dangerous temptations.

When I got to Houston, I found a different channel into these ideas of power and function, found I could "go pro" in rhetorical studies (the study of argument and persuasion), and found my next-generation mentor, the historian of rhetoric James L. Kastely, who prefers to go by a sole initial. J's course in the history of rhetoric brought together old familiar characters like Saint Augustine and Plato and Aristotle, added a few writers I hadn't really studied before like Machiavelli and Kenneth Burke, and re-contextualized them all for me in terms of the theory and practice of persuasion. As a mentor, J was the kind of sagacious, bearded father-figure I suppose I had always hoped to find in the academic world, and it turned out that he was a Vietnam veteran, too, a combat medic who went into Cambodia with the 1st Air Cavalry Division.

I suppose you could say that I actually did my Ph. D. in literature and rhetoric with a minor in creative writing, because J ended up directing my dissertation even though it was a creative work. In the kind of dramatic flare-up that creative-writing programs are famous for, my original director, a fiction writer who was actually hired mainly to serve as the chief administrator of the Creative Writing Program, resigned the night before my oral examination. I never looked into the details, because academic politics were and are generally low-stakes, arcane, and irrationally personal (one of my colleagues described the creative-writing world as the ego-circus of rock-stars but without the money), but I was left with no one to chair my dissertation committee. J was on my committee and it made sense that since I looked up to him as a mentor anyway he should become my director. The exquisite American poet Mark Doty was the faculty writer on my committee, and he was the exception that proved the rule about creative writing faculty—he was committed to his work, even beyond the normal commitment of faculty writers to their students; he lived up to the obligations of faculty to serve the program, department, college, and university.

Steven Liparulo

What I really learned from J can be pretty neatly summed up in the title of his 1997 book: *Rethinking the Rhetorical Tradition: From Plato to Postmodernism.* In several important cases, that meant translating the work of old friends from philosophy to rhetoric. As an undergraduate I had read Aristotle as the comprehensive brain-iac, a scholar from classical antiquity instituting the systematic study of biology, ethics, poetics, and more. It turns out, though, that if you start with Aristotle's *Rhetoric*, he ends up sounding a lot like Coach Bill Belichick: it's all situational. Aristotle's definition of rhetoric, as the ability to see in any given case the available means of persuasion, implies that in some situations only a limited choice of means will be present, or maybe none (Bud Adams had probably worked his way down to none). Like Foucault says, though, there's always something to do, even if it's to decide to wait until the situation changes. Practical wisdom from Coach Aristotle.

J's class started with, and lingered for a long time over, Plato's most rhetorical dialogue, the *Phaedrus.* The dialogue includes an explosively poetic description of the movement of the soul in love, a fit of madness rocked by shuddering, swelling, melting—in my marginalia, I invoked the sultry tones of Marlene Dietrich crooning "falling in love again, never wanted to, what am I to do, can't help it." The *Phaedrus* mainly concerns itself, however, with the political problem of seeking to attain action from an audience of non-lovers (again, Bud Adams might have benefited from a little Platonic thinking). The dramatic setting for the dialogue is at least implicitly seductive, as the older Socrates walks outside the walls of Athens with the young and attractive Phaedrus. Initially, they discuss a recent speech by Lysias in which the speaker attempts to persuade an attractive young man that the non-lover is the best partner—an openly exploitative approach to the erotic. Eventually Socrates' sense of shame overwhelms him and he turns their discussion to the higher-order concern of how the passions can be manipulated. The whole explosive erotic epiphany of the soul in love is actually an image of danger—being ruled by the passions results in divine madness. In contemporary Christian terms, Socrates is not far away from saying that disordered passions—embracing and following disordered passions—is a root of sinful behavior. The *Phaedrus* is a classic in both the rhetorical and philosophical traditions because it can be read and re-read and re-thought over and over again, addressing questions of audience and persuasion and love and passion, never quite holding to a stable interpretation, always available to new exploration.

While reading Saint Augustine as rhetoric, instead of philosophy, still offsets a few degrees from the author's aim at theology, it comes much closer, since this Platonic conception of rhetoric focuses on the movement of the soul. We studied a text I hadn't read before, *On Christian Doctrine,* and in its treatment of how a Christian reads and interprets Scripture, which includes both literal and figurative language, I found a powerful idea: "in the consideration of figurative expressions a rule such as this will serve, that what is read should be subjected to diligent scrutiny until an interpretation contributing to the reign of charity is produced" (XV. Three). When I first read it, this "rule of charity" was but a drop in a doctoral flood of new and recycled ideas about persuasion and interpretation, imagination and feeling, but in the long haul it provided one of the most important principles for living in a fallen world. It used "charity" in the Pauline sense as a specific form of love: "So faith, hope, love [charity] remain, these three; but the greatest of these is love" (1 COR 13:13). When in doubt, in a world full of danger, do what adds to the world's supply of love.

In J's course, I was also introduced to Machiavelli's *The Prince,* a game plan for rulers navigating the transition from a fairly determined feudal world to a more modern landscape of rhetorically manipulated appearances, which I found best treated with what we might call, with suitably academic long-windedness and endlessly punctuated sentences, "Belichickian situationality": I want to be able, in certain situations, to think like a Machiavellian, to game-plan like a Machiavellian, but not *to live* like a Machiavellian, more feared than loved. I would really like to live under the reign of charity. What would that look like? I don't think it would be trying to be cool to fit in. I don't think it would entail griping about what Bud Adams was doing to pro football in Houston, nor bitching and moaning about how other people thought about and wrote their stories. I think the point of a reign of charity would be going beyond those petty things. If so, I would be a long time getting there.

• • •

"I'm going to get something out of this deal, too."

November 9, 1996: Homecoming. Houston 56, Southern Mississippi 49, Robertson Stadium, Houston.

For whatever disappointments might have been entailed, whatever adjustments in expectations, one thing survived this deal I'd made to move on to graduate school at the doctoral level: I still loved to teach, even if it was now only a part-time job, and not particularly remunerative. I still loved to contribute to the intellectual growth of young people, and teaching writing in college, the work meant sponsoring growth in a transformational process—writing isn't just something done at the end to wrap up research and learning, it is an integral part of both. As it turned out, though, my expectations about "moving up a level" to teach at a university, at least to teach first-year composition at the University of Houston, might have been a little optimistic. A metropolitan public university in a very large international business hub in a border state, the U of H drew students of remarkable diversity (in the 21st century, UH would become the second-most ethnically-diverse research university in America, after New Jersey's Rutgers). This diversity applied to their academic preparation as well as their cultural heritage, with some students well prepared for college writing and others barely meeting high-school standards for competence, not much different from a lot of the students I had been teaching at Norwich High. That range of abilities made teaching the first-year composition courses surprisingly challenging, and I was lucky to have the experience I did to handle it.

Farewell to Football?

A lot of my colleagues were new to teaching and didn't manage their time very well, and when you added in their preference for partying on the weekends, that meant that I could only find a few of my fellow graduate students willing and able to enjoy the free college football games that came with our student ID's. By November, we'd gotten those things sorted out and I went to one of the most exciting football games I've ever witnessed with a guy from Pittsburgh.

It was Homecoming weekend, and the Southern Mississippi at Houston game marked the return of football to campus, because in 1996 the Cougars began splitting their schedule between the lifeless Astrodome and the relatively ancient Robertson (formerly Jeppesen) Stadium. This game had all the advantages: for an evening game in November, the conditions were ideal, clear and a little cool; late in the season, both teams were playing for a shot at the Conference-USA title and a bowl game; both teams could rack up the offense, so this wouldn't be a dull Jeff Fisher affair. Instead, it proved to be a barely-controlled detonation, as Houston tallied 577 yards to Southern Mississippi's 472 in winning the game in overtime, 56-49. The Cougars set four school records that still stand as of this writing, three by running back Antowain Smith, who scored 36 points on six touchdowns, five of them rushing.

The fourth record was set by Charles West for longest punt return in school history, an 87-yarder late in the fourth quarter, the most exciting play for which I'd ever been in the stands—add Robertson Stadium to the Houses of the Holy. The return was slow to develop, as West initially snaked back and forth across the field hesitantly until finally turning up-field and kicking in the after-burners, the crowd excitement building the whole time. Though the attendance was announced as a meager 18,107, it felt to me a lot more like the spontaneous simultaneous eruption of a million souls in football communion. The Cougars had come from behind to tie the game at 42, and this unexpected return for a touchdown gave them the lead, and everybody in that old relic of a stadium was on their feet cheering. All except the guy from Pittsburgh.

He was looking something up in the program and couldn't be both-ered to join in the fun. I smacked him on the head and asked him, "what on earth is wrong with you?" He said he was trying to figure out if this stadium used to be Jeppesen Stadium. "What difference does that make?" I wondered, ignorant at the time of the history of Houston foot-ball. Well, we were graduate students, here to do research.

Of course, he was right, as I would later discover through my own research. This old place, that to me looked as much like a rodeo arena as a football stadium, was the first home of the Houston Oilers and *had* been the site of that epic double-overtime game to decide the AFL title in 1962. (Just for irony's sake, I can report discovering that the same weekend in December 1962, the public was called upon to vote on an-other bond to cover additional costs incurred in preparing to build the Astrodome; Gast, p. 104). The AFL All-Star game *had* migrated here in 1965 after the players found New Orleans intolerable, and that had been one of the last college or pro games played on this field for decades, as the Cougars moved indoors to the Astrodome and the Oilers parked at Rice Stadium for a couple of years before finally landing in the dome themselves. Having shelled out a lot of money to go to a dreary Oilers game in the Astrodome earlier in the season, with that 49ers guy from California, I was ready to confess to the guy from Pittsburgh that college ball at "The Rob" was altogether the better way to go.

That 1996 Homecoming game, further research would also support, could be told as a tale of two Cougar running backs headed in different directions. Antowain Smith, the senior starter who set those three scor-ing records that night, would begin a long NFL journey the following year when he was drafted by Buffalo (he would start his career playing in Rich Stadium, where I had missed out on my chance to rock out with Led Zeppelin). Smith's career would wind its way to the Houses of the Holy in two Super Bowls with the dynastic Patriots: SB XXXVI after the 2001 season (which was briefly interrupted by 9/11), played in the New Orleans Superdome as New England beat St. Louis; and SB XXXVIII after the 2003 season, back in Houston at Reliant Stadium, which hadn't been built when Smith was running for the Cougars, as New England beat Carolina. The other running back for the Cougars, Ketric Sanford, was in his freshman year of scholarship football in 1996, and he fumbled early in the Homecoming game and didn't play much after that. That wasn't his only miscue that season, but he would find his way and eventually take ownership of several school records.

Sanford came from the small Texas city of Corsicana not even sure if he wanted to play college football. He was more of a soccer player, but football offered scholarships, and therein lay the beginning of the deal he would make with the University of Houston and with football. In his first semester, that fall of 1996, football gained the upper hand, as Sanford played well enough to earn the spot as Smith's understudy in the Cougar backfield. He didn't do so well in the classroom—when he *was in* the classroom. "Having that freedom," he told me years later, "doing real well on the field, I didn't go to a lot of my classes that first semester." Not surprisingly, his grades suffered, and he ended up on academic probation and had to pass something on the order of 24 credit hours in the spring to regain his athletic eligibility. He did more than pass, though, finding untapped resources and achieving a 3.2 grade-point-average. "Spring semester confirmed that I could do it. It taught me a hard lesson that you need to be more focused, had to have some sort of plan in place."

The balance was never going to be easy. While on the field his focus led to a career that makes him the school record-holder for career rushing attempts, rushing yards, and all-purpose plays, along with the season record for kickoff return average, carrying out the plan academically and socially proved very challenging, too. As Sanford once told his father-in-law, Guy Brown, who played NFL ball for the Cowboys from 1977 to 1982, "I went to college thinking that I'm here because they want something out of me. I'm going to get something out of this deal, too." While the Cougars got all of those yards out of him, Sanford had to settle sometimes for courses that he didn't really want just to meet the enrollment requirements for athletic eligibility while he couldn't take the economics courses he would have preferred because they conflicted with football practice or weight room workouts. A generation earlier, Rufus Cormier told me, he had faced the same quandary as a scholarship athlete at SMU, briefly considering majoring in chemistry until it occurred to him that football practice and chemistry labs were likely to conflict. Sanford also didn't want to miss out on the whole range of experiences of college life by remaining self-confined in the athletic complex like a lot of players tend to do, self-defined as a jock. He wouldn't wear his athletic gear outside the facility. "If you didn't know me, you wouldn't know I played football. I wasn't an athlete, I was a student that was there because of athletics."

Everyone makes their deal, and sometimes things turn out pretty well. Rufus Cormier didn't major in chemistry at SMU, but he still ended up winning the award as outstanding senior student with a degree in Anthropology—good enough for entry to Yale Law School, on his way to becoming the first African-American partner at Houston's Baker Botts law firm (and other students found ways to balance science majors with football—a backup quarterback on Cormier's team ultimately became a dentist). Ketric Sanford did earn his degree in Economics and makes use of his education as Chief Financial Officer at Great Southwest Fire & Safety in Dallas. Neither made a living playing professional football, but college football was an essential part of the deal that shaped the lives they are living. Neither is certain that college football today is entirely worth the price it demands from players. Cormier is wary about the unrealistic expectations players have and how much time and effort they put into the sport when "the odds are against them playing pro football." Sanford is even more direct and personal: when asked if he will let his sons play college football, he replied that "if they don't have to, there's no need for them to. At some point [my wife and I] have to give them the option, but if it was solely up to me, I wouldn't." He's convinced that young men need to be part of a team, but any kind of team will probably suffice, while "in college, it's tough to do, to do well academically if you're playing football."

Farewell to Football?

So what is football doing on campus? After completing undergraduate and master's degrees in Binghamton, at a university that didn't even field a football team, and earning my Army commission through ROTC at Cornell, a school where football generated no discernible idolatry, I was finally at an institution with a "college football tradition," Cougar pride including Andre Ware, the first black quarterback to win the Heisman Trophy, and in 1996 I was starting to see that there's more to that question than first appears, or that there are more answers than I expected. Football is doing all kinds of things. In the academic spirit of scholarly research, I can compare some of my observations since then with Easterbrook's critical findings in *The King of Sports.*

College football definitely provides excitement to its fans, gets them raving like me at that 1996 Homecoming game, and the NCAA like the NFL has done an outstanding job of transacting that excitement into hard currency. Easterbrook reports that the University of Georgia, whither my football journeys would take me in 2013, "*cleared* $53 million on its football program--$75 million in revenue against $22 million in costs" in 2010 (p. 82, emphasis mine). College football may exploit athletes, and it certainly makes money off the labor of football players without directly paying them salary or wages. Nor does college football necessarily contribute much to the rest of the university—players like Ketric Sanford have to make a concerted effort to live the life of the college student, and many choose to stay somewhat cultishly isolated. As Easterbrook concludes, "at many big-college sports programs, the athletic department is structured as an independent organization that leases campus space and school logos, then operates a tax-exempt business over which the school's president and board of trustees have little control" (p. 87). And while Georgia may actually *make* money through their football program, at Houston like at most universities in America, the revenue stream runs in the other direction, the university having to subsidize the athletic department. (According to the most recent figures published in *USA Today,* as of this writing the University of Houston subsidizes more than 53% of its athletics budget from student fees and other institutional support as well as state money.)

As I later learned from Ketric Sanford and Rufus Cormier, college football offers players tremendous opportunities, but it takes a player capable of swimming upstream to get the full academic benefit of the athletic-scholarship deal. Easterbrook found James Gayle playing defensive end at Virginia Tech. Gayle's uncle Shaun played defensive back on that 1985 Chicago Bears team that obliterated the Patriots in the Super Bowl with Dave Duerson and Jim McMahon, and in 2012 Shaun Gayle joined the head-injury lawsuit against the NFL. James Gayle told Easterbrook a story similar to the one Sanford told me: "Football made me a better student. I was mediocre at grades until I learned that needing a good GPA was for real, that GPA would help get a scholarship" (p. 296). Sanford and Cormier and Gayle are still the exceptions, in the aggregate, as Easterbrook reports on a 2010 study that shows that "the average graduation rate for Division I football players was 55 percent, compared to an average male graduation rate of 68 percent at the same colleges" (p. 114). Apparently, it's kind of tough to get the most out of that deal.

In 1996, I wasn't in any position to come to any firm conclusions regarding the role football should play on college campuses, or whether the demands were worth it to the players, or what should be done about all the money college sports were probably taking away from academic programs, or how cities like Houston should deal with NFL franchise-free-agency. Those explorations were just beginning, and meanwhile I had my own deal to try to transact, and that whole creative-writing/academics balance wasn't really working out so great for me, as it turned out. I was, in some sense, both out of place and not a whole person. In that early rush of enthusiasm about starting the doctoral program, I had taken advantage of ready access to the university library to read around liberally in the collected works of C. G. Jung, a founding father of psychoanalysis who, with Sigmund Freud, had pioneered the exploration of the human unconscious. I remember being thrilled to find him writing generously about the transformational symbolism of the Catholic Mass, and more generally was intrigued by his concept of the shadow, a kind of personification of the unconscious which, because it operates in the darkness—sometimes the darkness of repression—has a free hand to create both meaning and mischief. I thought—or maybe, better, sensed—that he was probably on to something.

CHAPTER 9

— • • • —

Just Getting There, Part I (1999)

"He had an immense self-importance; he was unable
to picture a world of which he was only a typical part—
a world of treachery, violence, and lust in which his
shame was altogether insignificant. How often the priest
had heard the same confession—Man was so limited
he hadn't even the ingenuity to invent a new vice: the
animals knew as much. It was for this world that Christ
had died; the more evil you saw and heard about you,
the greater glory lay around the death. It was too easy to
die for what was good or beautiful, for home or children
or a civilization—it needed a God to die for the half-
hearted and corrupt."

(GRAHAM GREENE, *THE POWER AND THE GLORY*, P. 97)

• • •

NOVEMBER 7, 1999: Detroit Lions 31, St. Louis Rams 27, Pontiac
Silverdome. The St. Louis Rams had something special going in 1999,
one of those stories the sports media love to tell. A team rallying around
a guy who just wouldn't quit. Best of all, they were playing exciting football: The Greatest Show on Turf.

The Rams came into their Week 9 match-up with Detroit at 6-1
(they'd had their bye week very early in the season), and they were lighting up the scoreboard, having tallied 40 points or more twice and more

than 30 an additional three times. Their lowest total so far came the week before, only 21 points in their first loss of the season—against Jeff Fisher's Tennessee Titans. That would hold up as the Rams' lowest score throughout the regular season. Fisher did his best to make the Greatest Show on Turf boring.

The Rams were led by quarterback Kurt Warner, a big-armed deep passer who through his career would set records for accuracy as well. Warner's enduring appeal originated somewhere beyond the numbers, though, and he was living out one of the great underdog-triumph stories in American sports. Time and again he had been passed over: third on the depth chart at second-rung University of Northern Iowa, he only got his chance to start as a senior; undrafted by the NFL, he was cut after a brief try-out during Green Bay's training camp; after starring in the Arena Football League, just a step or two away from professional wrestling when it comes to athletic credibility, Warner was signed by St. Louis, only to be relegated to exile in NFL Europe. With fervent faith as a convert to evangelical Christianity buoying his spirits against the tide of setbacks, Warner continued to believe in his ability, putting in the work needed to be ready when the opportunity presented itself.

That opportunity would come in the 1999 preseason, when Rams starting quarterback Trent Green went down with a knee injury and Warner took over the high-flying offense dreamed up by "mad scientist" Offensive Coordinator Mike Martz. With Marshall Faulk, arguably the best all-purpose back ever to play in the NFL, threatening defenses whether running the ball or catching passes, and Pro-Bowl wide receiver Isaac Bruce leading a quartet of wide-outs who would catch more than 30 passes each in the coming season, the Rams took advantage of the fast track inside St. Louis's Trans World Dome to become the top-ranked offense in the NFL that year. Warner stepped into a situation he had spent his life preparing for and rose to the challenge, winning Most Valuable Player awards for both the season and the Super Bowl.

I watched that Rams-at-Lions game, two Astroturf teams playing in the Pontiac Silverdome thirty miles north of Detroit, on television in Martinez, California, on the Oakland side of the bay. I was visiting my nephew, Matt Benson, and we were celebrating a family milestone. Matt was in the Bay Area in charge of a big cabling installation job, and his wife Kelly had given birth in September to their first child, a son they named Jaia. Born to educated parents imbued with the ironic humor of their generation, Jaia had already accrued a noble nickname: Sir Pooperton. Matt and Kelly were far away from family out there on the west coast, so I had decided to combine two objectives into one road trip: I visited Erin, a good friend from the Houston creative writing program who had won a Stegnar writer's fellowship at Stanford, and after a couple of days she ran me across the Bay Bridge to Martinez, to pay a call on the furthest west branch of our expanding family. (My middle sister's oldest daughter Courtney had married a Marine and gone west, giving birth to the first of the next generation, a son Michael born a couple of years earlier on the inland Twentynine Palms Marine Corps Base in southern California.)

I enjoyed being back in the Bay Area, having visited my old Binghamton housemate Michael Lederer down the peninsula on my way to Korea fifteen years earlier and a few more times thereafter, growing fond of the usual San Francisco charms, the hills and fogs and cold summer nights wrapped snugly around a funky friendly small city. Erin, who had come into the Houston program a year after me, was hedging bets on her future, the fellowship at Stanford the western point of a triangle connecting (or dividing) the graduate writing program in Houston and medical school in her native Wisconsin. Even though she was quite successful, already, as a poet, she never really took the writing entirely seriously, so she was in effect just hiding out in San Francisco until she started her "real life" as a doctor—her mother was a physician, and I think that's what her family expected of her. OK, I was somewhere in-between myself, taking a time-out, game to spend a few days hiding out, visiting City Lights Bookstore, founded in the 1950's by Lawrence Ferlinghetti, one of my all-time favorite poets, checking out the sea lions on the waterfront. We commuted from her very-downtown apartment—it was on Geary, if I remember correctly—to the cheery, sunny Stanford campus in her incongruous Texas-plated pickup truck, which she had sensibly purchased with the fruits of another writing competition she had won. I probably told her the story about how Michael Lederer's father, who had taught at Princeton and Yale before moving west, decided to quit his job as a professor of political science at Stanford on the day he read in the news that the Palo Alto trash collectors had settled their labor contract to end a strike—and the trash men would be making more than Professor Lederer! The lovely Stanford campus was as brilliant as I recalled from previous visits, all those arches and red tile roofs, and the student body as diverse and happy and friendly as could be, tooling around merrily on their happy-shiny bicycles. Somehow, it made my blood run cold, as if I could hear the coded whispers of a secretive elite conspiring to keep me out. Erin's fellowship called for a minimal teaching commitment, and we were free late in the week to trip up the Pacific Coast Highway for a picnic and cold dip in the Pacific at Point Reyes. It did my heart good to see a friend who was like me exploring the in-between, and it would be just as great to see New York family, I reflected as we crossed the Bay Bridge in Erin's Texas truck.

Truly on the other side of the bay, Matt and Kelly lived in a nondescript apartment in a nondescript complex which I guessed was convenient to Matt's job site. I couldn't think of any other reason to pick that particular place, which I could plausibly imagine as the site of an occasional gang-related shooting. I'd always thought the world of Matt, who was the first of his generation, my oldest sister's son, and visiting him and his wife in the first blush of their parenthood, with the prospect of sharing a cold beer and a steak cooked out on the grill, seemed like a pretty good way to wrap up the weekend. As we tuned into a football game that started at 10 o'clock in the morning on the west coast, we kicked off a rite of male bonding fairly rare in a family that decidedly tilted toward the distaff. Maybe it was for the best that we were on the coast, far from family, seeking room to breathe and redefine ourselves on a neutral field. Home turf was swampy and reeked of failure.

I had certainly factored in the distance when I made my decision to pursue my doctorate in Houston. Earning bachelor's and master's degrees an hour bus-ride away from my family, and teaching at a high school where both of my oldest sister's children were students, I'd spent a fair portion of my life close to family, and it wasn't always pretty. I had also swung out wide on the trapeze of travel during my Army service, from the American south to New England to Korea and to Europe, and found those distances sometimes felt liberating. At least I'd seen a range of possibilities.

The Army was a flat-out adventure, though, while Houston and The Program was ... something else, a major career choice, something like a football coach replacing his quarterback at halftime, not entirely a positive development. By 1999 I wasn't utterly certain that it was a mistake, but I had been mistaken in some of my assumptions, that much was clear. The results weren't encouraging. I had the freedom to travel to the Bay Area because I was taking a break from the creative writing program after three years so that I could try to really *write*, a paradox that didn't exactly speak well to the utility of my graduate *writing* program, or at least to my fit with that program. I had gotten a good start on a novel that I called *Catholic Divorce*, a medical mystery set in a small town pretty similar to Norwich, but then started to feel like the fragmented lifestyle of the graduate student/teaching assistant would act as a drag on the steady grinding fiction-writer's work of revision, so I had taken a leave of absence (I have always been tempted by the demon who advocates running away). At least I wouldn't have to take classes and write papers and plan lessons and grade papers, but I couldn't really figure out how to open up a lot of time for writing, since I would have to earn my living by the sweat of my brow. I took a full-time accounting job to make ends meet, which meant that I only had a few hours a day, early in the morning, at lunch, maybe in the evening (never my preference), and what I could manage on the weekend to devote to the writing. It was a compromise yielding only the most marginal of advantages.

Farewell to Football?

I didn't really know how to work like a writer, though. That had been a major weakness of The Program from my perspective, the fact that the emphasis was mainly on the product, and usually the isolated short story that could be covered in a single workshop session, and not on the process or project-management, which is a big part of writing books. My ambition was to write books.

I felt like I went on leave with half a plan. I had some idea of the end product I wanted to arrive at with *Catholic Divorce*, what kind of book I wanted to write, something akin to the big Victorian novels but set in contemporary context. I wanted the main characters to deal with emotional and spiritual conflicts rooted in major social problems, a story with a strong reality principle. I dreamed up a married couple of doctors whose love had gone cold but who stayed together in part because of their high-school-aged daughter and in part because of their Catholic faith (hence the title, slang for a married couple who continue to live together but not as lovers). Dr. Husband was a pathologist, and hence a little dark and ruminative, while Dr. Wife was a family practitioner, an exceptionally smart woman whose challenge was constantly dealing with rather dim everyday people who suffer bowel disorders and need to reduce their blood lipids. The main industry in town had shifted from commercial pharmaceuticals, which employed hundreds of locals, to secret chemical research, which employed very few and of an often-unpleasant secretive/governmental/technocratic character. I introduced adventure into the plot with a rebellious high-school kid who broke into the chemical plant and let loose test-lab dogs, but ultimately I had a hard time getting it all to come together—it lacked a compelling "story logic" connecting all the dots. It's not enough to have an idea, it's not anywhere near enough to *want* to write a certain kind of book. I did not have all the tools necessary to get where I wanted to be. I look back now and see that mainly it was a practical problem of research, and I needed to get out of the house and do the right kind of research, interview sources with expertise and experience in medicine and research and chemical-weapons programs and matters of that sort to drill down far enough into the information to tap into a fully-connected story. I also needed to know myself better as a writer, and to be much more honest with myself overall, confess to my sins and my suffering and take ownership of my disordered passions, in order to write with integrity. At the time, I just felt seriously out of place, as if I had ventured well beyond my capabilities, and I didn't really know how to proceed. Even now I'm not sure I could have ever achieved an authentic voice for such complex and accomplished characters.

The novel and its process was a mess, a confrontation with my own shortcomings, and there is no denying that the leave of absence was a tentative step in the direction of quitting, a step on the way to the swamp to which the demon beckoned me. That was, unfortunately, one of those "lessons" I had learned experientially through my family life, no chalkboard or paper-and-pencil test required, that when things get difficult, you should just give up, just drift into the swamp and then some time later start complaining about how hard it's going to be to get out of there. The way I remember it, distorted according to the shape of my own character, my three older sisters went through endless dramas of "breaking up" with boyfriends, and as they got older, divorcing husbands. My three sisters had seven kids by six different fathers, that part is a fact. Over and over again, bad choices, abandoned. It never seemed like they had any idea about making it work or staying with it. Nothing seemed to last. I had fought against that quitting tendency to complete my undergraduate degree, after abandoning my first academic major and trying to abandon Binghamton by unsuccessfully applying to transfer to an Ivy League school. I'd fought to earn my commission (it was never easy getting on that stupid bus, especially when badly hungover or burnt out), to serve out my active duty contract, to complete my master's degrees. I had given in a few times, too, quitting on Buffalo before I ever started at the university there, quitting on high school teaching after only four years, quitting on the only serious love affair of my life after a couple of years. The demon got on the scoreboard. My family was riddled with divorces, in some ways the ultimate in quitting, but I hadn't even gotten far enough to get married. Something was cold and hard in my heart and I hadn't hazarded enough of an exploration to see a way beyond the limits it imposed on my emotions. I had really never committed myself completely to anything, and with only a watery and lukewarm faith (baptized Episcopalian in my late twenties, I had never been active in the church), I don't know that I understood what that would look like or how it would work. The idea of an undying faith in a *Father?* That was tangled up in all the wrong associations of men and husbands and fathers in my family. According to the women close at hand in my life, men were mostly crap.

And yet, I was spiritually curious, like the World War II paratrooper Ike supposedly asked, "do you like jumping out of planes?" The kid answered, "no, sir, but I prefer serving with men who do." I was curious about what deep faith would look like and in Houston I had taken up a form of church tourism. Through the softball team affiliated with the creative writing program, I had gotten close to a poet who had also taken a degree in religious studies at an Ivy League divinity school. I don't recall exactly how it all came together, but we got in the habit of every month or so going to a different church for Sunday services, from a Catholic Mass in Latin to the Metropolitan Community Church, a broadly-tolerant hybrid of former Catholics and Protestants. The poet would explain to me the differences in belief and practices, and afterwards we would discuss our reactions over breakfast. She had been raised Catholic, but because she identified as a lesbian was no longer practicing and had taken her faith elsewhere. I could somehow sense that Roman Catholicism was the baseline against which the other churches were measured for her. She was a true believer (and acted on her faith, serving as a hospital chaplain among other acts of mercy), and she faced a conflict rooted in the reality of her emotional life. She loved who she loved and doctrine was not going to change the truth of that love. She wasn't the only gay Catholic I met through The Program, either (I first heard the name for my novel from a gay poet), and it made a strong impression on me that these good people I'd met had such love for a church that I thought defined their love as sin. More than ever, I was curious about what a life lived according to faith would look like, but was I curious enough to do more than just think about it? Not quite ready for commitment in 1999, not in this millennium.

In my journal, as part of the process of drafting my novel, I tried to imagine that most Catholic of ritual ordeals, Confession, no doubt over-dramatizing it as a medieval torture scenario, locked into a sweaty box with a stern and verbally-acute priest, most likely a Jesuit, an *inquisitor* ready to catch up the penitent in lie after lie. And what would I confess, if it were me instead of my protagonist in the box? What counted as a sin? That as a child I felt the seemingly endless and senseless stirrings of sexual desires? Where did these dirty thoughts and feelings come from—would I have to explain to the priest why I felt the rising of the sex-demons in my loins when my grade school teacher fiddled with the buttons of her blouse? How could I explain the connection between that pleasant view and the hideous picture that flashed up of foul obese nether-flesh from further back in my memory? Would I have to account for the rare and abrupt appearance of some devil tempting me to angry physical violence against the loved one who had stepped in for my mother on countless occasions because Mother had to work—how many sins were packed into that little scene? Would the priest force me to figure out who was that man in the cellar? Would the priest drill me until I finally told him all the secrets, leaving me fully exposed and with no chance for any happiness in life, so vile had my transgressions been? I didn't get very far with that confessional exercise, and did not return to it. The book suffered from this tendency to quit in the face of the really hard work.

I guess I was curious, too, visiting Matt, wondering if he was going to break the family cycle and make a go of it as a dad and husband. I had turned forty that year, and was starting to look to the next generation to see if maybe they would do a little better than we had done. The odds were really stacked against him, as his mother and father split before Matt started school, and his mother made no secret of her contempt for his father, who had been an abusive alcoholic in the days of that first marriage for both of them. I had been a witness to a few of those dark episodes, caught in the middle of family melodrama extended across generations.

Here's a plot for a bad, sad novel: In the late 1960's my mother had married for the third time, to a man she knew from the start had a major drinking problem. In fact, their "meet cute," to use the movie term, had come when she saved his life in an Elk's Club kitchen after he, the excessively-sampling bar-tender, had passed out and swallowed his tongue and she, trained as a nurse but working as a waitress, had opened the airway. It was their cute idea to let me get drunk on New Year's Eve, 1968 (when Rufus Cormier was running down Steve Owens in the Astro-Bluebonnet Bowl). In the early 1970's, hopped up on some hastily-sketched dream for a new life they had cooked up over highballs (maybe stirred by the demon who advocates running away), we had all packed up, dysfunctional family on the go, and moved to Florida, where the marriage unraveled across fifth, sixth, and seventh-grade for me. When things reached their foolish peak, my mother had packed up us remaining kids, oldest sister having married "abruptly," as those things happened in those days, and we returned to upstate New York—by bus, no less, a horrid odyssey, arriving just in time for another dismal winter to start.

Unable to make ends meet, my mother had farmed me out to Matt's mother and father (quite literally, as Matt's father was running the family dairy farm), where intersecting family patterns were playing themselves out in the occasional drunken nights erupting into what as a society we refer to as "domestic violence." *Wife-beating* is what it was back then, and I guess I thought I had to put up with it, since at 13 where else was I going to go? It wasn't like we sat down and had a family meeting about the situation. Eventually, after bearing him two children, Matt and Stephanie, my sister finally had enough of Matt's father's resentful drunken husband routine and began her own struggling journey as a single mother before the kids started elementary school. Not too long after that, Matt's father gave up drinking and got his act together, marrying again and starting another family, though I didn't know much about that until fairly recently.

Despite a rough start, Matt also had some advantages which were quite evident by the time I visited him in 1999. He was very bright, tall, good looking, and had been well-liked at school, selected as his high-school class's speaker at graduation. He had also pushed past the quitting point a few times playing sports, staying with basketball all through high school, even starting at times. I was honored that he had completed his undergraduate degree at my alma mater in Binghamton. He wasn't afraid to work hard, and had enough of a sense of adventure in his soul to ramble far afield. He met his wife in Missoula, Montana, of all places, and now his work had led him to the coast, where he was the boss-man on site. I guess I wouldn't bet against him.

I found out later that where I made up for lost ground through military initiations and academic mentorship, Matt had benefited from a few key episodes with baseball and basketball coaches, including his dad. What Matt remembers most about having his father as his Little League coach was the ferocious chewing out he got from his dad when he didn't follow through on a commitment to play in an all-star game. Matt was probably following our family protocol—*never mind, give up, whatever,* but his father insisted on a different code concerning commitment. You don't quit in the middle of things. Matt's high school basketball coach made a similar impact, pushing him and his teammates past what they thought were their limits during conditioning drills, and then forcing Matt to own up to his decision-making mistakes on offense—he wasn't going to start if he didn't make better passing choices. It was harder for Matt to get past these tempted-to-quit moments than for some of his teammates, since he didn't get a lot of support from home (no one was waiting to pick him up when the bus got back to school from away games), but their impact on him was apparent to me in 1999 when I visited the brand-new father on the other side of the bay.

Farewell to Football?

He was a good host, it turned out, and an interesting young man, someone I could have a real conversation with (he knew the temptations of the road and that he was probably going to have to bust some butt on his crew sooner or later concerning behavior, and for a moment we were like fellow officers after a few beers griping lovingly about the dang enlisted men). His wife was smart and cute and just far-out enough to be credible as a Missoula native (the coolest guy I knew in The Program had come from Missoula), though I don't remember much about her—symptomatic, I'm pretty sure, of my own cold-hearted short-sighted selfishness, like she was someone in a story I wasn't willing to do the work to get to know and provide with an attractive and distinguishing trait, and thus she would end up a flat character incapable of carrying on any important function in the story. Ultimately her function would almost certainly be as grist for the family gossip mill, a gruesome fate when the claws came out and the whip came down. Jaia was a lovely baby, hale and ruddy, though he sure could cry! They all major in wailing and bawling, those newborn, and he seemed healthy enough to live up to his Poopy nickname—eat and sleep and poop, that's the baby lifestyle, easy enough to sketch in a few words. Outside of the literary limitations, Sunday turned out to be a good day for Uncle Steve to impose on a dynamic young family to watch a good football game on TV.

You never know how these NFL games are going to turn out. There's a lot of excess and illusion in pro football, a lot of pumped up music and noise in the stadia, a lot of hype in the media, but the one thing that really isn't fake is the competition of the game on the field. While the Rams were the media darlings of the 1999 season, for good reason (their quarterback the subject of a *Sports Illustrated* cover story that asked "Who *Is* This Guy?"), the Detroit Lions were struggling to figure out just who they were, too. Hall of Fame running back Barry Sanders had surprised the football world by announcing his retirement just prior to the 1999 season, and the Lions had to improvise a sudden transition from a running team to a passing team. For all that, they came into the game against the Rams at 5-2, and darned if they didn't pull off the upset, 31-27. Somehow, they held Marshall Faulk to 15 yards rushing on 11 carries, and even though Kurt Warner threw for three touchdowns, so did the Detroit quarterback combination of Gus Frerotte and Charlie Batch (whom my guy from Pittsburgh in The Program used to coach in junior-high basketball).

St. Louis would only lose one more game the rest of the season, though, while Detroit dropped to 8-8, "good enough" to make the playoffs for a wild card game they lost to Washington. The Rams won a wild shootout with Minnesota, 49-37, to get their playoffs started with a bang. (Jerry Ball, who played on both sides of the line during Beaumont West Brook's "five in a row dome show" playoff run in 1982, started that game at defensive tackle for the Vikings.) The Rams had to squeak out a close one against Tampa Bay, 11-6, to make it to the Super Bowl. Head Coach Tony Dungy's Buccaneers kept the lid on Warner until the fourth quarter, when he finally connected for a touchdown to Ricky Proehl.

The Super Bowl provided a rematch of the Rams against the Tennessee Titans, whose four decades of peregrinations had led them first as the Oilers through Houston outdoor venues Jeppesen Stadium and Rice Stadium and thence indoors to the Astrodome, whence they journeyed on Bud Adams' magic franchise-free-agency carpet ride to a single season as the Tennessee Oilers outdoors on turf in Memphis, another season as the Tennessee Oilers in Nashville at Vanderbilt Stadium, and ultimately to a new permanent name and home as the Tennessee Titans playing at a Nashville stadium variously captioned Adelphi Coliseum and LP Field. Somehow it seems appropriate that the Titans would culminate the most successful season in franchise history, their only appearance in a Super Bowl, in a dome, in the bland confines of Atlanta's Georgia Dome, taking on the most quintessentially *dome/turf* team in NFL history, and another franchise-free-agency refugee outfit, the former Los Angeles (and before that Cleveland) Rams. The first Super Bowl of the new millennium, and suitably postmodern.

I was back in Houston for the Super Bowl, watching it on TV at a party hosted by some guy from The Program. I was halfway through my leave of absence, and secretly maybe a little surprised that the world hadn't ended with the advent of the new millennium (secretly disappointed?). I had not taken any chances and had hunkered down on New Year's Eve Y2K—no party for this paranoiac! No, I stayed at home and drank alone and pretended to confess my sins, or tried to confess my sins without knowing exactly what counted as sins and how they should be confessed.

Forgive me, Lord, for bad stewardship of resources. (Is that a sin? It should be.) I have taken out loans to pay for my education and I have made bad choices about how to spend that money. I've indulged in pornography and other sinful habits. I have turned away from people who love me and people I should love and care for and turned toward illusions, selfish sinful illusions. I have sought pleasure and found only momentary relief from boredom and fear. (Is the sin in the intention or in the outcome?)

Forgive me, God, for I have sinned, turning away from the truth and the gifts that I have been given and taking up an empty pursuit of acceptance. I have tried to fit in and be cool, and if you really know all things, Lord, you know that I was never meant to be cool. Forgive me, Lord, for making a fool of myself. (Forgive me, too, if making an inside joke in Confession is also a sin.)

I found that as I tried to flesh out the list of my sins, what I thought would be an endless litany, it became pretty clear that there was really just one sin, over and over again, if I understood sin at all. I was selfish, self-absorbed, self-centered. I had formed at least a vague idea of how a good and virtuous life should be lived, some concoction of the applied wisdom of Socrates and Jesus Christ and John Lennon, and I had come up short in execution, time after time. I knew better and I failed.

I didn't know what I was supposed to do once I'd completed the inventory and laid bare my sins, but I admit I felt a little better prepared to face the end of the world if it should come. I had reached out toward the truth.

A month later, in the Super Bowl, Jeff Fisher's Titans came up literally a yard short, as on the last play of the game St. Louis linebacker Mike Jones stopped Tennessee wide receiver Kevin Dyson at the one-yard line as time expired. Tennessee had followed the blue-print laid out by Detroit earlier in the season and held Marshall Faulk to 17 yards rushing on 10 carries, but Kurt Warner lit up Fisher's defense for 414 yards and two touchdowns.

The winning margin turned out to be a 73-yard pass from Warner to Isaac Bruce with less than two minutes left to go in the game. The guy just wouldn't quit.

CHAPTER 10

— • • • —

The Adventures of Cardboard Tim in Territory Held Largely by the Devil (2004)

"Satan does not tempt us just to make us do wrong things— he tempts us to make us lose what God has put into us through regeneration, namely, the possibility of being of value to God."

(September 18 passage from *My Utmost for His Highest*, by Oswald Chambers)

• • •

SEPTEMBER 18TH, 2004: Georgia 13, Marshall 3, Sanford Stadium, Athens, Georgia. Saturday was a "splendid" day for a college football game in Athens, Georgia (it even said so in the official game book). The sun was out and the temperature at game time would hit 74 degrees, with low humidity and a lightly gusting wind. Tim Loonam was enjoying every second of the day leading up to the 1:00 kickoff. He was alive on that campus in Athens, mind, body, and soul, flesh and blood, too, and compared to where he'd been spending his time lately, Athens was splendid indeed.

The morning had run according to the script for an official campus visit for recruits. Tim and his family were treated to the same seductive luxuries as all the other families of the young men the University of Georgia was considering feeding into its football pipeline. They enjoyed the lavish breakfast, with dozens of chafing dishes offering a variety of

sumptuous fare, heaps of eggs and grits and sausage and bacon and bis-
cuits, syrup and gravy to ladle over the top, all you can eat. Their pulses
raced as Bulldog football highlights were projected on the big screen—
recruits, the siren of the video highlights sang into the ears of every ambitious young athlete in the room, *this can be your image, larger than life,
if you'll take the challenge and commit to our program.* It probably feels like a
whale of a bargain when you are gorging on all that great free food and
then tan and smiling Coach Mark Richt offers up his humble low-key
blessing before turning up the volume a bit and sounding more like the
hard-charging college football coach the university pays something like
a million dollars a year, turning on the charm that convinces families
that here in Athens is where your sons should play their college ball. Tim
and Betsy Loonam sat eating breakfast in that crowd with their son and
daughter both, and son Jack really loved football. He was 11 years old.

After breakfast, the Loonams were privileged to join the horde of
recruiting families in the caravan of buses that took them down to the
entrance to the Athens Colosseum—Sanford Stadium. They got to join
the Dawg Walk, the procession of the gladiators into the arena, recruits
coming in ahead of the stars of the spectacle, the Georgia football team.
They we allowed to stroll the sidelines of the immaculately groomed
field as the teams began their protracted warm-ups, punts booming and
passes *thizzing* through that splendid fall air. The schools really pour it
on with these recruits and their families because, let's face it, it's an arms
race. Mike Shula at Alabama and Nick Saban at LSU and all the other
head coaches at all the other Big Time Programs are pouring on the
charm and lavishing the recruits with all the seductive allures the law
allows—and sometimes, let's admit it, a little more, recruiting violations
not unheard of in the NCAA, after all. College football is a highly competitive environment, and the game comes down to players, so college
football is really all about recruiting. Offer these kids scholarships and
hope that they don't let it go to their heads and that they stick with the
program for a couple of years when all they'll get to do is practice and
work out until they finally might earn a chance to play in the games, and

then hope they perform as well after three years as they did on all the high-school game film all the coaches looked at in making their recruiting decisions. That's the bargain, hope that you get some football out of the kids and that the kids know enough to get some education out of their scholarships. Honestly, in the whole meat market of the racket, that part is optional. Not everyone has the drive for academic achievement like Rufus Cormier from Beaumont, and not everyone gets the jolt of reality spurring him to perform in the classroom like Ketric Sanford from Corsicana. This is the SEC, and kids can disappear into the meat grinder.

Tim Loonam no doubt reflected on the nature of bargains as he strode down the sideline to see an old canine friend, Uga VI, the Bulldog mascot who owns a modest little home just outside the end zone on the plain of Sanford Stadium. Tim's connection to the university began in the mid-1990's when he decided to become a veterinarian and was accepted into the vet school, and as part of his rotations through the Doctor of Veterinary Medicine program he sometimes cared for the English bulldog, a direct descendant of the first Uga, who debuted between the hedges in 1956. That DVM program was really some kind of a bargain, because it meant Tim, who had been the Medical Services lieutenant going out on patrols with me in the Korean DMZ in 1985, had returned to the Army after nearly a decade of civilian life making a good living in medical sales. He had been selected for an Army Health Professions Scholarship, and it entailed a four-year active-duty commitment in exchange for a four-year full-ride scholarship for veterinary school. Kind of like ROTC all over again, or maybe something like those Division I scholarship athletes.

It's funny how these deals turn out sometimes. After graduating in Athens on a Thursday in May of 2000, Tim started his veterinary practice in uniform at Fort Jackson, South Carolina on the following Monday, and the whole set-up wasn't really all that Army—he and the family didn't even live on post. It sure seemed like a pretty good bargain, as Tim started looking ahead to his civilian future with a profitable small-animal practice, maybe in the Asheville area in North Carolina, and he even told some of his yuppie civilian friends who needled him about the dangers of the military, "guys, you just don't understand—Army veterinarians don't go to war."

Not until Thanksgiving of 2003, that is. The war in Iraq, begun with such promise for "shock and awe" and prematurely celebrated as a "mission accomplished," had turned into a bit of a problem after all, a counterinsurgency operation for the Americans, who had disbanded the Iraqi military without a very sound plan for preventing large contingents of soldiers disappearing into the countryside to join up with insurgent groups. "Hailed as liberators," Vice President Dick Cheney had predicted (maybe with a demon as ancient as the Roman Empire whispering in his ear), but in the event, not so much. It turned out that when the bond of tyranny that Saddam Hussein had exerted over the Sunni-Shiite-Kurd conglomerate was broken, things tended to fly apart. Whether termed freedom-fighters or jihadi or terrorists, a lot of bombers started plying their trade against Americans in Iraq, and as a very small part of the administration's vast and essentially incomprehensible "strategy," their postmodern mosaic of building things here and blowing things up there and training people here and killing people there, and spending billions everywhere, the American command had decided to deploy military working dogs (MWD) into combat for the first time since the Vietnam War. These dogs could sniff out explosives with extreme prejudice, and deployed properly, could save a lot of lives. Dogs of this sort are like race-horses, high-strung and finicky, and they require a high level of veterinary care, especially in the hostile desert environment of Iraq. Apparently the Army had a very special veterinarian in mind for the job (or at least the story fell together as if there had been a plan). Dr. Tim Loonam, Ranger-qualified Bulldog. Just 98 days before Major Tim Loonam was scheduled to complete his active-duty tour, paying back his scholarship, the "needs of the Army" intervened with wholly other plans. Well, something or Some One intervened.

Farewell to Football?

After his brief visit with Uga VI, Tim returned to midfield, where his wife was chatting pleasantly with Coach Mark Richt. Tim had to wonder at the kind of intervention that put him between the hedges in Athens, at the heart of SEC football on game day.

A week or so before this September 2004 game against Marshall, Bulldog Tim Loonam was engaged in that most Army of tasks—waiting (typical Army troop humor, spray-painted on the wall of a bombed-out building in Baghdad: *You're not in Iraq, you're not in Kuwait, you're in Iwait*). Waiting for a plane to get out of Iraq and start his two week Rest and Recreation mid-tour leave, Tim happened into the line of fire as a hose evacuating the juice from a Porta-Potty went astray, dousing his field uniform with the foul-smelling brew. Forty hours later, still wearing the same uniform, Tim was reunited with his family at the airport in Columbia, South Carolina. His eight-year-old daughter Katie thought Daddy smelled a little ripe. That's what war smells like, honey. A few days later, better rested and casually dressed for game day in white shorts and a Georgia-football print short-sleeved sport shirt, Major Tim Loonam was being introduced to the recruiting breakfast by Coach Mark Richt, receiving a standing ovation. Coach may well have hailed the major with the highest compliment that can be applied at the School of Athens: Damn Good Dawg.

The Georgia head coach, tipped off by friends of the Loonam family, had been occasionally emailing Tim in Iraq, and he invited Betsy and the kids to join him and the team for spring practice, where Jack spent about twenty minutes alone with the coach watching special-teams practice from end-zone seats at Sanford Stadium. Given the occasion of Tim's mid-tour leave, Richt brought the Loonams into the heart of the Georgia football family, treating 11-year-old Jack like a blue-chip recruit. As the coach told me later, "I love our armed forces and what they do to protect our country, and whatever I can do to try to bless them, that's what I try to do." I assured the coach that as far as I could tell, Tim and Betsy and the kids felt altogether blessed.

Georgia won that game, 13-3, scoring the only touchdown, a first-quarter rush for two yards by Michael Cooper. The Bulldogs doubled up the Thundering Herd in total yards, 371 to 160. Thomas Davis, currently still active in the NFL (he was named the 2014 Walter Payton Man of the Year), led Georgia's defense with 7 total tackles, a sack, and 3 QB hurries. The win gave Georgia a 3-0 record to start the 2004 season, and they had an open week before they would host LSU in Athens and thrash Nick Saban's Tigers 45-16. They would finish the season 9-2 and beat Wisconsin in the Outback Bowl 24-21.

Tim Loonam's R&R leave would fly by very quickly, and soon he was headed back to Iraq, where the prospects for victory, or even success, seemed increasingly discouraging.

I met Coach Richt in 2014 at a toney steakhouse just across the street from the ballpark in downtown Houston, where he was about to pitch to Georgia alumni, over some good food and after showing some exciting highlights on the big screen, about how they should throw money at his program. He's a nice enough guy, took time out of his busy schedule to talk to me about Tim and Jack Loonam (telling me that over time, walk-ons tend to "wear out, wear down, and quit," and he admired Jack for never quitting), and he's done pretty well as a college football coach, and better than most when it comes to putting emphasis on the academic opportunities that go along with college football. Still, I have to respectfully disagree with most of what he had to say about the armed forces, especially when it comes to that second Bush war in Iraq.

Tell me how that defended our freedoms, coach.

No, the way I saw it, looking back and somewhat zealously applying my newly-adopted "judge for yourself what is right" standard, President Bush and Vice President Cheney and Secretary of Defense Rumsfeld, just men and sinners like me, had likely given into the sinful temptation and illusion that wars can be good and necessary, the most basic and dangerous of temptations to think that they could outsmart war—Rumsfeld certainly thought that, with all his Pentagon blather about "transformation"—and in effect outsmart God; they all seemed to think they knew better than God. God had told us pretty plainly that "thou shalt not kill," but these guys acted like they had found the loophole in that commandment.

Beyond that I thought that they had probably figured out a great business model, this American Way of War as I understand it—start a popular war that provides cover for the massive transfer of wealth from taxpayers to lucky contractors who happened to be in on the game. It wasn't all that subtle—even the enlisted soldiers could see it. While he was deployed in Iraq, Tim Loonam wrote to some friends that "the joke among the troops here is that this isn't our war or the coalition's; it's KBR's ... we're just providing security for them! Some days it seems I see more KBR contractors out working than troops." Of course, KBR is also sometimes called Kellogg Brown & Root, a huge multinational corporation that Dick Cheney ran for years while the Republicans were out of the White House, and one of those contractors *lucky enough* to land big deals for logistical support of the war. For a while, like the good folks who cooked up Enron, Bush's closest advisors seemed like the smartest guys in the room, just taking advantage of an opportunity that history presented to them. After 9/11, Americans were pretty favorably disposed to wars, and so was the media. I'll always remember the story of the "embedded" journalist—a great euphemism for "seduced," isn't it?—who got so excited by the early stages of the war, when it was mobile and armored and pornographic, that he died of a heart attack.

As far as I was concerned back in 2003, the fix was in, and war was all that was on the menu, so I protested the war, perfunctorily and briefly, most overtly on a splendid sunny Texas afternoon in the late winter when there was still the slightest chance that the invasion of Iraq might be prevented, then saw that it was a done deal, and so turned to the work that I was doing at the University of Houston and got on with life (the fact that life goes on as usual "on the home front" is a part of the American Way of War, too). At the time, I didn't even know that Tim Loonam was back in the Army.

• • •

Sergeant Rex and the War of the IED's

Tim returned to Iraq in 2004 to continue a personal military mission that either entailed running down a virtually endless and hopelessly vague "to-do" list or, conversely, amounted to simplicity itself. He might be the dean of a veterinary school, might get to do some biomedical research; he would certainly have to take care of some animals, humanely euthanize others, make sure vermin didn't spread from the garbage dumps, inspect the food, perhaps assist in triage medicine ... or he might just try to get the working dogs into the fight.

By the time Tim got to Iraq in spring of 2004, a lot of the civilian infrastructure had been broken for a while, disrupting everyday necessities like electricity and running water and sewer service, creating ongoing threats of outbreaks of preventable diseases. Army preventive medicine units like the detachment in Baghdad with which Tim sometimes coordinated had their hands full trying to "break the chain of disease transmission" on American military bases. Jason Pike, an Army officer who once served in my old unit, the 10th Special Forces Group, commanded a preventive medicine detachment tasked with a similar mission in Afghanistan and likened it to the work of "your public health department." Like Tim's veterinary-medicine detachments, the preventive medicine soldiers had to travel extensively to provide support to far-flung commands, and sometimes their missions overlapped when wild and feral animals posed a threat to public health. Army veterinarians were responsible for putting such animals to death. Tim's duty to inspect military food also directly supported the preventive medicine mission. The American Way of War involves a lot of logistical tail, including shooting the occasional rat or weasel.

Tim's most challenging responsibility was providing veterinary support for the military working dogs, a daunting challenge because the mission was being worked up on the fly. The American command was revising strategy in the face of a deteriorating situation in Iraq, and they had to devise a response to the emerging insurgency groups that took advantage of readily available American munitions and ordnance wastefully strewn across the country to fashion what became known as IED's—improvised explosive devices. Somewhere along the chain of command, someone realized that the dogs the armed services bred and trained to sniff out explosives for their base security mission could provide similar and vital support to combat operations in Iraq, and through a similarly vague evolution, Major Loonam came to realize that his duties included helping to get dogs into the fight, using his rank and ingenuity and persuasive skills to advance the K9 cause. Upon deployment, the Ranger-qualified veterinarian had been astounded to find that his planning guidance amounted to "figure out your job when you get there." Rangers Lead the Way! He had to start by finding out where all the military-working-dog teams had been deployed.

In the course of his early travels to locate his resources, Tim got an up-close object lesson in the war of the IED's when he and his driver, Pete Meyers, headed out of Balad in a HUMV as the second vehicle in a 75-count convoy. They were right ahead of an SUV with some more of those KBR civilian contractors (retired special forces operators in this case), and about three miles into their trip felt the world explode around them. Tim thought at first that their vehicle was on fire because it seemed like the cockpit filled with smoke. Actually, the concussion from the explosion of four buried bombs had aerosolized all the dust in the vehicle when the insurgents set off the IED, probably targeting the SUV directly behind Loonam and Meyers. The insurgents likely knew that those soft-skinned civilian vehicles usually carried the high-value targets. Later investigation made it pretty clear that the bombers had used four US 105 mm artillery shells (easy enough to find for your enterprising guerilla in Iraq) and buried them too deep, causing the explosion to discharge most of its energy straight up. The presumed target, the civilian SUV, was only slightly damaged, and despite the dust, Tim and his driver were unhurt. Their vehicle suffered a casualty, though, as the box of Oreo cookies the driver was munching on got annihilated—all but one, which Meyers found wedged between his legs when they finally stopped and got out of the HUMV at the rally point. The Miracle

Oreo became a talisman or sacrament for the driver, and whenever he prepared for future convoys, he would hold up the relic cream-filled-sandwich-cookie as a required item on the pre-convoy check-list. Tim later compared the function of that cookie to the memorial stones the twelve men carried out of the River Jordan, commemorating how the Lord had made possible the crossing described in Chapter 4 of the Book of Joshua, enduring evidence of God's covenant with them. Sniffing out explosives like those used to rig the IED that wasted those Oreos, ideally before the bomb-makers could ever fashion their evil devices, was the primary mission of the dogs Tim came to support.

Marine NCO Mike Dowling detailed the introduction of military working dogs into Iraq in his 2011 book *Sergeant Rex,* a process fraught with major problems. The hot dusty environment in Iraq put a tremendous strain on the animals, German and Dutch Shepherds and Belgian Malinois who wore heavy coats and whose most essential function required constant sniffing. Keeping these keen, high-strung dogs healthy was challenging enough (considerably harder work than getting old Uga VI ready for game day), but deploying them properly sometimes meant confronting the assumptions and prejudices of high-ranking commanders who didn't understand what the dogs could do or didn't trust the enlisted handlers to take on risky work. In his book, Dowling recalls a briefing from Colonel Joseph Dunford, who commanded the Fifth Marine Regiment (and as of this writing is serving as the Chairman of the Joint Chiefs of Staff). Dunford claimed that "K9 teams have been talked about at the highest level of U. S. military command. We see you as the key to combating the IED threat here in Iraq, and we see you as vital to limiting casualties among both the marines and the Iraqi civilian population" (p. 96). Despite this clear command emphasis, enterprising enlisted men like Dowling still had to work their way into the confidence of senior NCO's and officers to convince them that the dogs had a far greater impact when they went out on combat patrols "outside the wire" rather than standing static guard duty at base gates.

Farewell to Football?

In *Sergeant Rex*, Dowling describes how intense and downright crazy the action got outside the wire, narrating the scene as he and Rex join a mission headed for the cauldron of Fallujah, his memory aided by a video he shot with a little Sony pocket camera. As they wait for the convoy to get under way, Dowling films brief interviews with Marines, one of whom predicts that Rex and all the Marines are going to die in the battle. Dowling writes, "I stop filming. That interaction sums up what a great deal of the tour's been like so far. It's been disjointed, it's made little sense, and at every turn it's been pretty much bordering on the insane" (p. 193). At my remove, reading this almost a decade later in the tranquility of my Houston home, I'm struck by a strange and vivid memory: *The Exorcist*, the 1973 movie that scared crap out of me when I first saw it as a scrawny ninth-grader, starts with a dog-fight in Iraq. While we think of this grisly tale of demonic possession taking place appropriately enough in Georgetown, in the darkest heart of all evil, our nation's capital, both the novel and film begin with a prologue in northern Iraq. A series of disjointed and uncanny fragmentary scenes there lead the Catholic priest Marrin to a desert confrontation with a statue representing the demon Pazuzu ("personification of the southwest wind" according to the text), while a pair of wild dogs scrap in the blazing desert sun. In the movie, we'll see that demon again in Georgetown. As for Dowling and Rex, the Marine prophet proves false, as they survive a wicked firefight. Of course, a lot of Marines *did* die in Fallujah after a pitched battle that all started when some of those private military contractors got killed.

Dowling told me recently about the overriding faith and confidence with which Tim Loonam went about his work supporting the dog handlers in the field in Iraq. Dogs like Sergeant Rex are notoriously aggressive, especially when veterinarians approach intent on poking at sore spots and, in perhaps the most cringe-inducing scene in *Sergeant Rex*, draining their anal glands (pp. 177-178). Dowling told me, though, that "Tim was not hesitant with the dogs or the handlers. He had confidence in the handlers to be able to restrain their dogs and protect him while he did the inspection. He did his health checks very quickly but was thorough. I knew that if anything happened to Rex out in the field that needed immediate medical attention he would be in good hands if Tim were the one to treat him." Among other items checked off his "to-do" list, Tim had set up a complete animal surgical suite at Alpha Surgical Hospital on the Al Asad air base, and just like American soldiers wounded in battle, military working dogs were sometimes medevacked there for treatment.

Getting the dogs properly into the fight was an ongoing challenge for Tim and all the dog handlers, and late in his deployment Tim's frustration reached a climax that was triggered by a preventable tragedy emblematic of the American war in Iraq. On December 21, 2004, a suicide bomber blew himself up inside the dining hall at Forward Operating Base (FOB) Marez outside of Mosul in northern Iraq. It was an outstanding mess hall, Tim told me, the kind of big, expensive, and permanent KBR installation that results from war-by-contractor, and he had enjoyed some fine meals there visiting a veterinary-medicine team stationed on the base. The bombing killed 14 people, mostly American military, and wounded more than 70. At the time, Tim was working out of Al Asad air base and was starting to feel kind of bitter about how the whole situation had devolved. The military-working-dog teams were going stale because they couldn't lay hands on vehicles to get around the massive base in the middle of the desert west of Baghdad, even while a racket in contractor-provided "non-tactical vehicles" supplied wheels to privileged base occupants. When it became clear what had happened in Mosul, Major Loonam requested—make that, *demanded*—an office call with the "mayor" of Al Asad, the installation commander, a Marine colonel. On the ego-fumed stage of military theatrics, it turned into a tense scene.

"Colonel," Tim began, possibly angling his left shoulder forward a little, to ensure that the Marine office could see his Ranger tab, to subtly emphasize that the colonel was not just dealing with some *pogue* medic, "I can stop the bombing in Mosul from happening here. We have a dozen working dogs with their handlers on this base but they aren't able to do their job."

"And why is that, Major?" The Marine was a notorious butt-chewer, and Tim couldn't be certain he wouldn't erupt into some kind of Jarhead *get-your-fricking-lazy-enlisted-men-and-their-fricking-overrated-dogs-off-their-butts* soliloquy.

Tim decided that if he was going to get busted for insubordination, then God had no doubt determined that was his mission for the day.

"They need a ride, sir."

The colonel paused behind his hard-edged glare at the Army veterinarian, perhaps considering all the vehicles tooling around the base carrying people who couldn't do squat to prevent terror-bombing. Shoot, the colonel didn't really know what half those mother-loving civilians even *did* for a living.

The colonel interrupted his own silence to call in his lieutenant-colonel deputy. Maybe he had seen the gleam of a zealot in the eyes of this Damn Good Dawg braced up at attention in front of him.

"Let's get this officer some vehicles."

• • •

A Saint in the Desert

When I was an undergraduate studying literature at Binghamton University in the early 1980's before I started down that dusty Army trail that led through ROTC and on to Korea, where I met Tim Loonam, I took a literature course with Richard Pindell, a creative-writing and English professor who used to write a quote on the board before every class. When we started reading *Wise Blood*, a novel by the Catholic writer from Georgia, Flannery O'Connor, he quoted this from her *Mystery and Manners:* "I have found, in short, from reading my own writing, that my subject in fiction is the action of grace in territory held largely by the devil" (p. 118). That last part stuck with me, maybe as a kind of contrasting parallel to Hemingway's formula about men and courage and grace under pressure. I don't think they were using the word "grace" the same way. I didn't really know much about grace in those callow undergraduate days.

In 2004, Tim Loonam had taken as his personal mission to live like a saint in the desert, but he was finding Iraq to be territory largely held by the devil.

By the time Tim had begun his tour of duty as an Army veterinarian at Fort Jackson at the beginning of the new millennium, his Protestant faith ran deep and strong, and so he and Betsy treated the devastating news they received around Thanksgiving of 2003—that Tim would not be processing out of the service, that they would not be buying that veterinary practice in North Carolina, that Tim would be going off to war—as a challenge to their beliefs. Do we really believe that God's will is playing out in our lives, or is that only when things are going well for us? Are the days of trial in the desert gone by like old-west cowboy myths or is faith a living thing still tested through ordeal? Tim remembers praying every early-winter morning that year as he commuted to Fort Jackson from their home on Lake Murray, and it was essentially the prayer of Christ in the Garden at Gethsemane, that "if it is possible, let this cup pass from me; yet, not as I will, but as you will" (Matthew 26:39). *Lord, I don't want to go to Iraq, but if you want me to, I'm going.* Tim accepted this radical change in plans and girded himself for the trial, committing himself to reading a Proverb a day as well the daily devotional in Oswald Chamber's *My Utmost for His Highest,* which Tim describes as simply a book about what it means to be a saint (a sample from the passage for May 22: "The things that happen either make us fiends, or they make us saints; it depends entirely upon the relationship we are in to God"). With these daily readings and prayer at every meal, Tim felt that God would be next to him.

Tim's faith helped him minister to others quietly and confidently, leading by example. Dr. Heidi Squier Kraft wrote about her experiences as a Navy psychologist helping U. S. Marines and other combatants in Iraq deal with the stresses of war in her 2007 book *Rule Number Two,* including a poignant episode in which Tim helps a female Marine sergeant regain a sense of purpose in life through the gift of a dog (pp. 188-192). Dr. Kraft told me more about Tim's impact on her. "I gained strength from being around him. He gave me strength with his smile, his faith, his easy comfort in his own skin." Still, her job was to worry about the struggles of others, and Tim faced some unique challenges. "I worried about him," she told me, "being one of one, a vet, an Army officer in a sea of Navy and Marines. And then they kept sending him away and we wouldn't know when he left or when he would come back. He was gone when we got our orders to go home."

When Tim was in residence at Alpha Surgical Hospital at Al Asad air base with Dr. Kraft, he helped with triage medicine when heavy casualties came into the hospital. The worst day saw 25 casualties come in at one time, and under stress like that, no one was checking to see what kind of doctor this Army Ranger major was—he held up under the strain and pitched in. Tim felt that he was there to do whatever he could to help, and besides, as a veterinarian he had seen a whole lot more trauma than an obstetrician or psychiatrist, who might also be called upon to work triage, so he just functioned within the excellent military medical system, a hallmark of the logistics-intensive American Way of War. While warriors like Marine Mike Dowling were out at the sharp end of the spear figuring out how to fight the evolving war in Iraq, the medical specialists knew what they were doing and had all the resources of the wealthiest nation on earth to save as many lives as possible.

Still, there was something absurd or pointless about a lot of what happened over there, what the Apostle Paul called the foolishness of this world, casualties that served no earthly purpose, and some of those stuck with Tim. When he told me about a Marine air wing that found an old MIG fighter jet from the first Gulf War out in the desert, I could sense the implied exasperated question running through his mind: *Really, God, this is your will?* The maintenance unit of the wing was packing up to head back to the States and decided that the ejector seat from that MIG would make a cool addition to their trophy room back home.

Somehow they botched the job of disarming the propulsive charge under the ejector seat, and it went off, beheading one Marine and severely burning another. I have to wonder if God's message wasn't crystal-clear: *Stop being so stupid, stop making pointless elective wars.* That's just me, I guess. I wasn't there.

I look back at it with the detachment that makes the moral judgments seem easy or clear, and maybe with the severity of the recently-converted zealot. As far as I can tell, those men and women running that war, sinners just like me, really became insidious through the choices they made. Those "leaders" may well have calculated that deploying accomplished American women to places like Alpha Surgical Hospital in the midst of the war the leaders had chosen could help sway the sentiments of the folks back home about how our *brave lady warriors* are facing up to adversity in "the war," as if the war just existed as this thing where some people had to go and "do their part." Those "leaders" really shaped the story (many had learned how during the first Bush Iraq War). You have to figure the dogs serve the same purpose in manipulative narratives like that—everybody loves a good story about a valiant dog. (Here's a challenge, to judge for yourself what is right: read through Kraft's and Dowling's books and show me where either author has anything to say about what the war is supposed to accomplish, and I bet all you will find is fairly clear talk about Americans taking care of each other and making it home alive, which aren't strategic war aims.) Those "leaders," sinners just like me and you but in better position to make world-wide mischief, put brave or foolish young men and women into battle so that we—an *assumed* we, the government in the name of the people—can spend a lot of money on the logistical tail that supports them—including state-of-the-art combat surgical hospitals to care for their needlessly and thoughtlessly broken bodies, facilities bought at boutique prices and deployed at travel-agency costs. From my perspective, judging for myself what is right, hoping I haven't lost all compassion in my zeal to be right, those brightest-guys-in-the-room were majoring in stupid, but they were making a fortune doing it.

Farewell to Football?

Tim Loonam had to face far worse trials than stupidity. Early in his deployment, Tim had to endure the quintessential trial of the true believer, the confrontation with evil incarnate. The New Testament tells us that Jesus begins his public ministry with a retreat into the desert after his baptism in the River Jordan by the wild-man John, and he is tested by a figure variously described as the tempter, the Devil, or Satan. Fasting and alone, Jesus must face these temptations while his humanity is weakened. In March, 2004, Tim Loonam was a couple of months into his ordeal in Iraq, his mission unclear and seemingly ever-changing, his accommodations minimal at best at Camp Anaconda in Balad, north of Baghdad along the Tigris River (one of six places in Iraq where he would "live" his nomadic existence).

Feeling old and useless and alone, but fighting the urge to self-pity, he decides to take the mile-long walk to a Protestant chapel service on the base. Along the way he is confronted by a Filipino Muslim, one of the large contingent of Third Country Nationals brought in to provide logistical services as part of the whole war-by-contract business model. At first the Filipino is enthusiastic and friendly and smiling, but once he has engaged Tim in conversation, the humanity seems to drain out of his eyes, leaving Tim staring into a void of pure evil. The guy has turned belligerent, too, pointing to Tim's Bible and proclaiming how offensive it is to him, how wrong its teaching, seeming to threaten to either take the Bible out of Tim's hand or to strike him. The temptation working upon him, Tim sinks into despair, wondering how he'll ever get through a year of this—wondering how he'll get through the next hour, let alone the rest of the day. *My God, why have you forsaken me?* (Matthew 27:46)

But readers of the Bible know that the story doesn't end there. That's just a moment of human temptation, when we can choose to abandon our faith and wallow in our misery—free choice of the will means we are free to fail (the theological point behind all those horrific gymnastics of affliction in *The Exorcist* is that the Devil will do anything he can to make our existence so miserable that we will choose to turn away from God and stop believing in His love). We can also choose the way of faith, the path through temptation and suffering and toward salvation, and Tim finds his way back down that road this day in Iraq. Holding on to a shred of irrational hope, gripping his Bible like his memorial stone from the River Jordan, perhaps visited by grace, he makes his way into an old bombed-out Iraqi Air Force building and a conference room set up as a chapel. And can it be (maybe a little hard to make out with eyes clouded by dust from the desert)? At the altar is Lieutenant Colonel Al Lowe, an Army chaplain whose dog had been Tim's first surgical patient when he started his veterinary practice at Fort Jackson. In that simultaneity of spiritual life, past meets present to enliven the future of the mission. Tim still has a lot of work to do. The Devil had seemed to be standing in the way of where he needed to go, but that was really just illusion, all that the Devil has to work with.

• • •

Cardboard Tim

While Tim was enduring his trial in the desert, his family and friends at home kept him close to their hearts in a most singular and ultimately All-American manner. In addition to the usual traffic in letters and cards and emails, along with the occasional phone calls, the Loonam circle created a life-size image that they called Cardboard Tim.

Family friend David Youngerman came from a background in marketing and knew where to get those cardboard cutouts made, like the figures of Bartles & Jaymes that used to stand up near the coolers in supermarkets to advertise the wine-coolers. He selected a nice photo Tim had sent of himself in his full desert combat gear—but with a characteristically toothy, Glenn-Frey grin—and had it made into a full-sized cutout. Cardboard Tim. A marketing ploy used to express fondness and love in the face of absence.

Farewell to Football?

Photorealism: Cardboard Tim with Dr. Tim Loonam,
Athens, Georgia, September 2013.

Soon Cardboard Tim was showing up all over Athens. As Youngerman told me later, "the many adventures of Cardboard Tim took him everywhere and he did a lot of normal American things, like flipping burgers, laying on the couch watching TV, going to football games. While Tim was sacrificing for his family and country in Iraq, his alter-counterpart was experiencing the rewards of his sacrifice. Ironic, huh?"

Perfectly ironic.

Cardboard Tim was a smiling icon, someone's idea of a hero. What you couldn't see in the photorealism of that cardboard cutout was the pain in his eyes as he watched the stupid world repeatedly blow up little parts of itself. You couldn't see the guilt he felt for subjecting his family to both the absence and the anxiety—would Tim be the next casualty? would Dad come home in a tin coffin like coffee in a can?—and for what?

So that he could go to veterinary school and become the DawgDoc? You couldn't see the shame he carried as a dupe thrown into a morally compromised environment as part of a devil's bargain. You couldn't see the saint mourning in the desert for the opportunities he had missed to bring God to those who needed Him.

Cardboard Tim just played his part, more propaganda for the American Way of War.

The real Tim, his spiritual director Perry Bower assured me (in the very first interview I recorded for this book), came home a changed man, an evangelist transformed like Paul on the road to Emmaus. Encountering that man, standing in the place of Christ in this fallen world, would be an unforgettable step on my own spiritual journey.

CHAPTER 11

• • •

"I" Is for "Ike," Like the Hurricane (2008)

"We probably got away from the run game too quick in
the second half."

(TEXANS HEAD COACH GARY KUBIAK AFTER SEPTEMBER 21,
2008 LOSS TO THE TENNESSEE TITANS)

• • •

SEPTEMBER 21, 2008: Tennessee Titans 31, Houston Texans 12, LP Field, Nashville, Tennessee. As they headed into the locker room at halftime of their game at Tennessee, the Houston Texans almost certainly felt guardedly optimistic. Football games have been known to take as many turns in plot as a five-act Shakespearean play. The Texans weren't out of it yet.

Sure, they were down 21-12, but there's more to the score than just the numbers. The Titans had scored three times, and the Texans had scored three times, too. The Titans scored touchdowns, while the Texans scored two field goals and a touchdown, but then rather ominously missed the typically-automatic extra point. Houston had their running game going, rookie Steve Slaton already over a hundred yards, with a couple of long-gainers that showed off his burst through the line of scrimmage. They must have been thinking, we're still in this game, we've just got to execute, extend drives, make the big plays when needed, make the little plays that set up the big plays. We're not going to get blown out like we did in week one at Pittsburgh. That seems like a lifetime ago.

Texans fans, with that disordered identification that afflicts American fans of all sports, must have been thinking "we've" ridden out the initial storm and, indomitable as ever, we're back to football. Sure, maybe "we're" kind of shaky out on the field, but who wouldn't be a little out of synch after a really freaky ten days that saw a hurricane blow out the original plans for a game against Baltimore last Sunday, leading to an early bye week instead? Like good Houstonians, we've faced up to adversity, and you know what? We're still in this game.

But any optimism had to be guarded. The quarterback was not playing well—again. Matt Schaub had squandered the Texans' first two chances. He threw consecutive incompletions to stall the first drive of the game, and then wasted a golden opportunity after Houston cornerback Jacques Reeves intercepted a Tennessee pass, throwing yet another incompletion on a deep shot and then getting sacked to kill the drive. At least the Texans scored, a Kris Brown field goal, but neither fans nor head coach Gary Kubiak could be happy with Schaub's balky start. He only made things worse when the Texans got the ball back after a long Titans drive paid off with a rushing touchdown. On the first play of the Texans drive, Schaub finally completed a pass—to Titans defensive back Michael Griffin for an interception. What a disaster!

Kubiak had to be seething on the sideline. The coach was all in on this, Schaub was his *solution* at quarterback. Kubiak had backed up quarterback John Elway and held for kicks for the Broncos team that lost consecutive Super Bowls in the 1980s (one of them to Parcells and Belichick and Simms and the Giants), and then had coached Super Bowl winners at San Francisco (as quarterbacks coach of the 49ers team that demolished San Diego in January 1995) and Denver (as offensive coordinator when the Broncos won two straight in the late 90's). He had taken over as the second head coach in Houston Texans history in 2006, and in his first year had realized that the team wasn't going to win with former #1-overall draft-pick David Carr at quarterback. In the off-season, Kubiak had gone out recruiting and secured through trade the Atlanta Falcons' backup to Michael Vick, Virginia alumni Matt Schaub. In 2007, the former Cavalier had proven an upgrade over Carr (whose career, most observers agree, had been ruined by the Texans' inability to protect him, as he set records as the most-sacked quarterback in the NFL two of his first three seasons), but Schaub had also missed five games with injuries and had thrown as many interceptions as touchdowns. The jury was still out on this solution, to say the least. To start 2008, against Pittsburgh Schaub seemed to combine all the worst elements, throwing two interceptions to a single touchdown and getting sacked five times, as Houston got blown out on the road, 38-17.

Still, in Tennessee the Texans fought their way back, making good on a long drive in the second quarter that paid off with a Slaton rushing touchdown. Warming to his work, Schaub completed three passes and missed on two, while Slaton chugged along on short-gainers that kept the chains moving. Culminating a 12-play drive that ate up more than six minutes, Slaton ran it in for the touchdown from six yards out. But then, as if to tamp down any enthusiasm the road team might have generated, Kris Brown missed the extra point. The Titans led, 14-12, and came back to score a touchdown on the following drive, the way that a playoff-bound team playing at home should, and thus the score stood at 21-12 as the Texans, no doubt guardedly optimistic, headed into the locker room at half-time.

High above the field, in luxury boxes, the owners almost certainly experienced the game in different emotional registers. Bud Adams, one of the charter members of the "foolish club" that founded the upstart AFL almost fifty years before, had finally gotten what he wanted in Nashville, the revenue-generating luxury-box-rich stadium that he had demanded and Houston had refused him. The Oilers, rechristened as the Tennessee Titans, had even made it to the Super Bowl, coming up just a yard short of victory against Kurt Warner and the St. Louis Rams. Houston's Bob McNair had shocked the football world in 1999, when his bid for the 32nd NFL franchise surprisingly beat out the proposal from Los Angeles, the heavy favorite. McNair had put together the deal to build Houston's Reliant Stadium, which a coffee-table photo-book published to commemorate the launch of the Texans claimed cost $367 million to build, with the Texans putting up $85 million, the rodeo $35 million—and the public $250 million, a whole different quantum from what the public had last spent to appease football ownership—in the neighborhood of $67 million in 1987 to keep the Oilers from leaving the Astrodome for Jacksonville, and the $180 million range that Bud Adams demanded but didn't get in 1996. The stadium, a retractable-roofed behemoth that rises up like the Hindenburg taking flight above the decrepit Astrodome, had seen a tremendously exciting regular-season inauguration in 2002 when David Carr led the Texans to defeat in-state rival the Dallas Cowboys, but Carr's struggles in the following seasons and the lack of any offensive punch beyond superlative wide receiver Andre Johnson ultimately resulted in McNair firing defense-obsessed head coach Dom Capers and taking the risk on first-time head coach Gary Kubiak, a native Houstonian and an offensive specialist. Now, in September of 2008, the stadium's fate was somewhat uncertain.

Hurricane Ike, a gigantic tropical cyclone which proved to be the costliest ever to wreak havoc on Texas, had blown through town late on a Saturday night and torn off five panels from the signature retractable roof of Reliant Stadium, canceling initial plans to move the Texans game against Baltimore to Monday night. The engineers were still checking out the damage to determine if the stadium was safe to host events (in photos from above, the Hindenburg now sported a gap-toothed smile). For now, the Texans were on the road and uncertain what they would be coming home to.

But first, they had a football game to complete. They were still in this contest against their former Houston selves.

• • •

"All in one place together" (Acts 2:1)

In those dread latter days of early September, 2008, there really was a sense of "we" in Houston, a very real sense of community, and we really had ridden the storm out together.

Farewell to Football?

We had watched the massive cyclone approach, killing people in Cuba and Haiti, feeling a dizzying mix of terror and elation as it became clear that Ike was likely to hit Houston right on the button. We had stocked up on food and water and batteries and begun the nervous but exciting ritual of waiting, watching the psychedelic monster on TV screens, that spinning vortex Spirograph black-light poster of a storm churning through the Gulf of Mexico, a trippy pulsing graphic freighted with dread like Scotty Ferguson's spiraling nightmare in Hitchcock's *Vertigo*—this monster had killed more than 70 people in Haiti, and it appeared to be heading right for us. We couldn't look away as the robotic newscasters blathered on and on, probably hoping in their hearts that something big was going to happen and make their careers, a hope poised in tension with the worry that they would cry wolf and the hurricane might peter out and they would look ridiculous. Maybe somewhere in there they felt a little concern that harm might come to their fellow man, but I wouldn't have bet on it.

All in one place together, at first, we were, until we splintered into a wilderness of individualities.

The hurricane came upon us monstrously slow, belting Galveston on Saturday morning and slowly making its way inland toward Houston, the weather turning more and more hostile as darkness fell, a haunting low-pressure calm ratcheting up the anticipation until the strong driving wind started to whistle its way up the scale. We still had electricity to watch the disaster unfold on TV. The worst of the storm hit my neighborhood overnight, wind roaring like a freight train, yet everything holding up. The subdivision where I lived, Sharpstown in southwest Houston, had been built in the mid-1950's and had proven capable over the years of taking a few punches.

We became *me* in a single explosive snap as a transformer blew up and the power went out, and then I was singular, remarkably, howlingly, achingly alone. In that thunder-clap moment, when with a distinct ripping sound the electricity surged and then went out, we became I—"I" for Isolated, Individual, separated from the sea of humanity all around by the darkness and the roaring winds lashing rains, the tearing sounds now of trees twisting and being wrenched, limb from limb, crashing into the ground or onto roofs or through windows, who could tell in that unrelenting darkness. I would sneak a peek out the windows every few minutes, wondering if there was anyone else out there, hoping this wouldn't be the moment when the winds would surge and the windows explode. No lights, nothing to see, only the terror of imagination.

While the hurricane roared, no one was going to venture out of doors. Once the storm subsided, the first of the groping outward was very local, reconnaissance and damage assessment, then maybe a quick check on immediate neighbors. Sunrise saw the end of the storm in my part of town, and I quickly realized I had been freakishly lucky. While trees were down in both front yard and back, neither had struck the house. My roof was intact, and no windows had been broken, and thus my house had held up its end of the bargain, maintaining its barrier against the outside world. On the list of necessities, I could check off shelter.

It turned out I was mostly lucky. I had water and natural gas, which for me meant hot water as well as stove service. What I lacked was electricity, though an initial inspection didn't disclose any lines down. It would probably just be a matter of restoring the service, though there was no telling what damage had been incurred up the line. Let's just hope that in the wake of the storm the weather might give us a break from typical September heat, because no electricity meant no air-conditioning, which in Houston is a frightful prospect.

By Monday evening, the following day, I had gotten a handle on the situation, cleaned up what I could. Some enterprising neighbors had come by with a chain saw and for a fee cut up the ash tree that had fallen in my front yard. I had even gotten my car out of the garage and ventured afield far enough to find a liquor store open to sell me a bottle of wine and a cigar, which I enjoyed as I listened to the Monday Night Football game on the radio on my back deck. That was a welcome break from the survival drama of Hurricane Ike, a good old-fashioned NFC East shootout between Dallas and Philadelphia that the Cowboys ended up winning 41-37.

Farewell to Football?

That game included a long delay for a replay challenge of an apparent Eagles touchdown, when rookie wide receiver DeSean Jackson appeared to flippantly drop the ball out of his hands before crossing the goal line, a stupid, insolent move that typified the talented young wide-out from Cal-Berkeley. The delay gave me pause to reflect.

The weather was surprisingly cool for September, down into the mid-60's by the time the game got going, well below average, and I felt glad to be alive, glad my house hadn't been demolished, glad to have football and food and drink. But there was something else, some mystery in the air in that darkened backyard still cluttered with downed branches, still reeking of wet leaves and flooded ground. What on earth was I doing here in the Houston suburbs? If I had died in the hurricane, none of my neighbors would have known my name or whom to contact to come fetch my body.

I'd only moved into the neighborhood a few months before, having bought the four-bedroom single-story house in Sharpstown as a rational solution to a challenging economic equation: where does the curve of what I can afford intersect with the curve of where I can stand to live? Houses in the artsy Montrose district, where I rented apartments throughout my graduate program and first few years of employment, were way beyond my means. There were plenty of easily affordable properties in the greater Houston metro if I wanted to make epic commutes or live in gangster-infested neighborhoods. Sharpstown was the point of intersection, affordable at the high-end of my budget and not utterly horrible, but it turned out to be a pretty joyless solution. I got to calling it the land of the Moustache Heroes, the realm of the hard-working multi-ethnic middle-class, "single-family residences" with half-a-dozen or more vehicles squeezed into the driveways, and I was pretty sure there weren't many intellectuals or writers on the block. Not that I was the friendly guy to drop in on my new neighbors with a 12-pack of Bud Light to introduce myself. But so what? I'd gotten the last of the mortgages before the housing market collapsed.

On the radio, the commercials finally ended and the official made the call: the runner fumbled the ball at the one yard line, no touchdown.

Oh, well, the Eagles just gave it to Brian Westbrook, who ran it up the middle for a touchdown. How hard is it to gain a single yard?

• • •

Coach Zeno

The following Sunday, in the game against the Titans, the Texans really had a good thing going to start the fourth quarter, a sustained drive, what the Texans under Kubiak were supposed to look like: the Gulf Coast descendant of the Mile High variant of the West Coast Offense that Bill Walsh had actually started dreaming up in Cincinnati long ago. Mixing up the short passes with runs using the zone-blocking scheme. Targeting six different receivers, with completions to four. Schaub even ran it once, for six yards.

But then Kubiak started getting involved, started *thinking things over*, calling a time-out to ponder a fourth-and-three call at the Titans 17. I don't like this, I don't trust Kubiak *thinking about football*. He'd already messed up a play call on fourth down in the third quarter, gone for it and failed, as Schaub completed a dump-off pass to Slaton for one yard when they needed four. That was SO Kubiak. And now the head coach and play-caller was calling a time-out, and that only tends to make things worse.

Kubiak has a little problem, in my estimation, when it comes to *thinking about football*. I'm just a fan, and don't have any privileged access to the whole process, but I know something about pedagogy and cognitive function and to me he seems prone to a football strain of magical thinking, not seeing the game and its outcomes in terms of cause and effect but instead heeding magic formulae. *Run it this many times and you will win*, is one of his oft-professed articles of faith, when in fact it's the other way around—teams tend to run a lot *when they are winning* because they get the early lead and then use the running game to wind down the clock and reduce the chance of turnovers. The running's an effect, not a cause. Coach Kubiak also shows a tendency to call plays short—call for two-yard passes when the team needs five, expecting the receiver to make the first down rather than running a route to be at or past the sticks upon reception, like the one-yard dump-off to Slaton when the Texans needed four. I mean, I'm just a fan, but don't they game-plan this stuff? I tend to get my mind wrapped up in this spiral of thought as I get upset, almost perseverating during times-out in critical game situations. I'm in this no-man's-land of the half-informed fan, so far obsessed by the game that I can't help thinking about it, but not versed well enough in the process of game-planning and play-calling to know what's really going on. Doesn't that big laminated menu of play-calls Kubiak fusses over have a section for short-gainers or something, plays put in and practiced specifically to gain five yards? Why does it always seem like he's trying to figure it out on the spot, with that painful wince in the rictus of which Coach tends to look like a dog trying to expel a peach seed?

At this point in my life, though, I have no way of really knowing how these guys plan and think, don't have that level of access to the coach. I have been reading more in depth about football and coaching, and hope maybe someday to get a chance to interview coaches, maybe even write a book about football, but that's all in the future—here, I'm just another griping fan. *Stupid Kubiak's like Zeno, always getting halfway to the goal line!* I'm just caught up in a great American illusion of false identification with sports, like self-aggrandizing literary Romantic Fred Exley in *A Fan's Notes* almost having a heart attack from watching the Giants play football on TV. We're fans, we're nuts, and what we think about "our" sport reflects the image we prefer for ourselves, and some of us want to be sports intellectuals. Just to take one example, this *New Republic* writer in 1999 described an American sports family-spat enacted by literary standard-bearers, contrasting George Will's cold anti-romanticism concerning baseball in *Men at Work* (1990—a book I'd read and loved when it came out) with David Maraniss's depth of rumination over the Jesuitical mysteries of Vince Lombardi's Packer Sweep in his then-recent *When Pride Still Mattered*: "Baseball fans assume their game is intellectually sophisticated because they can understand it. Football fans know their game is intellectually sophisticated because they can't" (Plotz, p. 50).

Sure. I'm such a Big Brain I don't know what on earth is going on out there.

But why does it matter how Kubiak thinks about football? Why do I get physically upset over play-calls watching a game on TV? Why does football seem to be so important? It's an old trick, really, the kind of behavior and attitude in the Pharisees that brought out the human anger in the Jesus of the Gospels, the judging of others ahead of judging self, the criticism of the mote of dust in the eye of the other rather than pulling the beam out of one's own eye. If I spend my time and energy criticizing Coach Zeno for how he thinks about football, I can avoid examining my own conscience, my own plentiful disordered thinking and passions—the classic trap of the Pharisees: criticize the lack of virtue in others as if that would add to your own virtuous standing.

I just know that in the fourth quarter at Tennessee, Kubiak screwed it up again. After the first time-out, a great play. Schaub hit Andre Johnson for 13 yards, making it first and goal from the four, but then the drive started to feel darkly familiar to this pessimistic fan, like some reincarnation of Zeno's paradox, a slowing down and diminution. One step up and two steps back. Slaton runs for three yards, OK, that's the typical yield for a running play, especially in the red zone, where things get tight. Now they're on the one-yard-line, just a yard to go for a touchdown. How hard can it be to gain a single yard? Kubiak calls for a pass and Schaub misses. Zero yards. Then, somehow, Schaub throws a completion to Kevin Walter—and the Texans *lose* a yard! Going backward. So it's fourth and goal from the two, and Kubiak calls another time-out (that's another mistake, by the way, for the receiver to not only lose yards but not to get out of bounds when time is short). He's *thinking this over,* and mulling the vast array of choices on his Waffle House laminated menu of play-calls. And danged if the idiot doesn't settle for the most obvious play there is in this situation, a run up the middle, and coming off a time-out, and trying to run against a defense coached by Jeff Fisher, who knows something about coming up a yard short of the goal line. A run up the middle for one yard. And they needed two. So the Texans spent 8:07 time of possession on 15 plays and gained 66 yards, but ended up with no points, two time-outs burned, score remaining 24-12.

A guy who regularly posts to the *Houston Chronicle* NFL blog likes to call Kubiak *Mediocrates*, the Greek household god of almost-right. Yep, I'm a fan, I'm nuts, but he's epic: Coach Zeno and *Mediocrates* all rolled up in one.

If I had been at home I certainly would have stood up and shouted obscenities, and might even have thrown something. In those days, I got kind of overwrought about these things, overly passionate about a stupid game coached by a stupid Aggie with a tendency toward an "antic disposition" when the game got tight.

But I wasn't at home. The power was still out and I hadn't opted to rent a generator like a lot of my neighbors had and so was watching the game on campus at the University of Houston, where I worked at the UH Writing Center. The university is really a city within the city and generates its own power, and so since a couple of days after the hurricane went through town, I'd been going in to the office to charge up the batteries on my cell phone and lap-top computer and to get on the Internet and enjoy the air-conditioning. There wasn't much work to do, since school was closed all week, so the whole thing felt like a week-long weekend. And then when Sunday rolled around and the power was still out at my house, I went to the Writing Center with a bottle of white wine that I chilled in the refrigerator, to enjoy as I watched the Texans on the TV in one of the classrooms of the Writing Center.

By the time Kubiak went for it and failed in the fourth quarter, I was enjoying the wine a whole lot more than the game.

• • •

Writing Is Thinking

This is where my choices had led me. I was the associate director of the Writing Center at the University of Houston, and if you have to have a job, it was a pretty good place to be. We were more than just a tutoring shop, as we also developed writing support programs for colleges and departments. Writing is pretty important to student success in college, and we had taken as our motto, "Writing Is Thinking." That's how we worked, to get students to think through the writing that they are doing and to go away with a plan for improving it, not just to help them "fix" the problems in what they've done. We did tutoring, and lots of it, thousands of scheduled interactions per year, but we also did assessment and developed curriculum and programs to support student writing.

This was a career choice for me, and it entailed a pretty severe compromise. After completing a doctorate in creative writing, what I would really have liked was a job teaching writing, but most of those positions are at small colleges in the hinterlands, a long way in most cases from NFL franchises, not to mention symphony orchestras, opera, or theater. I also didn't have the publications record to qualify for those creative-writing positions. Instead, I took advantage of an opportunity to work as an administrator when the Writing Center was just getting reorganized, after flooding from Tropical Storm Allison in 2001 wiped out an earlier version, which was, somewhat typically, located in the basement of a campus building.

The direction the Writing Center took in rebuilding reflected its new leader, Marjorie Chadwick, who was somewhat of an outsider on campus. A native Houstonian whose father, Red Bourne, had played college football and was one of the first referees in the old AFL, Marjorie graduated from the University of Houston in the days when the Cougars played their football games at Rice Stadium (before they moved into the Astrodome). She had made a career as a teacher and administrator in Houston public schools, returning to UH to complete her doctorate in the mid-1990's. When she took over the Writing Center in 2000, it was not as a faculty member but as a full-time administrator, and the Writing Center was not subordinate to the English Department but instead stood as an autonomous department of its own, with substantial quarters above ground. Dr. Chadwick would run the center with a small staff of full-time administrators directing the work of a couple of dozen undergraduate tutors, what we called Writing Consultants. All of these decisions would make for a rather unique Writing Center, divorced from the faculty concerns with research and tenure and focused on delivery of individualized services directly to students, and I consider myself lucky to have been one of those full-time administrators hired in the first couple of years of the new regime.

I had a full-time job, meaningful work, benefits, the chance to stay at a research university in the country's fourth-largest metro, but what I didn't have in sufficient quantity was time to write. That was my compromise. After the project-management experience of completing the novel *Catholic Divorce* while on leave of absence, I had written a second book, a literary detective novel I initially called *Turbulence*, later *Blood Halo*, as my dissertation. I had tried to revise and market the book after I graduated, but had found myself in that old familiar swamp again, running out of energy for and belief in the project, sensing that something was off—not just in my writing but in my life. By 2008, I wasn't really writing much.

Instead, I had embarked upon a campaign of what I thought at the time were "solutions" to my lowering discontent. I set about cleaning up my financial situation and had upgraded my car and then decided to make my move into what President Bush called "the ownership society," buying a house. The American Dream, and because I was a veteran I would be able to get financing without a big down payment. Somewhere in that list of things to do was find a church, but I hadn't gotten around to it yet. My sense of priorities was, as they say, what it was.

I was feeling some pretty intense existential urgency in those days, feeling like life was getting away from me. Only a year before, my oldest sister had died, ending a long suffering decline plagued by a variety of mysterious debilitating ailments. At one time the soul of hospitality, she had become by the end a bitter recluse, refusing visits and isolating herself. This was part of our family legacy, these disordered passions: my grandmother had struggled with vicious anger that played a big part in ruining several marriages; one of my uncles sank into isolation as a depressed alcoholic, by turns angry and abject; my father had been rescued from wet-brained isolation through the merciful intervention of my sisters, but only lasted a year after they brought him north from Florida. My sister's death was unbelievably melodramatic in its timing, too. She went into a coma on the weekend when her son, my nephew Matt, was getting married for the second time, and then died just after, her shadow almost literally hovering spectrally over the nuptials. I made it for the funeral but not the wedding. It was April and it could have been spring, but instead we were hit with a late snowstorm. When I got back to Texas from her funeral, I started watching this new TV series called *Mad Men*, which I praised for telling secrets from inside the house of debased American masculinity, the drinking, the sexual obsession and contempt for marriage, the depression at the core of consumer-oriented marketing—spend your way out of the gaping maw of the certain destination of death. I loved it, thought it was the smartest thing on television.

Death and marriage, and I was just an onlooker, still as much a curious spectator as when I had visited Matt when Jaia was born in 1999—*what's it like to be married, to have kids of your own, to share your life with others?* I felt like I hadn't done anything yet, none of the really important things in life, and I think I fell for an illusion, the trap of trying to solve spiritual problems with material means.

In a matter of months, from May to September, 2008, my "solutions" had taken me from a neighborhood where I'd lived for a dozen years and still had a few friends (surprising few, though) to a subdivision where I knew not a single one of the Moustache Heroes up and down every street, but where I could afford a mortgage, and then I had seen an economic collapse chop down the market value of that house well below what I owed on it the same week that a hurricane tried its best to blow away that house and every house in the whole city of Houston. The newest of the Houses of the Holy, Reliant Stadium hadn't yet been declared safe for future contests, and my street in Sharpstown was without power indefinitely.

So I was watching the Texans play the Titans on TV in the Writing Center at the University of Houston. And they were blowing it.

Farewell to Football?

With 2:30 left in the game, the Texans still had a long shot to come back and win the game. They had the ball, down 24-12, with good field position thanks to a defensive stand and a penalty against Tennessee on the punt that gave Houston the ball. 22 yards to go and the Texans could get back in the game with a touchdown and two-point conversion, which would only leave them down by four points.

"We" have to score, and quickly.

But "we" blow it. After a good start, two pass plays that advance the ball to the two yard line—into what I might call the "Zeno Zone," where Coach Kubiak seems to have a special genius for slowing down and even going backward—the negative plays come in rapid succession. Steve Slaton runs off tackle for a loss of one. Matt Schaub is sacked for a loss of five. Two straight failures by the offensive line. And then the crowning glory for how to lose a football game on the road: Schaub drops back to pass, puts up a weak throw across his body in the general direction of Andre Johnson on the left, and it's picked off by the scrappy little Titans cornerback Cortland Finnegan. Not just intercepted, but run back for a touchdown, run back for a 99-yard touchdown. 99 yards! The field is only 100 yards long!

You can't lose in any more demoralizing fashion than that, blowing a close game on the road with an essentially unforced error that not only takes away your chance of winning but puts more points on the board for your opponent. A defensive score, the crowd goes wild, the crowd has *forever* to go wild, since the defender has to run the entire length of the field. It's an elation bomb like a walk-off home run in baseball. Schaub slinks to the sideline, where Coach Kubiak is waiting, stunned look on his face, the hungry kid who just realized the bully stole the sandwich out of his lunch. You see him shaking his head, muttering, probably laying it all on the quarterback. You can't do that. You just can't do that at this point in the game.

I am beyond stunned, not even bothering to rise or swear. My rage is molten, but at some point I realize that this is bigger than a football game. I have lost control completely here, lost control of everything. The power is out at my house. The economy collapsed when I couldn't even watch it on TV. I'm trapped, underwater, it's going to be years before I can even think about getting out from under this mortgage. *Mortgage,* from the Old French for "dead pledge." This dead dread thing that has swallowed me whole.

In a panicked moment of choking anxiety, I am confronted with a vivid flashback of the one event more than any other that forced my campaign for solutions to this debacle, a nadir moment: late in May, in my old apartment on Hawthorne Street in the Montrose district, I'm drinking alone and the college student upstairs is having a party, a lot of people making a lot of noise right over my head, pounding into my brain the dreary music of every failure in my miserable life. They're young, they're alive, they've just graduated from college—it's *that* summer for them. It's starting to get late, late for me, at least, late for an old man lonely and bitter in the isolation his choices have led him to, an old man drinking down the poison of victimology—why does everything bad happen to me? (Inside the Haunted House of Debased Masculinity: *Is this how it went for Gus before my sisters found him and rescued him—an old man full of rage drinking alone? Is this the secret that Uncle Clint brooded over, that there's finally just nothing to it in life but bad things endlessly piled up, endlessly replicating?*) A rage is growing inside me as if I'm possessed by the demon of envy that can't stand young, energetic, beautiful people disrupting the gloom—but for just one moment of clarity I realize that I still have a choice and that this is a bad situation and that I should be careful—*you can't do that.* Then that moment passes and I have chosen to become a stupid raging downstairs neighbor banging on the metal fire-escape stairs with a baseball bat, a grumpy old man telling the kids to get off his lawn only without any of the humor of that cartoon cliché. With menace, in fact. *You just can't do that.*

I don't end up achieving the results I hoped for, and in fact spend some time that night, when I should have been sleeping, could have been sleeping had I exercised my free choice a little more wisely, talking with police out on the back deck. "This is not who I am," I tell them, but of course, this is exactly who I am, but I would rather not face that fact. I get off with a warning, but it's nothing like a victory.

I'm trapped with a dirty little secret, *another* dirty little secret, and I don't feel I have anyone to turn to, and I would be mortified to tell anyone this secret anyway. So I do the only thing I can imagine, speeding up the house-hunting process I've already embarked upon and very quickly commit to the best compromise I can find as far as the affordability/acceptability equation. I make my dead pledge.

I buy my house and trap myself in with my secret, and even though Hurricane Ike huffed and puffed and tried to blow my house in, the house wouldn't give in and these secrets stay locked in my heart. If a hurricane and the collapse of the American economy couldn't do it, what would it take to break through into the light of the truth?

CHAPTER 12

• • •

Just Getting There, Part II (2010)

"Strong feelings are not decisive for the morality or the holiness of persons; they are simply the inexhaustible reservoir of images and affections in which the moral life is expressed. Passions are mainly good when they contribute to a good action, evil in the opposite case. The upright will orders the movements of the senses it appropriates, to the good and to beatitude; an evil will succumbs to disordered passions and exacerbates them. Emotions and feelings can be taken up into the *virtues* or perverted by the *vices.*"

(CATECHISM OF THE CATHOLIC CHURCH, 1768)

• • •

NOVEMBER 7, 2010: San Diego Chargers 29, Houston Texans 23, Reliant Stadium. It was a good game. It just wasn't enough.

The Texans under Gary Kubiak had methodically installed a proficient NFL offense and manned it with some solid players to complement superstar receiver Andre Johnson. Undrafted free agent running back Arian Foster had initiated his second year as a pro with a bang, threatening an opening-day record for rushing as he gained 231 yards on the ground and Houston beat Indianapolis 34-24 to start the 2010 season.

But by the middle of the season, the Texans were stuck in a .500 rut because their defense was terrible, had been terrible since Kubiak appointed first-time coordinator Richard Smith to lead the defense when Kubiak first took over as head coach in 2006, and had stayed terrible when Smith was eventually fired and replaced by another first-time coordinator, Frank Bush, in 2009. Some Houston "theorists" (people who gripe on football blogs) believed that Kubiak didn't want any competition at the top and so hired "buddies" to coach the defense, with the sad results they were always in the bottom half of the league in all the basic measures of what matters most on defense—how many yards and how many points they gave up. There's an old football adage that defense wins championships, and that may or may not be true, but it's certain that defense can lose you plenty of games if it keeps giving up plenty of points.

At home against the San Diego Chargers in the middle of the 2010 season, a familiar pattern played out in Houston. Foster scored a couple of touchdowns on the ground and kicker Neil Rackers successfully booted a couple of field goals and the Texans led at the half, 20-14. But on the other side of the ball, Chargers quarterback Philip Rivers, who'd already been to two Pro Bowls in his career and would go again after the 2010 season, was lighting up the Texans pass defense (which would finish the season worst in the league in yards given up through the air and second-worst in passing touchdowns—the things that matter most). The mouthy quarterback from North Carolina State would finish the day with four touchdown passes—all of the Chargers' scores were touchdown passes as San Diego ended up winning, 29-23.

Still, for a fan it wasn't so bad. The day was *splendid*, sunny and fair, with temperatures in the mid-60's, which meant the Texans finally took advantage of their retractable roof and let the sun shine in on NFL football in Houston. This was a bit of a tricky subject for the team, with some personal history for me: I'd been in the stadium for my first regular-season Houston Texans game in 2005 when management thought they could out-smart the Super-Bowl-bound Pittsburgh Steelers by opening the roof to the roaring sub-tropical heat and humidity of the Bayou City in September and forcing the Steelers to wear their black jerseys. The strategy backfired on every level. Pittsburgh trounced the Texans 27-7, the Steelers sacked David Carr eight times (Troy Polamalu got three), and the fans stewed in their own sweat as the home team floundered on the field. After that, with some guidance from the NFL offices no doubt, the Texans announced a "roof policy" that said panels of the retractable crown would only be wheeled opened if the temperature was between 50 and 80 degrees Fahrenheit, and if there was little or no chance of rain. So the roof was rarely open (except for that hurricane year, 2008, when storm damage meant they couldn't get it shut), and while the field was allegedly "natural grass," grown outdoors and trucked in on pallets for game day, a lot of the games had the same sterile feel as in the Astrodome. Knowing that it was all governed by an NFL-approved *policy* just sucked out the cheer more fully.

But not today. Today the roof is open and the sun is out and I have family in town and we are sitting in the front row at mid-field. My nephew Matt and his son Jaia have flown down from Albany, NY, for a football weekend and my friend Warren Rawson has gotten us choice seats by way of the pro-football writer and Hall of Fame voter John McClain of the *Houston Chronicle*. I am close enough to the field to be heard by coaches and players if I choose to holler, and I choose to holler.

Farewell to Football?

With Jaia and Matt Benson at (then) Reliant
Stadium on a splendid fall day, Houston, November
2010. Photo Courtesy of Warren Rawson.

In the first quarter, Matt Schaub throws a pass to Jacoby Jones, a gangly but speedy receiver the Texans had drafted out of small historically-black Lane College in Tennessee. Jones has it on his hands but drops the ball, and, not a fan of this skit, I holler at him as he skulks over to the sidelines while the field-goal team takes the field: "Skillet Hands!" It's an old, stupid football epithet from the same genus as "butterfingers," infused with special poignancy for Jones, who apparently went through a growth spurt in high school that saw him sprout up to 6' 3" in height but without comparable growth in his hands. His hands are *objectively* small for a man his size, and I'm a stupid lout for pointing it out.

I'm not sure how much of that I knew at the time, but I know that he heard me, because he tore off his helmet and stared me down in what is usually termed "Murder One." I thought for just a second he might come up the wall and take a Lambeau Leap at me. We were that close to the field! More than anything, though, I felt scalded by his gaze, since justice was on his side. What was I thinking? What kind of example was I setting for my 11-year-old nephew, sitting beside me in the midfield sun?

Only two days earlier, we'd been in the stands at the old Robertson Stadium (the same one that used to be Jeppesen Stadium when Abner Haynes was calling Red Bourne's coin-toss and kicking to the clock) for a University of Houston game. We really didn't know what to expect on the field, since the Cougars were without gunslinger quarterback Case Keenum, injured in the third game of the season against UCLA. Not to worry, though, as the Cougars and the University of Central Florida (what? Knights) staged a shootout, each team going over 500 yards of total offense as UCF prevailed 40-33. It was a great night to be out at the ball park, fall-cool—which means evening temperatures in the 60's—and old-school in the stadium that dated back to the days of the New Deal. It might have been nicer, though, if a fan right next to us had exercised a little restraint on his use of profanity to comment on the game. Even after I asked him to cool it, *there's a kid here, buddy*, he asserted his right to be a foul-mouthed jerk, and so it went, the beer going in and the cursing coming out.

By 2010, I had started to really reflect on what can go wrong around football, the excesses and illusions and the disordered passions of the fans. Here, I might have been wondering: *What's up with that? Why does football so often bring out such random low-boil hatred and profanity—not even snarling, just swearing, almost a random breakdown of one level of socio-linguistic inhibition? Why do people so often take football games as the occasion for amateur-hour drinking? What is this guy even doing here? What combination of conflicted loves and hates get you to the ballpark only to grouse about it obscenely the whole time, to yell mercilessly at the players, who are, from what the coaches tell me, doing the best that they can?*

In his harrowing "fictional memoir," *A Fan's Notes,* Fred Exley describes a tragi-comic encounter he has with a Norman-Rockwell family of "spectators" at the Polo Grounds for a New York Giants game, and he ends up cussing at the handsome, even-tempered father who tries to tell him that it's nothing to cry about, "it's *only* a game." At his alcoholic, self-pitying best, Exley muses: "My irritation had nothing to do with these dead people, and not really—I know now—anything to do with the outcome of the game. I had begun to be haunted again by that which had haunted me on my first trip to the city—the inability of a man to impose his dreams, his ego, upon the city, and for many long months had been experiencing a rage induced by New York's stony refusal to esteem me" (p. 70). The muse of football's disordered passions finds her bard in Exley.

I know how that goes from personal experience, been there, done that, but like the Beatles song says, "man I was mean but I'm changing my scene, and I'm doing the best that I can." I'm trying to learn to restrain myself, and I'm not doing it on my own anymore.

On campus, not only where I currently worked but where I had taken my doctorate, I no doubt felt called to a higher level of decorum. On our way to the old football stadium, I had seized the opportunity to try to initiate Jaia Benson into the world of higher education by escorting him and his father up to the library where they shelve the dissertations. I pointed out to them, here's what you do to earn a Ph. D. You write one of these. Here's mine. Jaia's question was exemplary in its clear simplicity: How many pages do you have to write? To him, at 11, I'm sure it looked like a lot of other things you do in school—this many homework problems, this many pages in your report, this many experimental tries at your hypothesis. How many pages in a dissertation? I'm sure my answer sounded like an old man's worn-out trick: as many as it takes. Like I was trying to con Sir Pooperton.

The college game had more of a family feel, too, because I had arranged to meet up with my colleague Veronique Tran and her husband, along with their two sons, roughly Jaia's age and similarly fiercely athletic. Veronique and her husband are part of the vast Southeast Asian community in the vicinity of Houston, which has the second-largest Vietnamese population of any American city—a few years after I'd made the move to Houston, I counted and found that there were eight pages of Smith's in the phone book and five pages of Nguyen's. Their sons Liem and Hiep, though, are all-American in their love for football. They may well have idolized Dat Nguyen when they were growing up, as he was the first Vietnamese football star in the United States and a decidedly local hero, a standout linebacker who played high school ball in Gulf-Coast Rockport, then in College Station at Texas A&M, and finally in the NFL with the Dallas Cowboys. Like Nguyen's family, Veronique's parents had left Vietnam when Saigon fell in 1975, and like me she had earned her doctorate at the University of Houston and worked as an administrator at the U of H. Like my nephew Matt, and my niece Courtney in upstate New York, and parents all across America, Veronique was facing the Football Question: how do I balance my desire to support my kids in their athletic endeavors, recognizing how important team sports can be in growing up, with my deep-rooted concern for their safety? For the Trans, the compromise was clear—the boys could play football in junior high, but not in high school. In their case, their physiques and skills would end up better suited for basketball, anyway.

Beyond their concerns about safety, "sports families" also face economic challenges about how much parents should spend to transact their children's athletic potential. The first major economic temptation dangling out there for most is the college scholarship, the dream that The Kid will have his education paid for by athletics. This may seem more realistic than the truly far-off hope that The Kid will make it to the lucrative League, the NFL, where the "rookie minimum" salary as of this writing stands at $435,000, but in fact the pyramid also narrows severely from high school to college. As Mark Hyman notes in his aptly titled *The Most Expensive Game in Town: The Rising Cost of Youth Sports and the Toll on Today's Families*, only 5.8% of high-school football players end

Farewell to Football?

up on college teams, and not all of them earn scholarships (p. 97). A niche industry has risen up to exploit those scholarship illusions held by many sports parents, offering help for aspiring athletes to prepare them for the recruiting and try-out process. With so much at stake, why not spend a few hundred—or a few thousand—dollars on a couple of camps and clinics to help The Kid maximize his chances of getting one of those full-ride scholarship packages?

I asked Matt Benson about this recently, and his answers seemed reasonable to me, and properly grounded. He was willing to spend substantially, more than $10,000 as it turned out, to pay for sports travel when Jaia's youth-league baseball team went on a winning run that saw them victors of successive tournaments in Albany, Brooklyn, and Pittsburgh to advance to the World Series in Monterey, California. That was for the kids to compete and play as a team. Matt wasn't going to spend much on individual camps and clinics, although he admits that if Jaia starts to generate scholarship interest from colleges, he might consider spending frugally on carefully-targeted preparation. His examination of conscience comes down to a couple of bedrock principles: pragmatic cost/benefit analysis, and parental best-practices, engaging the sensible Jaia in a running dialogue about what The Kid wants to do. These seem to me like good antidotes to the obnoxious and joy-sapping "Helicopter Parent" tactics that a lot of "sports families" have adopted to try and run down an often-illusory dream. (The camps and clinics may not make a lot of economic sense, anyway, since the college coaches I talked to in the process of researching this book told me that they rely almost exclusively in recruiting on what they themselves see on tape and measure in clinics, and on what they get from high-school coaches.)

On that cool Friday evening on campus at the University of Houston, while the adults talked at half time, Jaia and Liem and Hiep threw the football around in a little open area they found outside one of the corners of the stadium, and while you could tell they were having a good time, you could also hear in their voices that this was serious play. The

261

brothers, especially, would get on each other if they dropped a pass or threw wildly. *Come on, man! Bear down!* I'm sure that at some point, each one of them hit the ground hard, and might have been tempted to get up a little angry and sore, but nothing came of it. They were just athletic kids, and highly competitive, having fun and imaging the days ahead when they would be in the spotlight, whether on a football field or basketball court.

Matt told me later that a turning point in Jaia's competitive athletic life came when he was four years old (four!), playing in a basketball league for five-year-olds. Jaia was disgusted with the level of effort from his teammates and decided he wanted to quit, right then and there, in the middle of a game. Matt took him into the locker room and explained to him how this worked: if you want to quit at the end of the season, fine, but you don't quit in the middle of a game. Listening to my nephew, I was learning a lesson, not just about Jaia but about Matt, too. In my generation of the House of Women Who Divorce, the advice might have run completely opposite: just give up, if it's too hard don't bother, get a divorce, break up with that team. Quit. Something more than basketball was at work here.

Back at the Texans game on Sunday, the home team had a chance late in the game, but Andre Johnson dropped a pass—it would have been a tough catch, but it was briefly on his hands. This time I did a better job of resisting the temptation. Ah, crap, I thought, and didn't even say that. "That's the NFL. Game of inches." It's a great day to be at the stadium.

Things had gotten better in the anger-management department because I had begun an initiation into self-mastery and a training in human freedom. Due to the family visit and the NFL game, I had a week off from adult catechism at St. Thomas More Catholic Church, but I knew that next week I would be back to my pursuit of a more faithful life. This wasn't something I was likely to quit.

• • •

"An Apprenticeship in Self-Mastery"

This whole process of entering the church really began with hospitality, with me welcoming my mother into my home. In the spring of 2010, a little crack must have opened up in that hermetic selfishness of mine that even Hurricane Ike had not breached. I realized that one benefit of owning your own home is you can entertain guests. It dawned on me that I could entertain and accommodate my mother—no easy feat given her health condition by this time. She'd had four heart attacks since the 1970's, and in 2002 had nearly died, requiring quadruple-bypass surgery. There was certainly some urgency in inviting her to visit me. Who knows how many years we have left? It would be a major chore hosting her for a week, but some little corner of my heart actually warmed to the task of *doing things* for my mother. There was also that little matter of the commandment to "honor thy mother." This was more than just passive-aggressive trans-actional maneuvering to show her that I have a life of my own, look at me, I own a house and when you come to visit, you get your own room! Not boasting like that, this was tinged, however lightly, with that genuine open-heartedness that Peter alludes to in his first letter: "Be hospitable to one another without complaining" (4:9). It wasn't much—we cooked to-gether in my kitchen, watched *Gone with the Wind* on Blu-Ray, visited some of my friends, made like tourists at Space Center Houston—but it broke the ice, and when my mother had flown back north, in this new spirit I went looking for a different kind of home, a church.

I settled on St. Thomas More, a Catholic church not far from me, as my starting point based on a kind of peculiar litmus test. I had decided that I wouldn't even consider any churches that didn't engage in prison ministry (maybe it went back to my very first teaching job in that base-ment of the sheriff's department). Somehow it seemed to me that this would separate the blood from the water, so to speak, the spiritually hot from the lukewarm. St. Thomas More scored on that account, and of course had the advantage of being named for one of my literary heroes, the author of *Utopia* and the subject of *A Man for All Seasons*. So I began the opening stage, called Inquiry, and was immediately blessed.

Deacon Ed Stoessel conducted the Inquiry sessions with his wife of 48 years, Cathey. Inquiry was a weekly Wednesday evening meeting in the religious education building at the church, and people interested in joining the Catholic faith would come in and pose questions that Deacon Ed would do his best to answer. He did pretty well, and in the process I learned a few lessons in the Catholic faith that weren't found in his words but in his character (appropriate to Christianity, which is a personal encounter with the risen Lord more than a philosophy). He'd earned his Ph. D. in theoretical physics, and was retired after a career as a research scientist and manager in the international oil industry. He knew his faith very well, and tended to answer the questions he was posed with admirable sincerity and compassion.

I reached an early turning-point with Deacon Ed and with the church when I asked him about homosexuality. I have friends and family who identify as gay and lesbian, have wondered at times about my own inclinations, and I had to know what the church was going to expect from me regarding something that I thought, from the outside and with no real basis, Catholicism condemned. This was on the order of a "deal-breaker" for me.

In so many words, Deacon Ed made it clear that our first response to anyone must be to seek to love and accept them. The church doesn't necessarily want to deal with people in terms of labels, but it does recognize that some people are drawn to same-sex love. I was surprised to find out that homosexual desire is not actually a sin, but that acting on that desire could be sinful. Deacon Ed concluded that probably my entering the Catholic Church would not have much impact on my relationships with people who identify as homosexual, and that I wasn't expected to shun them or to try to convert them, either. I should try to continue to love them, or really try to love them even more with a better sense of how love comes from God through us to others, but I should also recognize that like every human being, they were struggling with their own temptations and sins.

At some point, this became very clear to me: all sexual activity outside of marriage, not just homosexuality, is considered sinful. It took a long time to sink in that because I had never been married, all of my sexual experiences had been sinful—I had never experienced the joy of sexuality as God intended it. As one of the disciplines in John's Gospel laments, "this saying is hard. Who can accept it?" (6:60). This was going to be a hard teaching to accept, the ground of my history shifting beneath me, what I thought I knew proven to be mere wrong opinion (however widely shared that wrong opinion is in American culture, which more and more tends to an open-ended moral relativism that implies "it's all OK, everyone's doing it, there aren't really any rules so long as no one gets hurt"). I was going to have to make major changes in my life, reassess what mattered or what I thought mattered, take a shot at detaching from those loose ideas about "relationships" and pleasure and the activities and pursuits that go along with those ideas, take as many shots as I could, keep trying, engage in and commit to a process of trying however many times I failed. I'd spent my whole life either trying to or claiming to try to deal with addictions, to resist temptations without number, to quit smoking, to get my drinking or my weight or my temper under control, and so I had some idea of how difficult and relentless the process would be. But maybe I was looking at it wrong, making it some ritual ordeal or torture, maybe if I understood *why* I should resist, beyond superficial utilitarian reasons, maybe I would find patience and perseverance in that. This is really what faith means, to believe that God will provide for us in our needs, even when we don't know how that will work.

I was moving out of the shadows of ignorance into the light of truth.

The next stage in the process of entering the church was adult catechism, or what the reliably grandiloquent Catholic Church calls the Rite of Christian Initiation for Adults, ominously abbreviated as RCIA. You'd think I was back in the Army with nomenclature like that, and in fact, my sponsor was a retired Army sergeant-major. This stage was a lot more like the college routine: we met each Sunday after Mass for two hours, one each studying the Bible readings for the day and covering a topic from the Catechism of the Catholic Church (sample topic: The Real Presence). It was pretty highly-organized, but it was also pretty highly-populated. It took a lot of people to bring us candidates and cate-chumens into the church, and that sense of community and family made a really strong impression on me. I started noticing how many people worked together to conduct the Mass, for example, people of all ages, races, and economic classes, all united by a singular purpose. To praise God. It was a mysterious kind of teamwork I hadn't really experienced in my life.

In my catechism classes, I started noticing something else, this word "freedom." The word represented a big concept in the Catholic faith, part of the trinity of "truth, freedom, love" at the core of the belief sys-tem and ethics of this religion (the core of the *experience* of Christianity, of course, is the encounter with the three-personed God—Father, Son, and Holy Spirit). The way that people were using that word in church settings made me realize that throughout my life, most people were us-ing the term "freedom" as if it meant something entirely different. I was on my way to breaking open a lie at the heart of American culture. In some senses, it came down to prepositions: I had spent most of my life in a big herd of people seeking "freedom from," freedom from stupid laws and restrictions, freedom from fear, freedom from want, freedom from outside interference while we sought our autonomously-chosen plea-sures, while in the church people really meant the *freedom to* love God with their whole minds, souls, and hearts, and with all their strength. To achieve that freedom to love God, we have to work out how to detach ourselves from the disordered passions holding us back.

When you connect freedom with sexuality, you end up with chastity, and when I read what the Catechism had to say about that, I found my-self in some strange new land, some Utopia where everything I thought turned out to be something different: "Chastity includes an apprentice-ship in self-mastery which is a training in human freedom. The alterna-tive is clear: either man governs his passions and finds peace, or he lets himself be dominated by them and becomes unhappy" (CCC 2339). If this was true, then among other things the scales had fallen from my eyes and I had cracked the code on Hollywood Humanism.

Farewell to Football?

Around the time I was going through adult catechism, I had been casually studying the film career of Montgomery Clift, who, while compelling in his on-screen intensity, was a strange figure to end up as an American movie star, however briefly, a tortured semi-closeted gay man who drank incessantly and frequently compounded the intoxication with drugs, until his self-destructive habits destroyed his appeal as much as his famous car accident destroyed his handsome face. Clift, along with James Dean and Marlon Brando, was part of that mid-century American cinema that honored transgression above all things, elevated and idolized the Self above all things, rebels indulging in a kind of perverse strain of Hollywood Humanism. Brando plays a character in *The Wild One* who is asked, "what are you rebelling against?" "Whattaya got?" he replies. As I was studying the catechism, I was starting to realize how—hidden in plain sight, broad daylight—there was a distinct cultural conflict between these opposing value systems and the meanings they applied to the essential experiences and choices in life. In Hollywood Humanism, the only truth was feeling, love was expressed and fulfilled as sexual desire, and the only path to freedom was transgression. Without God, there was only this ever-shifting subjective sentimentality, and the tragic fates of transgressive heroes like Clift suggested how poor a basis for life this mistaken perception of freedom really was. The alternative really was clear.

But the way of the Lord would be hard. Chastity a training in human freedom? This saying is hard indeed. But I had guidance along the way—I was amazed to find in the Catechism a more frank and truthful description of the complexities of human desire and disorders of human passions and sexuality than I'd ever encountered anywhere else in my literate and educated life. I also had plenty of company. St. Thomas More Catholic Church describes itself as "a family of families," as is the one, holy, catholic, and apostolic church, and I was beginning to realize that the fellowship went deeper than just our autonomous consumerist choices to "buy into" this church. Every time we celebrated Mass, together we acknowledged our sinful nature. Of course I had known that about myself, but for the first time in my life, I also knew that it wasn't an excuse to retreat into what Walker Percy often called "the sucking hole of self." I could do something about it.

• • •

"27 Toss"

A year later, Jaia Benson would play his greatest game of football ever, a real lesson in self-mastery, and it was still just not enough for the win.

It's a cold rainy autumn night in Brent Steurwald Stadium in Clifton Park, NY, and Jaia is celebrating his 12th birthday with his teammates in the Shenendehowa Junior Plainsmen youth football league. Jaia's playing a great game at linebacker, but as we say in Texas, he's fixin' to play an even bigger game.

The running back for Jaia's team, the Braves, takes the ball up the middle and ends up at the bottom of a pile, and there's a lot more talking than usual coming out of that pile, voices higher-pitched, not talking trash now. *Hotaling is hurt! Get some help out here! His arm is broken! REALLY broken!* When they get the kids unpiled, they discover the brutal truth, it's a clean compound fracture.

As the kids mill around waiting for the ambulance to take their friend off the field, Jaia starts to reflect on the situation from the sideline. He's shocked—hasn't seen such a serious injury up close before—and sure, a little scared. But then he remembers his pregame ritual, bowing his head under the goal post and asking himself, "what's my goal for this game? How can I make myself the best player today?" He'll be going into the game at running back, and he starts to think that his goal today will be to step up and take the lead and get everyone else to play the best game they have in them.

Besides, he thinks as he readies himself for play to resume, we've got the outside running game going. We've got the "27 Toss" working to the outside. 2: toss to the tailback, that's me. 7: take it all the way to the left, outside the end, where it's a footrace between me and the defensive back.

Farewell to Football?

If I try to take it up the middle—well, look what happened to Hotaling! If I try to take it into the 5 hole, that DB is going to meet me there. But if I take it all the way outside, 7 hole, I've got the advantages there.

And that's exactly how it went for the rest of the game. When the Braves had the ball, the "27 Toss" had all the advantages, and Jaia Benson must have carried for close to 200 yards. And still, it just wasn't enough for the win. That defensive back for the Comanches was just too quick, always catching up with Jaia before he could cross the goal line. The game ended in a scoreless tie.

The score never mattered less to Matt Benson than on that cold, misty night. "It was the greatest football game I ever saw him play," my nephew told me. "I knew he was playing with a level of fear and uncertainty that night, after having seen and heard what he did with that compound fracture. He grew up a little that night." Here was the drama of sports across the whole spectrum from comedy to tragedy to heroics on the artificial turf under the Saturday night lights in the stadium. The zany cop-show car-chase scene of 11- and 12-year-old kids in pads trying their best to run down the plays on a wet field, the realization of every parent's worst nightmare with a serious injury, the camaraderie of a team coming together to play for each other, to lift each other up and face their fears together.

And then it was all over. That game ended, the season played out to its conclusion, and then it was all over for football for Jaia Benson.

When summer came around in 2012 and Jaia saw football practice looming ahead in the hazy dog days of August, he realized that the joy had just been boiled out of the sport for him. He loved the games, loved the teamwork, but the thought of two-hour or even three-hour practices, in the heat, the boring practices running the same plays over and over again, 27 Toss after 27 Toss, mix in that tedium with the ever-present low-grade anxiety about serious injuries, especially concussions, and it all added up to a stark realization: he wasn't committed enough to football to put up with the practices. Football just wasn't that important to him.

The joy had gone out of it, and it was time to say farewell to football.

He had gotten out before he had gotten in so far that the choice would have been tortured. He hadn't quit anything. He had chosen to commit himself even more fully to baseball and basketball, sports where you played more games and spent less time practicing. Basketball especially was a game of creative freedom—the plays were just a basis for the game to come alive, different every time, different with each group of players, different against every defensive set. Football meant running Coach's boring seven plays over and over again, perfection meant compliance and conformity, and where was the joy in that?

Jaia was 12 and had bid farewell to football right when the joy went out of the game. Grown men had made different choices and sometimes found that when the joy ran out, they were stuck in a tough spot.

George Sauer, Jr., was an outstanding wide receiver on the 1963 Texas Longhorn team that John F. Kennedy would have visited had he not been assassinated in Dallas on that Friday afternoon in November. Sauer played six seasons with the New York Jets, Joe Namath throwing him the ball, and had himself a big game in Super Bowl III after the 1968 season, catching 8 passes for 133 yards as the Jets upset the Baltimore Colts. Sauer got out of football after only six NFL seasons because he'd lost the joy of the game. As he said at the time, "I like football. It is a framework around which you can see the dynamics of a player working together with other players, which can be a beautiful thing to watch. When people enjoy what they are doing it can be ecstatic. But the way it's structured, the intrinsic values of sports are choked off. It has been despiritualized, the profane applied to the sacred" (in Merchant, p. 44). He said farewell to football and went into writing and graphics work.

Bill Curry may be the most eloquent communicator of the modern American football experience ever, a mainstay for on-camera contributions to the NFL Network's *America's Game* and *A Football Life* series. He played 10 seasons in the NFL, played on championship teams in Green Bay and Baltimore, played for Vince Lombardi and Don Shula. He started at center when the Shula-coached Colts lost to Namath and Sauer and the Jets in Super Bowl III. He seems to have never missed a telling detail or incisive anecdote. George Plimpton recognized Curry's gifts and collaborated with him on a 1977 book, *One More July*, in which Curry describes the contrast between the joy of play and the grinding work into which the NFL has converted the game of football with the weird eloquence of William Blake contrasting Innocence with Experience. He recalls training camp late in his career, when he signed with the Houston Oilers, and how in the simmering Texas afternoon he was "groggy, almost dazed, and during two-a-days I always had a headache" (p. 70). On the way to the practice session one afternoon, he saw the high-school band that had their summer camp on the same college campus playing touch football, shirts vs. skins. "The kids were really having a joyous experience," he recalled to Plimpton. "And here I was, that sloshing feeling in my head, going over to participate in the same game, me, thirty-one years of age, high salary, family responsibilities, college degree, keen mind, broken nose, eloquence, ambition, and foolish ego—I was going over to play the same game, and yet I was miserable. I kept wondering: what have we done? What have we done with this game?"

Vince Lombardi, the Hall of Fame coach, might provide the best answer. In the book that W. C. Heinz wrote with Lombardi's help, *Run to Daylight!* (1963), the coach muses on how hard it is for him to celebrate a victory. "What success does to you. It is like a habit-forming drug that, in victory, saps your elation and, in defeat, deepens your despair" (p. 22). To narrow it down to a fine, sharp point, the coach wonders, "has this become a game for madmen and am I one of them?"

How do we judge for ourselves what is right?

CHAPTER 13

— • • • —

Veterans Day: Winning Ugly (2012)

" … this is the moral rule: *Love the truth of an object more than your attachment to the opinions you have already formed about it.* More concisely, one could say, 'love the truth more than yourself.'"

(Luigi Giussani, *The Religious Sense*, p. 31)

• • •

November 11, 2012: Houston Texans 13, Chicago Bears 6, Soldier Field, Chicago. By 2012, the Houston Texans were a good enough football team to warrant a few prime-time games on national television. With All-Pro quarterback Peyton Manning injured and out of the picture for the division-rival Indianapolis Colts, Houston had won the AFC South in 2011. The Texans even won a wild-card playoff game, with rookie sensation J. J. Watt returning an interception for a touchdown against the Cincinnati Bengals. What a scene that had been in Reliant Stadium: a big defensive lineman plucking the ball out of the air and gliding into the end zone! I was watching the game on TV with friends at the house and I thought of that description of the B-52 George C. Scott gives in *Dr. Strangelove*, a big plane like a '52, flying low, frying chicken in the barnyard!

The Texans had evolved into a winning team, at least when the stakes weren't too high. Coach Gary Kubiak had synthesized an efficient offense with quarterback Matt Schaub throwing selectively to wide-out Andre Johnson and tight end Owen Daniels, the whole offense predicated on the running game. Undrafted free agent Arian Foster had developed into an elite NFL running back in the Kubiak version of the West Coast Offense, which relied upon mobile line-men to flow off the line of scrimmage and create holes that Foster had to read and react to. This proved to be Foster's strength—his vision, and his ability to cut back, often breaking big gainers by re-versing the flow as defenders over-pursued. At its best, the Texans offense looked artistic and elegantly improvisational in slow-motion replay, a synchronized gallop of choreographed blocking with no cer-tain destination—the runner would wait for the play to develop and then exploit the gap wherever it opened up. You won at this kind of game by committing to the process, not the particular outcome, and by waiting to commit until the situation clarified itself. Foster was kind of a poetic soul who bowed Namaste ("I see the divinity in you") when he scored touchdowns, and you could see how this scheme fit his character.

The Texans defense finally had a winning mentor in coordinator Wade Phillips—a University of Houston graduate and son of the be-loved former Oilers coach Bum Phillips. (The Texans exuded a home-town covered-dish family-dinner feel; Coach Kubiak had starred in high school at Houston's St. Pius X and had served as a ball-boy at Oilers training camp.) Merging the talent the team had drafted like Watt and linebackers Brian Cushing and Connor Barwin with veteran free agents such as cornerback Johnathan Joseph and safety Danieal Manning, Phillips had finally given the Texans a defense that could offer the of-fense a fair shot at winning a lot of games. Occasionally, as with Watt's touchdown in the 2011 playoffs, the "D" could even pull off a big play of their own.

The Texans had become winners, and the NFL likes to put winners on TV in prime time. In 2012, the Texans were scheduled to play twice each on Sunday Night Football and Monday Night Football, and they also would play in the nationally-televised Thanksgiving Day game in Detroit. Heading into a Sunday Night Football matchup with the Bears at Soldier Field on Veterans Day, the Texans were 7-1, off to a great start in 2012, although that one loss was, rather ominously, a prime-time blow-out at home against the Green Bay Packers (Aaron Rodgers threw for six touchdowns). The NFL is a competitive environment of ever-increasing intensity, evidenced by the number of teams that spiral, year upon year of a particular coaching regime, up the levels of the playoffs. It's one thing, a difficult thing, to win in the NFL, and another thing entirely to win when the pressure is really on, in prime time or in the playoffs. The Baltimore Ravens, who would make it all the way to a Super Bowl win following the 2012 season, had begun working their way up the spiral of Super Bowl Mountain when they changed head coaches in 2009, making the playoffs every season since then, always winning at least one but not quite making it to the top of the heap, finding that winning in the post-season was even more daunting a task than winning a regular-season NFL game. The Houston Texans weren't there yet.

To see if they were even ready to win in prime time, I would have to travel a circuit that could stand for the whole story of my life in the Year of Our Lord, 2012.

My first lap was to early Mass at St. Thomas More and back. I had completed my Rite of Christian Initiation for Adults, had been shepherded through the Mother of All Vigils by our singing young priest, Father Christopher Plant, and had entered into full communion with the Church, and was now a regular Catholic, following the precepts and attending Mass and taking communion every week. I was starting to contribute to the Mass, too, occasionally serving as lector, reading either the Old Testament passage or reading from an Epistle prior to the deacon or priest reading from the Gospel. Before long, I would also serve as an Extraordinary Minister of Holy Communion, one of the dozen or so lay ministers who help the clergy deliver communion. Today, though, I was just a guy in the pew, attending to God's word, celebrating the mystery of faith, accepting the body and blood of Christ to participate in and benefit from His saving sacrifice. That was plenty, and thanks be to God.

Farewell to Football?

On the short drive home, snug in my car as a light drizzle fell out-side, I got to thinking about callings, two callings in particular. The first of those callings, to serve incarcerated veterans in a state prison unit south of Houston, would take me on my second lap of the day, absorbing almost half of my waking hours on Veterans Day. The second calling, a sort of ministry of words, had adjusted my professional path in life and diverted me from a potentially wasted journey down a road into the old familiar family swamp of "relationships." Thanks be to God, indeed.

While I was still in the adult catechism or "RCIA" phase of my initia-tion into the church in 2010, I had visited the Ramsey Unit of the Texas Department of Criminal Justice (TDCJ) with Deacon Ed Stoessel. I had considered prison ministry one of the essential tests of religion when I was "shopping," and so I joined Deacon Ed on one of his weekly Friday visits to the unit to see what this ministry was all about. Deacon Ed taught a class for Catholic offenders, a somewhat advanced class for men who might in the future become ministers themselves, part church history, part catechism, and part Bible study. He also conducted a prayer and communion service, and since at that point I was not yet in full com-munion with the church, I was the odd man out, watching imprisoned felons take the Body of Christ. As part of the start-up of the class, Deacon Ed introduced me and noted that I was an Army veteran. At the end of class, one of the offenders spoke briefly to me and mentioned that he was part of a group of incarcerated veterans on the unit, and that their out-side sponsor was struggling with cancer. Would I be willing to consider becoming a TDCJ volunteer and serving as their sponsor? I was willing to consider it.

Thus began a recruiting process. The offender who spoke to me at the meeting, who went by "Bill," though that's not his real name, began writing to me, sending me information about the group and also direct-ing me to the volunteer administration at TDCJ to find out more about the requirements to become a "regular volunteer." Always the servant leader, Deacon Ed also helped me with that part of the process.

What was going on here? What a wild coincidence that I would come along just at the time when they needed me! No, that's probably not a coincidence, and if I keep thinking about it in those self-heroizing terms, it's likely to be a temptation. They don't need *me*—that's vanity calling—they need someone to help them keep their group in operation, and if it happens to be me, then maybe that is God calling me to be about His work.

I realized that this was free choice of the will, and that this was discernment. I was being called to do God's work, and I was free to say no, could come up with a million worldly and selfish reasons to say no, but I was also free to say yes.

That's what I did. I said yes to the Veterans Incarcerated Group at TDCJ Ramsey, went through the necessary training and paperwork and became their outside sponsor. I would be spending the better part of my Veterans Day in 2012 striving to extend God's love from one world to another, from the City of Houston where I lived and the University of Houston where I worked and St. Thomas More Catholic Church where I worshipped to a "farm," a state prison unit near Rosharon, TX, where men served out their sentences for the crimes they had committed. I was hoping I would get home in time to catch the second half of the Texans game on TV.

Up until the last minute, I was actually planning to be out of the country for Veterans Day, in the Persian Gulf emirate of Qatar of all places, and that whole chain of events stems from the second major calling I received in close relationship to my initiation into the Catholic Church.

In spring 2011, as I was entering the last stages of "RCIA" and preparing for the "Mother of All Vigils" on the Saturday evening before Easter, when the church pulls out all the stops and welcomes its new members as part of the most fully elaborated services of the liturgical year, the candlelight and the incense and the priest chanting a minor-key dirge in unison with the pipe-organ, I got a tip from my boss at the Writing Center that there was someone she wanted me to talk to. A friend of hers who runs an art gallery had met a man who was considering writing a book and was looking for someone to help him. Marjorie asked me as a favor to look into it.

I was glad to, though I knew it was likely nothing would come of it. A few times a year, we would be contacted by someone who has an idea for a book and wants a professional writer to help them get it together. This results in part from confusion between the Writing Center and the Creative Writing Program, but in any case typically the person calling doesn't really have an idea for a book. If they are lucky, they might have enough material for a feature article, but it's more likely they have an anecdote or a set-up. Rarely do you run across someone with both the intriguing topic and enough narrative material for a real book. But there is no harm in making the exploratory phone call.

This time was different, alive with the promise of the one you've been waiting for. The gallery-owner put me into contact with the person I'll refer to simply as The Lucky Man, for reasons to be elaborated later, and in our first phone conversation I could tell that if nothing else, this was a serious man, intelligent, well-spoken, low-key, someone worth meeting just on the basic terms of fellowship. He was an executive in one of the major global energy corporations and, more to the point, he had a story to tell. In 2010, he had been working in Milan, and on a rainy winter evening he was hit by a car and almost killed crossing the street. This Lucky Man underwent brain surgery to treat his injury, was in a coma for nearly six weeks, and then made a full and miraculous recovery. He was in Houston on temporary duty, working his way back into shape before taking on another major assignment in the energy industry. As part of this recovery, the doctor who led the neurosurgical team in Milan and witnessed the miraculous recovery suggested maybe he should write a memoir to recover the events he had missed while he was in a coma—it was his story, but he wasn't there, hence the need for a collaborator. Could I help him?

If there was one factor more than any other that swayed me in this man's favor in considering that request, it was his answer to a question

I posed: do you have any book in mind as far as what kind of story you would like to tell? I had to ask him to repeat his answer—did he say J. M. Coetzee? He did, referring to the Nobel-prize-winner's novel *Slow Man*, thinking that the way it weaved its story together might be a good model. Wow. I was expecting the usual suspects, maybe Stephen King or Erik Larson—or even Stieg Larsson, but no, my potential collaborator cited a writer I had studied in a postmodernism seminar as a doctoral student. Another wild coincidence, or maybe the Holy Spirit at work again.

Still, this was a tough call, or I made it a tough call because I was still between two worlds, not yet in full communion with the church with one foot still in the swamp of family relationships. At the time when I started my contact with The Lucky Man, I had begun indulging in some vague forward-looking speculation: what if through the good work I've done getting ready to come into the church I've become the kind of person to *get into a relationship*? What if I were to put out feelers through people I've come to know in the church and maybe start looking to begin dating? That's not really nuts, is it? Well, yes, in a way, it is, because I am still the same person from the same family background. In fact, at the very time I was getting ready to enter the church and was contemplating collaborating with The Lucky Man on his project, a loved one in the family was embarking upon the worst kind of relationship—she was "moving in with someone." She never talked about love, it was more like a domestic partnership, some arrangement of convenience that didn't even seem convenient. It reminded me of a vulgar but true saying I had heard from one of my uncles: "Love will go where it's sent," he chortled sardonically on more than one occasion, observing the *relationships* around him, "even if it's up a pig's butt."

So I told The Lucky Man, if you can wait until after Easter, I will pray on this matter and give you an answer. A second discernment on a second calling, and again the selfish and worldly reasons to say no asserted themselves. *You take on this project and you are never going to have any time for yourself. You get into this collaboration and you give up all control of* *the process—this book is going to be all about <u>him</u>. Is this really how you want to spend the next year of your life?*

Yes.

Once I had passed through the Mother of All Vigils and taken the body and the blood in full communion, the vision of freedom was clear. What seemed like drawbacks became advantages, and I would learn a new way of writing and a new way of living through this process of collaboration. I could escape the sucking hole of self that subjective writing can sometimes become, I could at least seek an alternative to Hollywood Humanism in writing nonfiction, where the story is whatever happens. I could connect in a deep way with other people, with exemplary people—this was really the story of The Lucky Man's family and how they came together in the time of his dire need, and they are the salt of the earth, good American Heartland people with accomplished professional lives and deep strong roots in their families. I could use my gifts in service of something more important than myself.

And so I spent the next year working with The Lucky Man on top of my duties at the Writing Center, interviewing him on weekends, reading through all the documentary evidence he provided me, researching on my own all the background details on brain injuries and coma and recovery. We took a trip to Milan—my first visit to Europe since my Army days. There I met Dr. Claudio Betto, who was in charge of the wonderfully-named *Neurorianimazione* ward where my collaborator made his recovery, and we talked about how important the doctor's Catholic faith was to his commitment to his work. The doctor and I ended up exchanging books at Christmas time: I sent him Walker Percy's *Love in the Ruins*, and he sent me Luigi Giussani's *The Religious Sense*. The Lucky Man and I spent a weekend in Cleveland, visiting his family and some of the sights from his childhood, including Kent State University, where his father used to teach public speaking. One of his sisters told me about how Victor Frankl's *Man's Search for Meaning* helped her understand her brother and have faith that he would return to them—her brother's will was driven by his purpose in life, the meaning that he had always found in life, to love and take care of his family.

By the summer of 2012, I was ready to write, and took a leave of absence from the university to work on the book full-time. I completed a draft manuscript, and when the fall semester started, I was back at school. By then, The Lucky Man had moved back to the Middle East to take on a challenging assignment and didn't have time to do anything with the project. We actually made plans to meet in Qatar in November, to visit with some of my collaborator's colleagues connected to the story, but it proved impossible to arrange. So, by Veterans Day, I had basically put the project aside, waiting for the time when The Lucky Man might be ready to take it up again. But I had to consider that I had come out way ahead in the bargain: this had been a contract job, work for hire, so I had made some money writing, I had served a paid apprenticeship in the process of nonfiction writing, and I had met some truly outstanding people who, without necessarily knowing it, assisted me in my faith journey, showed me what love in everyday action looked like. Meanwhile, my loved one's "relationship" had proven disastrous, they had broken up and called it quits and she was back where she started, only a little more disillusioned. I can't say I was surprised, though I was deeply disappointed for her. Love hadn't really gone anywhere, or maybe it wasn't really love at all.

So my second calling had made very clear to me the importance of taking the time to properly examine these big choices in life, discern where the freedom really lies, and then to say yes to what is right.

On Veterans Day, 2012, I set out on the road in the late afternoon to attend to the further unfolding of my first calling.

Snug in my car against a gray rainy day, I drive south from Houston playing an audiobook about Lyndon Johnson's presidency on the stereo. Through all the steps and checkpoints of my journey, my mind is occupied with the world that Michel Foucault told me is always dangerous. I need to pay attention to my driving and keep an eye out for cops, as this is open highway on an unending flat plain, and it's easy to let your speed creep upwards of 80 without really noticing. Around me, the city falls away and I'm into farm country.

After an hour's drive, I pull into the parking lot of the Ramsey Unit, TDCJ, and begin an endless routine of checking myself out, jumpmaster instincts revived. Getting out of the car, I have to be careful about not taking anything in that could get me in trouble. Families visiting offenders have to follow arcane rules about money and food and pictures—phones and tobacco products are strictly forbidden—and contraband incidents are frequent. Basically, all I take in is my driver's license, one car key, and my paperwork for the meeting. I don't even wear a belt, since I would have to take it off going through security anyway.

Going through security, emptying and turning out my pockets, taking off my shoes, putting all my belongings in a basket, I am aware of moving back in time. While there is a metal detector, everything else about the little building on the inside of a double fence of chain-link topped with barbed-wire could have come out of the middle of the 20th century, old wooden desks and metal file cabinets, even a dial-up phone. Things are still done with paper and pen. The officer who is checking me in looks for a clipboard hung up on a peg on the enamel-painted cinder-block wall. I have to hope that all the paperwork I was careful to mail in weeks ahead of time has gotten there and been processed and sent to the gate. Otherwise, our Veterans Day guests won't be able to enter the unit. Once I've gone through the metal detector and been patted down by an officer, I have to be careful to put everything back in my pockets and also not to forget to sign in the volunteer's book, which seems to change location every couple of months, sometimes out here at the gate and sometimes inside the administration building. Prison is a bureaucratic world, a regime of surveillance and documentation, and there's a lot of signing in and checklists, and if I forget to sign in or fill out the paperwork wrong, I can lose my status as "regular volunteer."

I am careful to say my prayer. I always pray the "Come, Holy Spirit" in the walk of 50 or so yards from the gate to the administration building.

I don't want to go in there alone. "Come, Holy Spirit, fill the hearts of your faithful, and kindle in us the fire of your love. ...."

I don't want to go in there at all, but it's a calling and my desires don't count.

Inside the administration building, which resembles the business office of a mid-century American factory (which this prison is, a working farm and furniture refinishing shop), I am careful to use the restroom and get a drink of cold water from the fountain. If the warden is in his office, I like to stop by and say hello. It's part of my job as outside sponsor to serve as a liaison between the group and the outside world, and that includes maintaining cordial relationships with the unit administration, since they have final approval on who can come in for our monthly meetings. I don't care for the warden, a veteran himself who thinks that the offenders have dishonored their service, but that's not part of my job description anyway, my opinion doesn't really matter, but I am glad to see his office door closed and locked.

I buzz into the inner lock-up, which includes a short corridor with a barber shop off to the side, and reach the last checkpoint, where I surrender my driver's license as identification. I feel as though I've been stripped of the last layer of my civilized identity and as the final heavy security door slams shut behind me, I enter the world of the offender. Michel Foucault wrote specifically about the penal regime in *Discipline and Punish*, and I recognize the "discursive traces" of its purpose to enact domination and brutality on the prisoner's body under the rubric of a moral and legal order.

This prison is not necessarily a violent world—in fact, this unit, because it offers graduate-level education, tends to house an older, more-settled population—but it is an oppressive and demeaning one in the basic sense that what it calls out of the person incarcerated here is not freedom but obedience. From the warden on down to the most junior officer, their priority concern is with security and order. Prisoner welfare is not neglected, but it's not what the unit is all about. Prisoner rehabilitation is mostly an incidental matter for individual choice, with options for work and education and spirituality. Our Veterans Incarcerated Group falls under the chaplain's jurisdiction, and I have to coordinate with him, a Catholic deacon in this case, to set up the meetings.

I have found that there are, fundamentally, only two kinds of prisoners. The first, and fairly rare, have made what I think of as "the turn to freedom," owning up to themselves, their guilt, their agency, and their freedom. I recall reading in Victor Frankl about how men in prison (in Frankl's case, the concentration camp) maintain some degree of freedom, regardless of how degraded their circumstances become, so long as they believe they are free and exercise the freedom to choose how to respond to their environment. The board members who lead the Veterans Incarcerated Group tend to be men who have made the turn, and to the extent they can, they live the group motto: "Veterans Helping Veterans." The rest live the prison life, a deeply selfish and dehumanized existence, doing their own time, victims in their own minds, distorted in their thinking, manipulative in their behavior. *I didn't do it. It's someone else's fault. I deserve better than this and when the time comes, I will get what's coming to me, whatever it takes.* I have to remind myself that "my" group is also nothing but veterans, and so many of the members carry with them that jaded military attitude, that cynical line of BS. I need to be careful not to buy into that cynical line of BS.

As I enter in the Old Chow Hall, where we hold our monthly meetings, I need to be careful in my interactions with the offenders, seek to maintain detachment. I am here to help the group function. I am not here to be anyone's friend or advocate. I'm not here as a representative of the Veterans Administration and I am not here to distribute any benefits. What on earth am I here for?

Beyond the bureaucratic requirement that an outside sponsor be present for any prisoner organization to hold meetings and events, I have concluded that I am here to stand in the place of Christ. Just as the Son of God reached out from one world to another, so do I. I am a living enactment of love on the simplest level of bodily presence. I will come and visit the imprisoned, as Matthew 25 tells us we all should, to turn my face to them and say: "I see you and honor your humanity. I see the divinity in you, even if you refuse to see it in yourself."

Next month, leading up to Christmas, we will have a celebratory meeting where we invite back all of our guests from the year, play music, eat cake, and hand out gifts that the offenders have made in the shop as tokens of appreciation to people who came out of their way to visit the imprisoned. (For example, the neuroscientist David Eagleman, host of the PBS television series *The Brain,* responded to correspondence from an incarcerated veteran by visiting the unit a couple of times.) The group raises funds internally (offenders have banks accounts within TDCJ, and if their families can afford it, some end up with enough money to donate to the group), and we spend it on flowers for visiting women on Mother's Day and to provide T-shirts, socks, and soap to group members for Christmas. When the men line up to pick up their gift bags at the December meeting, I stand ahead of the pick-up point and shake every offender's hand. It's a bit like touching lepers, given the amount of contempt most people in our society direct at the imprisoned. In that moment, I am standing in the place of Christ, reaching out to the humanity that I believe still lives somewhere in even the most wretched of criminals. I am enacting our Lord's words when he said "whatever you did for one of these least brothers of mine, you did for me" (Matthew 25:40).

This month, it's Veterans Day. Even more than most meetings, this draws heavily upon the shared military experience of the one-hundred-plus group members. We have a color guard, which conducts drill and ceremonies and presents the colors, including the flags for all the armed services. We stand at attention as the band and choir sing the national anthem, and we recite the Pledge of Allegiance together. These are deeply ironic moments for me: I don't so much believe in the greatness of my country anymore, I loathe the idolatry of the military that has arisen in the endless wars of Post-9/11 America, but through my faith and the gifts of the Holy Spirit, I believe in the human potential of these men, and the shared military experience is one way for a lot of them to find their way back to a better part of themselves, perhaps their humanity. So I tend to feel a Walker-Percy-an twisting from my spiritual gyroscope as I stand at attention in a state prison unit surrounded by convicted criminals praising America. I'm reminded of the day when this calling began and the Catholic offenders consumed the body of Christ while I watched, on the outside looking in.

The ironies continue. An Evangelical group puts on the Veterans Day program, singing songs and making speeches. I've always been given to a sarcastic humor, and I fight the temptation to mentally belittle their show. One guy gives a speech about how he's not a veteran but honors those who are, in what I consider overly sentimental tones, and I cringe—it seems shameful to me that a grown man show so little tact or restrain in public. In my mind, full of my long-established opinions, they present a vision of a muddy-river Baptist Jesus whom I contrast with my own Catholic image of a bloody Christ hung up to die by the Roman Empire.

I don't know.

These particular Evangelicals show up where others fear to tread and witness to God or whatever they do.

I really don't know.

I know that when I journey from one world to another, it is to stand in the place of Christ. I have never had a personal encounter with Jesus Christ, as the Evangelicals tend to say, whatever that might even mean, but I have stood in His place many times, both here in the prison unit and in Mass on Sundays, proclaiming the Word and distributing the Host. Maybe finding a way into fellowship not only with criminals but even with Evangelicals is part of the Holy Spirit's plan for me this Veterans Day.

We live in a fallen world full of meanness and violence and injustice, and through encounters with the divine mystery we seek to find our way back to our home in God. The way isn't always pretty. Christ died on the cross to win redemption for us, and it was an ugly victory.

On the way back, snug in my car against a cold rainy evening, my mind emptied of all those cares and concerns, I can just listen to a football game on the radio. The Texans are playing the Bears in cold, rainy Chicago, and soon the void of my mind is filled with deeply rooted memories of cold and rainy December in 1964. Blanton Collier's Cleveland Browns, with the incomparable Jim Brown, are playing Don Shula's Baltimore Colts and the legendary John Unitas for the championship of the National football league in cold, damp Cleveland.

I didn't know that at the time. In December of 1964 I was a scared, lonely, very sick five-year-old in a hospital room in Norwich, New York.

It's strange how parts of our lives, whether we call them memories or not, ghosts or demons, float around in the mist and come back to us at odd moments. I was five years old and stricken with pneumonia and hepatitis, and I was very lonely at Christmas time. I've suffered from respiratory ailments all my life, no doubt sequelae to that youthful pneumonia, and sometimes when I'm sick and especially if I'm doped up with cough medicine, I feel that melancholy December come back to me out of the mists.

Tonight the football game on the radio comes and goes across the gulf coast plains, intermingling with the 1964 NFL title game in Cleveland, the Browns defense somehow mystifying the great Unitas, playing a coverage he'd never prepared for. How do I know this? I wasn't at that game and have only read about it, and yet it is as real as the day before yesterday, maybe more real because what was decided the day before yesterday? The clouds drift past in the dark that surrounds me, snug against the rainy night in my car, and the hospital room in Norwich drifts away, to be replaced by the prison unit I've just departed, foolish heroic tragic lonely men singing praise to the Roman Empire, and then it's not that at all.

The clouds drift past.

I know where my prison unit is located. A basement boiler room in an apartment building in Norwich, NY, in 1964. An old man, the building custodian, takes me down there to sexually abuse me.

I don't think he violates me, I think he just has me touch myself while he watches. I don't know what he does while watching. This memory has always been indexed in my mind with a singular image of *chiaroscuro*, the orange-red light of a furnace flame flaring out against the dusty gray-black basement darkness. I will never know for sure, because our minds react to traumatic shocks by shutting down, turning on the white noise. I have no direct evidence that anything ever happened, but I have all kinds of evidence that something had the impact on me as if this thing happened. If it was an illusion, it has been an effective illusion throughout my life.

Because I was young and didn't understand what was happening and didn't tell anyone and didn't process it, that abuse insinuated itself into my sexuality, defined the boundaries of my sexual person. I carried my prison cell with me wherever I went, wherever desire went, wherever love wanted to go (but didn't go because I couldn't let it go). I became trapped in that act, trapped in a selfish perversion of human physical love. My sexuality had been initiated way before my soul and spirit were ready to incorporate it into a fully ordered, loving, godly life, and the impact was that in some ways my emotional development got hung up at around the level of a kindergartner, that five-year-old boy in the hospital room at Christmas time. I got the pneumonia from coming home from school in the rain, soaked to the bone, but did I get the hepatitis from that old man?

I had been betrayed and the people who should have loved and protected me from an always-dangerous world had failed me.

My father had failed me, living at the other end of the country, seemingly as far away as he could get, in no position to protect me, and apparently not so inclined.

My mother had failed me, had gone off to work and left me with my sisters, who were too young to take on that responsibility.

That old man had violated me, taken away my innocence. He had failed the most basic test of a human being—what do you do in the face of temptation? He had given in and done a terrible thing to me.

These are hard sayings, but they are true. What's more important, and just as true, though only recently revealed to me, is that these were human failings, the everyday stuff of fallen lives, the sorrowful truths that even Our Lord experienced and learned through His Passion, betrayed by those He loved and rejected by the world He came to save. And yet Our Lord forgave them, and if I am ever to achieve real freedom, to move up that seven storey mountain towards freedom, I will have to find a way to forgive them.

The prisoner faces that question of freedom: am I exercising the gift of free choice of the will to decide how I will respond to my circumstances?

For most of my life, I had not been aware of the choice. I had gone along in life, only dimly aware that something invisible was hobbling my emotional and spiritual growth. I knew a lot, learned a lot and loved learning, did this and achieved that, and was even passionate about a few things, but at some point always found myself in a lonely hollow place without love or real connection. The sunny days of life would episodically give way to rain and the clouds would drift in, and I would be imprisoned in that hospital room again. Lap after lap around that mountain, never ascending.

As I got older, I would sometimes try to warm that cloudy rain with whiskey or other strong drink. I indulged other rainy day vices, too.

The Father of Lies tempts us to remain imprisoned, holding onto those grudges against all who betrayed us, tempts us to deny that freedom to choose our response, tempts us to believe ourselves hopelessly victimized by others. He tempts us, too, to maintain the illusion, especially in cases of sexual wounds through pornography, which sustains the illusion of sexual pleasure in the absence of loving connection. The lie is evident in one of the possible results, addiction to pornography, in which the yield of pleasure decreases even as the compulsion to indulge in it increases (this process is summarized in *The Brain That Changes Itself,* pp. 106-108). We aren't just helpless victims of that addiction, though—we choose the illusion.

I'm back in my car, snug against the rainy evening, listening to the Texans play the Bears on the radio. I only missed part of the first quarter before I got out of the unit and on my way home, and now, as the second quarter gets started, there's a long delay as a Matt Schaub interception is challenged on replay. The windy conditions are proving ruinous to the passing game: Schaub and Chicago starting quarterback Jay Cutler will each throw a pair of interceptions, and neither will exceed 100 yards passing. An NFL football game can prove to be a lengthy struggle, three hours or more, as long as a full-text performance of a Shakespeare play, often with as many plot twists and turns. How will the coaches respond to their circumstances?

I turn off the radio to avoid the endless inane commercials that drone on through the replay delay, and I give thanks that my faith has provided me with resources for responding to the temptations that seek to keep me imprisoned in my childhood sexual wound. I can pray that the Holy Spirit will assist me in forgiving those who have trespassed against me, just as I pray that God will forgive me my trespasses, a most important prayer as we pray that together every week right in the middle of the Mass. I can confess my sins and seek to discern the pattern to them, to see beyond the illusions that can blind me to the freedom I really possess. So long as I live in this fallen world, I cannot achieve perfect freedom, but I can choose to commit myself to the pursuit of freedom instead of pursuing power, wealth, or pleasure, the great illusions with which the Father of Lies goes about his business of deceiving us into giving up—freely—our gift of freedom. It's a hard struggle, but I am starting to believe in winning ugly, hoping to step up in my turnings round the seven storey mountain.

The football game seems even longer broken out into distinct segments—the part I missed while I was in the prison, the part I listened to indifferently on the radio driving home, the part I see on television. I get home while the game is still in the second quarter, and quickly catch a couple of key plays. Houston takes a 10-3 lead when Arian Foster makes an impossible leaping grab of a short pass at the goal line, stretching out horizontally, *flying* to the ball, snagging it with his fingertips mid-flight, somehow landing across the goal line and maintaining possession as he goes to the ground. They replay it and replay it and there's no way to say for sure that he *didn't* make the touchdown. Score! Beauty amidst a game played in ugly circumstances, a triumph for an undrafted player who refused to give up on his dream.

It gets uglier on the next series, as Jay Cutler takes a vicious hit from Texans linebacker Tim Dobbins. Though clearly dazed, Cutler stays in the game as the Bears and Texans exchange futile drives to close out the half. At half-time, they announce that Cutler suffered a concussion and won't return to the game. He stayed in the game for seven plays after the hit that concussed him, and in looking at the replay, you can see the soft-focus glimmer in his eyes that clearly indicates his brain had been traumatized. He threw an interception three plays later—who knows what he saw.

The NFL is in the midst of a crisis about concussions, and this game is an example of the challenge they face—the action moves at such a tempo, especially near the end of halves, with players coming in and out and coaches caught up in reacting to personnel and sets, the refs moving the chains and rotating in clean footballs, that there isn't always time to assess the situation adequately, and players aren't always disposed to self-report head injuries. The players are so big and fast (Dobbins weighs 230 pounds and is considered a small, quick linebacker, while Cutler is 6-3 and 220 playing quarterback) that the collisions can be monstrously violent, and the laws of physics just dictate that sometimes helmets are going to collide with helmets, and the brain—a couple of pounds of Jell-O sloshing around inside a bone box, as I discovered in my research for The Lucky Man's book—is going to be traumatized as a result. The NFL's bigger concern—player welfare being a genuine if limited priority—is controlling its liability for the after-effects of concussions. A group of retired players brought a class-action complaint against the NFL in 2011 to set in motion a process for determining what the league's responsibility would be for players who suffer adverse effects of head injuries later in life.

Farewell to Football?

For tonight, Cutler is out of the game, neither team is generating much offense through the air, and the Texans hold on to win ugly, 13-6.

After showering at half-time and enjoying a late dinner and glass of wine with the second half of the game, I'm happy to be home after a long day. Veterans Day, a national holiday, specifically observed on November 11 to commemorate the end of the ghastly trauma of World War I and to honor more generally all those who have served.

CHAPTER 14

• • •

The School of Athens, continued:
The Cost of an Education (2013)

"I was free. I had recovered my liberty. I belonged to
God, not to myself: and to belong to Him is to be free,
free of all the anxieties and worries and sorrows that
belong to this earth, and the love of the things that are
in it. What was the difference between one place and
another, one habit and another, if your life belonged
to God, and if you placed yourself completely in His
hands?"

(THOMAS MERTON, *THE SEVEN STOREY MOUNTAIN*, P. 406)

• • •

SEPTEMBER 7, 2013: Georgia Bulldogs 41, South Carolina Gamecocks 30,
Sanford Stadium, Athens, Georgia.

THURSDAY: I'm flying into Georgia, reading Morris Berman's
gloomy *The Twilight of American Culture*, which was written before 9/11
but nonetheless predicts a new Dark Ages for America just based on how
stupid we have become (later, in 2006 and 2013 he'll write the cheery
titles *Dark Ages America* and *Why America Failed*). In Walker Percy's *Love in
the Ruins*, Dr. Tom More, brilliant fallen inventor of the fabulous *lapsometer*, is always staying up nights drinking Early Times toddies and reading from (the possibly-notional) Stedmann's account of the Battle of

Farewell to Football?

Verdun, a great chronicle of the grand stupidity of European decadence in the early 20th century. Even with my crude and inaccurate meter, the sloshing of fluid in the semicircular canals of altitude-distressed inner ears, I can feel my own post-Millennial project at its tipping point. Travel is never pleasant anymore, since the airlines decided to just flat-out drop any pretense to luxury or comfort and get straight into the business of maximizing the profits of hauling meat-bags, but I feel a particular tension, knowing that my examination of conscience is likely to engage rich veins of material in the heart of Dixie, and knowing that I will either be up to the task or not. I'm not a working writer but I'm trying to pretend my way into becoming one. I also recognize that this is how it goes in the Apostolic Succession, that you prepare to meet opportunity, but in the end you don't worry because in the moment the Holy Spirit will tell you what to do and say (Luke 12:12). I've simplified this into one of the mottoes for my project: The Story Is Whatever Happens.

Have I prepared adequately since the interrupted Super Bowl? According to the strict protocols of football I've learned from the coaches, I've given it a shot: I've put in my game plan, working up the *Examen* questions that lay out my thematic ambitions, what I hope to accomplish. I've drafted an outline identifying important football games for significant biographical episodes, going back and forth between the games and the questions to see if I understand what my life has been about, what I think football has meant to me. I've started reading, with and without toddies, trying to get caught up so that I can talk about football without sounding like a complete idiot. In the very beginning, it all started with the Word, so I would imagine that writers always start with reading, that we always become to some extent a reflection of what we are reading, and on the literary side I've gone back and checked in on Thomas Merton's *The Seven Storey Mountain* and Frederick Exley's *A Fan's Notes*, a Trappist monk's conversion narrative and a manic-depressive alcoholic's memoirs of his disordered passion for football. There's Alpha and Omega for you. Morris Berman and the twilight of our culture, that's just pleasure reading in between.

I've learned something important from studying the football coaches and their game-planning processes, and what I understand is reflected in that motto that The Story Is Whatever Happens. The coaches don't force the issue, don't force their opinions, they let the game-plan emerge out of truthful analysis of their opponents, how *they* line up and what plays *they* like to run out of what sets, and how *we* can create opportunities to do what *we* do best. I've tried to trust my analytical gifts, to trust that the Holy Spirit will provide the wind at my back, and to go where the story wants to go, even if it's into the Christ-haunted heart of the Old South.

Most importantly, I've recruited my principal collaborators. My nephew Matt and his son Jaia are willing to give it a go, and I've already got their interviews in the digital can. Tim Loonam and his son Jack are also enthusiastic about the project, and that's why I'm flying to Georgia. The rest has been setting the line-up and game-planning and practice. This will be the first real game, and it's a doozy: South Carolina at Georgia for the Bulldogs' first home contest. SEC Game Day, between the hedges. The School of Athens.

"Come, Holy Spirit."

I'm on the ground in Atlanta on time, and with military precision and a few text messages, Tim is picking me up curbside, halting just long enough for a quick bro-hug, and then I throw my suitcase in back and hop in the front seat with my student's backpack. We've got a long drive on 285 and 85 ahead of us, and I have made plans to get as many interviews as possible with my old Army buddy. I had actually rehearsed the move to get the backpack out of the suitcase, and had mentally worn out the packing list to make sure that I would be able to start working as soon as I hit the ground. A big smile lights up my face as I see that Tim has printed out the list of questions I sent him. Rangers lead the way!

"Fill the hearts of your faithful, and kindle in us the fire of your love."

We're tooling north in Tim's well-worn Chevy Tahoe through a hot sunny fall day in big-pines country, and Tim begins unfolding his war stories for me, evoking Baghdad on the way to Athens. I notice a couple of things as I take notes just in case the incredibly-reliable digital voice recorder somehow fouls up, trying also to look up often enough to register how Tim feels about what he's saying. I notice that his Iraq tales involve Byzantine military-industrial complexity, multiple levels of overlapping command authority (even down to who owns the military working dogs and who has jurisdiction over their handlers—with predictable government precision, not the same), conflicting personalities leading to endless changes in plan—and an overall sense that the American Way of War, because it involves deploying and operating the logistical riches of Solomon, is hugely, perhaps inhumanly, bureaucratic, plagued by intrigue and in-fighting (I'm reminded of something that both Carl Gustav Jung and Jean-Francois Lyotard said about how the more the scale of a thing exceeds the human, the more that thing approaches the monstrous). I'd studied Eisenhower's World War II commands in relative depth, and knew that this was nothing new, but still found it somehow simultaneously shocking, exciting, and disappointing. I also notice that Tim's descriptions are vivid and clear and full of rich details (a big tent looks like a massive Hershey's kiss; an incompetent officer is a "booger-eatin' moron"). This is profoundly encouraging to the would-be working writer—as Tim speaks, I can literally see some of his phrases scrolling in quotations across the page and hear them translated into my own voice in paraphrase. Having already started my interviews for the book, I am becoming aware that some interviews are better than others, and that these are going to be solid gold. Tim is a man washed in the Blood of the Lamb who lives in this fallen world to hit the ball out of the park whenever he can, certainly whenever a friend asks it. And I'm no mere friend, I'm a fellow Ranger and brother Buffalo—his mother-loving patrol leader!

We find my motel, which because an SEC Game Day weekend is coming up and all the rooms at the inns in town have long been reserved is about 30 miles north of Athens. I check in, we further the unpacking, and then deploy for the final march on the college town. More interviews along the way, about how Tim was almost out of the Army and then they decided to run the "stop-loss" routine on him, extend his contract and send him to the war in Iraq, a veterinary Army of one. Lunch in town, some discussion of my evangelical mission in writing this book, and then we meet a few of Tim's friends, who talk about how they supported the Loonam family while Tim was deployed. Out to David Youngerman's house, where I meet the real Cardboard Tim, who because he is cardboard and a picture looks just like he did in the pictures.

It is a kaleidoscopic day that includes meeting Jack Loonam, who is coming from ROTC and wearing fatigues—because he is on the roster of an SEC football team as a tight end, I expected him to be bigger. He's an engaging, courteous, high-spirited young man with a frequently-flashing Irish grin, and we chat over dinner, occasionally interrupted as football teammates greet him in passing. The day ends with me back in the motel room, trying to keep up the discipline by writing a running-record journal of the day's events while watching the first NFL game of the season on TV. Recent tradition holds that the Super Bowl champions host the season-kickoff on Thursday night, but for some reason related to baseball, the Baltimore Ravens travel to Denver to take on the Broncos. Like the power outage in the Superdome, it's another little glitch for the Ravens, but this time it seems to make a big difference, as the Broncos pummel the champs 49-27. Peyton Manning throws for seven touchdowns. Welcome to NFL 2013.

FRIDAY: I'm on the job like a working writer, or how I would imagine one to work.

Tim has loaned me the Tahoe, so I am on my own, starting the day with this very hospitable tour of the athletic facilities at the Butts-Mehre Heritage Hall and Football Facility. It's largely a matter of subdivisions within the locker room, the scholarship athletes segregated from the walk-ons in the spirit of Old Dixie, very separate but of course equal. It goes further, with distinctions evident in the laminated game-day schedules hung from lanyards on all the lockers, identifying whether the player is dressing for the game or not, and thus which schedule he will follow. Subdivisions all the way down: scholarship or not, dressing or not, traveling to away games or not. (After the season, I'll run this by Houston Head Coach Tony Levine, who tells me that kind of thing doesn't fly with his team, which "represents" the second-most ethnically diverse research university in the country—but he gets fired after the 2014 season, so who knows what rules apply in the Cougar locker room today?)

Here in Athens, it's all very quiet today. The coaches, along with the players deemed worthy of the honor, are holed up in a team hotel, in retreat (what we used to call "isolation" when we were planning for special forces missions), conducting whatever Football Freemasonry or secular ritual is needed to get up for an SEC football game—a *rivalry game*, this is South Carolina, that's Saint Steve Superior on the other sideline! As a walk-on, but one who is dressing, Jack is not invited to the retreat and will join the team later for meetings. Getting this all to fit together must be work fit for a con masterminding a caper like in *The Asphalt Jungle* or *The Killing*!

I walk by and peek in on the extensive training facilities. Later I will interview Head Athletic Trainer Ron Courson and find out more about what Georgia football is doing to deal with the controversy surrounding concussions and traumatic brain injuries. It turns out the team is at the center of a very promising research project that puts motion-sensors in selected helmets (something like 25 of the 125 players on the team), recording all of the hits to the head taken by the player inside the helmet. Dr. Julianne Schmidt, one of the principal investigators for the research, and a protégé of Kevin Guskiewicz (identified as a "Dissenter" among the "Principal Characters" in the 2013 landmark investigative book *League of Denial*), tells me how it works. The team videotapes all the practice sessions, so the coaches are given "hit profiles" from the 25 helmets and can match up the hit recorded by the motion sensor with the tape of the play. Dr. Schmidt was an athletic trainer before earning her doctorate, admits she loves football (as does Guskiewicz), and believes "we have to be careful to preserve it." She and the other researchers hope that coaches will be able to teach safer techniques through this process. Riddell, which manufactures and sells football helmets, developed the motion-sensor system called HITS (Head Impact Telemetry System), but is not directly involved in the research.

I'm on to the academic support center, where I receive more of that great Georgia hospitality and still wonder, with all of this support, how do *any* athletes fail their courses and wind up ineligible to play their sports? Apparently they find ways. It's difficult for me to imagine the lives of scholarship athletes, anyway, kids heavily recruited by grown men lusting after their pass-rush skills or their recognition and anticipation in the passing game. How distorted can your adolescent thinking become when you are brought on campus to play football and then told you've got to make a good show of academic pursuits, too? How persuasive does the earnings benefit of a college degree sound when in your mind you are comparing it to Matthew Stafford's $13 million per year NFL contract? I reckon that there is a significant risk for excess and illusion, along with exploitation, in this big business of recruiting and educating elite athletes.

I jot down some notes along these lines over coffee and a snack as I get ready to visit the Military Building.

The Professor of Military Science (PMS), Lieutenant Colonel (LTC) Kurt Felpel, is dressed in civilian clothes because it's Friday and he works on the campus of a Division I university, so why not? Typical of most military officers dressing in "civvies," the colonel has the slightly dated look of a character in a situation comedy gone to syndication. LTC Felpel is an affable fellow, far more so than the PMS I talked to in Houston (I know what we would have called him back when I was on active duty and it doesn't rhyme with "swell guy"), and maybe that's because for Kurt this is the last assignment before retirement—he's getting out of the Army alive. He's just here to bring a couple of more classes of officers into the Army, no ambition beyond that. He seems comfortable talking about some of the more difficult realities of military life in the Age of Obama, pointing out how all the officers currently serving in the Army (89,000) could fit inside Sanford Stadium, with some room to spare, and even with all of the war-like "kinetic interventions" (or whatever the euphemism-generators in D. C. call wars these days) around the world, that number will continue to shrink. You might never fit all those officers in that little old Robertson/Jeppesen stadium they just tore down at the University of Houston, but the number will continue to shrink. LTC Felpel told me that only half of the officers commissioned through ROTC would be going on active duty. In my day the Reservist or National Guard commission was exceptionally rare. Once again, Jack Loonam will have to wait and see if he'll be suiting up or not. One thing was for sure: the Army was paying for Jack's education, but he has also paid them back with plenty of good publicity relative to his role on the football team.

I hijack a room in the Military Building and work my way through successive one-hour interviews with Jack, LTC Felpel, and Tim Loonam, and then my old Army buddy and I start the long stroll back to the Butts-Mehre complex where I parked. Along the way, overawed by the spectacle of Sanford Stadium, maybe imagining it full of Army officers (or maybe full to overflowing with the casualties of our current wars—a truly twilight thought, surreal, morbid, honest), I experience that epiphany about the School of Athens, Plato and Aristotle, the idealist and the realist. The working day has filled my mind with worthwhile stuff, full to overflowing, and the questions just have to come out, and come they will at the end of the day when I recollect in the tranquility of my motel room the spontaneous overflow of strong feelings worked up on the campus of the School of Athens.

What is all this commerce, all this jock aristocracy and jock money, all this media and sports journalism, what is all this business doing on a college campus? Why is the American university so willing to tie itself up in a web of hypocrisy, bleating about the "amateur spirit" and the "purity of the student *athlete" while the coaches and a few of the top administrators rake in salaries that far exceed the American president's? Why can't "college football" just cynically cut to the chase the way the NFL does—"we're the Roman Empire, so love us or be crushed!" Sure, the NFL secretes a little gooey veneer of greeting-card sentimentality (slogans like "together we make football"), but mostly it's just good old American mercenary greed, best symbolized by the shield frequently invoked by Commissioner Roger Goodell, a shield that no doubt helps him protect his riches, like the "$29 Million Tip" he earned for outmaneuvering the players union in the latest Collective Bargaining Agreement. All Hail Caesar, and let the games begin!*

I drive through a Burger King on the way back to the motel, and enjoy these ruminations over a Whopper with wine, watching college football on TV and running through my notes. Tomorrow will be Game Day.

SATURDAY: The big event arrives with the promise of an all-day ritual ordeal. I wake up early and I'm not in a big hurry to get out of bed so I spend some time in prayer.

Can I compare this day to Christ's Passion as a way of embracing it without celebrating its decadence? Is this arrogance or the essence of the Christian experience?

I pack what I hope will be everything I need for a working day at an SEC football game, something I've never done before. On my way into Athens I pick up sunscreen and bottled water, along with a few snacks to stuff into my student's backpack. It probably never hurts to treat any occasion as if it might suddenly turn into a war-zone/survival situation and plan according to the old-school Five Paragraphs. Do I have a map and compass? I do.

I use the map to find the parking lot for which Claude Felton in the Athletics Department set me up—I have a pass for free parking, and the lot is on the periphery of campus nearest my hotel. That will matter considerably after the game, when the unpiling can take hours. I begin my maneuver half-way across campus, moving south by east, destination Sanford Stadium. Already the roaring engine of SEC Game Day is starting to thrum, and it's only mid-morning. Kickoff is 5:30.

I find a nice place in the student union for a second coffee and snack, and make contact with Tim Loonam, just confirming that we'll be meeting at a tailgate party south of the stadium in a few hours (we reconnoitered the site yesterday afternoon). My next stop is the Colosseum itself, where I make my way up to the press box to check out my seats. The press box is almost like a separate building a half-dozen or more stories above the playing field. Claude has set me up in an auxiliary seating area next to the main press box. It's more than adequate, it's great, and before the game, I'll get a free meal. The weather is sunny and hot, and I'm starting to get a vibe that maybe this is going to be a special day.

On with the Athens Odyssey, on to an SEC campus tailgate party.

On the campus of the School of Athens I meet a man named Cicero. Of course I do. In fact, this is Cicero's tailgate party, in whatever sense anything as amorphous as a college football game tailgate party can be said to have a host. A man named Cicero, I come to find out, goes by Ro in our fallen world, and Ro's father played football at Georgia, so this whole thing is kind of a Dixie big deal. In the Old South, legacies matter and all that. I just don't know if this is the legacy of the Roman orator or of the slave-and-cotton market or of the Georgia segregationist Richard Brevard Russell or of the Heisman Trophy winners, Sinkwich and Walker. An educated fool, I tend to wander through a laminated consciousness of simultaneity.

I find Tim and meet his wife Betsy and daughter Katie. They are warm and hospitable, show me to the food and drink. I try to go easy on the drink since I'm on the job here and it's still a long time until kickoff. The drinking all around me seems to evoke the gloomy twilight spirit of Morris Berman into the party scene, and I see with his eyes for a spell. I keep hearing that Eagles song, "Heartache Tonight," with those brutal lyrics, "somebody's gonna hurt someone," keep thinking about drunken frat-boys and gang-rape and just how far from the Platonic form of a school we may have drifted, how close to the decadence of Cicero's Rome. Rivalry games usually inspire fights if not riots among the fans. Everyone is very nice to me, though, the kids shiny and pleasant and handsome, and I don't know why my mind always wanders into these dark alleys even when it's a sunny SEC Game Day in Athens. Maybe it's because I've watched a few SEC games on TV and by the time the game is on and the cameras are scanning the crowd, these same kids will tend to morph into drunken raving maniacs, faces painted, girls showing skin, boys flashing hand-signals that mean God-knows-what. School spirit is maybe just another name for disordered passions on SEC Game Day.

Were they partying in Jerusalem on that sunny spring day when Christ traveled the Via Dolorosa? It was a High Holy Day, and spirits ran high, Messianic fever disappointed into fury at this weakling Prince of Peace to the point that the Romans grew worried and prepared for their martial clamp-down.

Game Day means endless dilatory pageantry, hours of mobbed crawling steps leading into the stadium and the shared expectation of a football game sometime in our future. In Athens, the Dawg Walk is the big deal, and it makes me wonder how far over the border into Excess and Illusion have we stepped. The football team gets on buses at the Butts-Mehre Football Facility and drives a few blocks up the street, a little trip I casually walked in a few minutes yesterday, in order that the heroes of the day can get out and walk through the crowds for a few blocks leading into Sanford Stadium. Is this idolatry? It looks awesome on TV! All the big-time college football programs do it! Sure, it's an arms race, and Georgia just has to keep up!

I end up right in the middle of the crush, and what I notice is the other-worldly look worn by a lot of the players, facial muscles slack, eyes unfocused. Their coaches have screwed them up to the sticking pitch, ready to do battle. They are not literally entering the gladiatorial arena, but it is still a dangerous space. Somebody's gonna hurt someone, some of these *student-athletes* may be leaving the field on stretchers, some may be leaving the stadium in ambulances, and part of the blank, glazed-eyed look that some of them exhibit is that combination of fear sandwiched by the mastery of fear. I remember once encountering a highly-successful Houston Cougars running back in the pool locker-room back at my university and realizing how short he was—heavily muscled and powerfully built, but still a small man who would have to muster considerable courage to overcome the fear of running into the valley of the beastly big men of football, the six-foot-six 300-pounders who play in the pit. But these Bulldogs have also spent most of the last day and a half secluded in isolation like a cult, monastically focusing on a very narrow set of tasks. Their thousand-yard-stares may be partly the result of ongoing concentration and visualization of what they have to do, their version of memorizing and reciting the patrol routes and immediate action drills Tim Loonam and I had to hammer into the soldiers going out on patrol with us. Their coaches have ground away at them with details of their part in the game-plan, what it will take to achieve a grand version of what Coach John Pluta described to me simply as "Perfect Starts," drilling down into scheme and technique to try to find any small competitive edge, and now the players have to keep their minds calm and focused. I vaguely remember that look from when I used jump-master particularly complicated airborne operations, at night, say, with heavy equipment into uncertain terrain. I am a reminiscing old fool, and don't know if it's really like that or not.

I reunite with Tim and Betsy heading into the stadium tunnel. After we catch a few pictures with Jack, who is excited to be suiting up today and will get a little feature Tweet from ESPN showing the ROTC sticker on his Georgia helmet (the media is all-in on anything that connects the military and sports), along with other Bulldog players in the stadium tunnel, I part ways with the Loonams and make my way up to the press box.

Dr. Tim, Jack (83), and Betsy Loonam, in the tunnel at Sanford Stadium on game day, Athens, Georgia, September 2013.

It's a long hike up there, and then elevated, elite, I discover that there is a hologram on my press pass that opens the door to the press box, and I am in, a privileged insider.

Satan is with me, as he is ever and always where wealth accumulates and power is transacted and the temptation to exploit people for personal gain plays out amongst weak humanity, leading us to stand on the parapet of the temple, telling us, "If you really believe in your God, throw yourself down from here." God will protect you. Do I have the wisdom and the courage to reply, "You shall not put me to the test"? Will I just go along to get along, since resisting temptation seems like it might be kind of tough today?

Sometimes a door is just a door, and while I may be inside the press box, I may not be much of an insider.

The meal is a decent Georgia imitation of barbeque, brisket and beans and coleslaw, and I sit and chat with beat writers covering the game. They seem to take me at my word that I'm working on a book, and show almost no curiosity. I think that's the nature of their business, as sportswriters, not to be deterred from their predetermined certainty by curiosity or anything other than what they were expecting. They trade in opinions, they are full of opinions about players, and since half of them are from South Carolina (all men, half of them middle-aged, mostly obese), I solicit their opinions about players the Houston Texans recently drafted (Clemson's DeAndre Hopkins: you're going to love that kid; South Carolina's D. J. Swearinger: might have some trouble with him and his whole "swag" trip), and Jack Loonam's high-school teammate now playing for Steve Spurrier and the Gamecocks, Shaq Roland (waiting to see if he's the real deal, but he's in a good system to catch a lot of passes—best pure athlete to come out of South Carolina in a generation).

The time goes pretty quickly when you are chatting pleasantly over lunch in an air-conditioned press box, with all-you-want beverage service (non-alcoholic, of course). I occasionally think of Tim and Betsy out in the end-zone bleachers with the other parents, soaking up the sun and bombarded by all the noise from the crowd, school band, and stadium sound-system. It's like a mid-80's outdoor rock festival out there! Rock on, Journey! Rock on, Rush! Rock on, Tower of Babel!

At last, somehow, the National Anthem and massive field-filling flag and "salute to service" and fighter-jet flyover or whatever requisite patriotic ceremony all finally get behind us and the football game has started. I've never been to an SEC game before, but I've been to plenty of football games, so now I can relax. I'm in familiar territory. It's just football, just a game, running, blocking, passing, tackling, at least when the hype machine cranked up around it stops to let the kids play.

Georgia responds to South Carolina's opening field goal with a touchdown pass to tight end Arthur Lynch mid-way through the first quarter. It's a great old play that I remember watching the Dallas Cowboys run, often against my New York Giants, when tight end Jay Novacek would briefly block, fall down, then get up and drift out into the flat, where Troy Aikman would find him with a touch pass. Here it's Aaron Murray to Lynch, his friend and roommate, and it's six points for Georgia.

Lynch is one of Jack Loonam's friends who answered the questionnaire I sent out for my book. He's the student-athlete the NCAA wants the public to see: big, handsome, articulate—though subject to considerable ribbing from his Dixie teammates for his Massachusetts "chowdah" accent. He has already graduated and is working on his master's degree this semester. That will stop with the coming of the New Year, when he will concentrate on preparing for the NFL draft. A bright and gregarious young man, Lynch is known around town as "the Mayor of Athens." He plans a career in politics after football.

Later in September, I'll talk with Artie's mom, Carline Lynch, and find out that football is in their family. Artie's grandfather, Carlin, played end at Holy Cross under legendary coach—and practicing medical doctor—Eddie Anderson. Their family believes in what I come to call "the New England position" regarding football and concussions. No tackle football until age 14. Dr. Robert Cantu of Emerson Hospital in Concord, Massachusetts, another of the "Dissenters" from *League of Denial,* is cited in that book saying he "would call for a complete ban on tackle football for children under 14" (p. 292). He and other brain scientists believe that the human brain's development makes it particularly vulnerable to concussions prior to adolescence. Carline Lynch is a school nurse, and she tells me about seeing "first and second graders with their football pads on. To me it looked obscene—no way they should be doing that." Arthur Lynch didn't start playing tackle football until he was 14, and it hasn't impeded his progress; he was recruited by all the big schools, ending up with Mark Richt at Georgia, and he will be taken in the fifth round of the NFL draft. Carlin Lynch, a hall-of-fame high-school football coach with the fieldhouse at Dartmouth High School named after him, tells me in a separate interview that one of the additional dangers of youth football is that the coaches often have no training and "don't know beans," as he puts it in his salty New-England enunciation.

The Bulldogs add a field goal and lead the Gamecocks 10-3 as the first quarter expires. Then havoc breaks out and the teams combine to score 35 total points in the second period, a touchdown pass and touchdown run for Georgia and two touchdown passes and a touch-down run for South Carolina. The game action is exciting enough, but the assault that the stadium launches on the audience of 92,000 is completely over the top, and ultimately unneeded. During the ex-tended television time-outs, the huge end-zone hi-def TV scoreboard is ablaze with quick-cut flashing video images, rapidly intercutting from a TV feed of highlights from other games to advertisements to public-service-announcements to superfluous incitements to the crowd to "GET LOUD!" We ARE loud! The "music" is a postmodern night-mare pastiche of hip-hop, classic-rock, techno, and old-time college fight songs. The crowd does the wave, claps along as instructed, hollers whatever the screen tells them to holler! Game Day is insane, the very embodiment of the stupidity that will lead to the Twilight of American Culture.

> *"With loud shouts ... they persisted in calling for his crucifixion, and their voices prevailed. The verdict of Pilate was that their demand should be granted. So he released the man who had been imprisoned for rebellion and murder, for whom they asked, and he handed Jesus over to them to deal with as they wished."*

(LUKE 23:23-25)

I look over to the fellow sitting next to me and see that he is, like me, on the verge of cringing. What's up with this assault? The game is good enough, isn't it, without all this embellishment? Is anyone here for foot-ball? We manage introductions over the din. He's a sports-talk-radio producer from Atlanta, Alec Campbell, and like me is attending his first SEC football game in person. He mainly works the NFL Falcons games and produces sports-talk shows. Later, I will interview him and explore his perception of this insanity of college football, where "the game is the smallest part of the day." I find it peculiar, if admirable, that someone who deals in the daily cultural plague of *sports opinions* should have achieved such detachment from it. He thinks that in part the game-day experience functions as a fantasy for the fan, as a stepping out of normal life into a nostalgic "bubble of comfort, to relive old college days without repercussions." I suggest that maybe it's nostalgia for a past that never really existed, the kind of thing one probably has to do a lot of in what Flannery O'Connor called the "Christ-haunted South." Once in the stadium, he notes, after the endless ritual of tailgating, the crowd is then treated as if they can't be trusted to entertain themselves for more than a few seconds when the game isn't being played, so instead they are assaulted by "ear-splitting audio." His final verdict: "insane."

I tend to agree, as I survive the assault of the stadium mania through the less-tumultuous third quarter, as Georgia rebuilds its lead to 10 points. I am a little tired from an already-long day with a lot of walking in the Georgia heat, a little sleepy after the additional snack of half-time hot-dogs (I waited in line with ESPN on-air talent Brad Nessler and Todd Blackledge), a little disoriented in an unfamiliar environment (panic thought: *where did I park, how the heck am I going to get there, do I still have the stupid key to Tim's Tahoe, what do I do if something goes wrong with his car, how the heck do I get back to the motel, who will come claim my godforsaken body at the morgue if I am crushed by the crowd like a pilgrim on the way to Mecca?*). At times, in the midst of the ersatz chaos when the game is not happening, I'm ready to concede: college football as practiced by the NCAA and especially in the SEC is WAY TOO MUCH, an abomination against higher education, a step on the highway to American Twilight, a step on the Highway to Hell (Rock On, Tower of Babel!)! There's nothing inherently wrong with football or other athletic competition, if it is kept in perspective and doesn't turn into the exploitation of athletes and pursuit of wealth and power by a few elites, but where are we going to find that? Not at the School of Athens. Not back in Houston, either.

Is there an alternative to saying farewell to football? Is there an alternative to all this excess? Of course there is, I realize with a slight shiver against the warmth of early-evening, there's high school kids like John Pluta used to coach, playing football without excessive illusions like Mike Chase, my niece's son, who admits that if you're not willing to take the risk of serious injury you shouldn't play the sport but also sees the sport as a way of keeping his life organized and positively-focused. I'm withdrawing into myself even in the midst of 92,000 football fans, getting out a notebook to start putting words down, somehow startled to discover that the day is fading beyond the lights of the stadium, recalling that before I ever came to Athens I talked to another college football player whose approach to the game and all that surrounds it was entirely different.

I met Clay Buhler through his brother Wes, who worked with me at the University of Houston Writing Center, and discovered that Clay played Biblical football at Greenville College in Illinois. The coaching staff at Greenville treats football as an athletic experience taught through Biblical principles, embodying the "InSide Out Coaching" philosophy of author and former NFL player Joe Ehrmann, himself a Christian minister. When I asked Clay for pictures of his locker room and weight-training facilities, what he sent looked a little different from what I had toured here in Athens—they weren't scandalous or horrifying, torture chambers or rattle-snake pits, just regular, slightly-worn-down gym facilities that almost certainly smelled like sweat and bleach and Ben-Gay. There weren't any endorsement deals at Greenville, no scholarships, just college kids playing for the love of the game and a dedication to their ongoing relationships to a risen Christ. Their vision statement proclaims: "We will be a witness to the culture that it is possible to be fierce committed football players and play the game in a way that honors Jesus Christ."

Clay Buhler played Biblical football at
Greenville College in Illinois, 2013.

What Clay realized, and what I found reassuring if not downright revelatory, was that football can create a rich environment for ministry, since student-athletes tend to be so passionately attached to the sport, so willing and open to coaching. If the coaches see their work as ministry, and care about not just winning and losing but about the very salvation of their athletes, then all the things that go into making a successful football team, the hard work, dedication, selfless commitment, team-work, all of those good things can create a powerful Christian commu-nity. It's a lot like what Coach John Pluta described to me regarding his

Farewell to Football?

football teams at Norwich High School, though he could not explicitly coach Biblical football at a public high school, and that wasn't his inclination anyway. In a lot of ways, Clay Buhler pulled me back from the ledge concerning football—confirmed for me that if we judge for ourselves what is right, if we seek *to do* what is right, whether it be in football or missionary work or university administration, we can turn away from the excess and illusion and instead struggle and stumble in humility towards salvation. As Clay approached graduation from college, he began to realize that he would have those football resources with him the rest of his life. As he told me, "I am seeing just how much the skills and character required to be a great football player and teammate translate over into being a great professional, parent, spouse, and citizen."

While the game continues to go on around me in Athens, I write and I write, the spontaneous overflow of powerful feelings, hoping that it won't read tomorrow or next week recollected in tranquility like stoned rambling or drunken love poetry. In the ecstasy of the inspired moments, many a writer has wasted many a word on nonsense. You never really know what will come out. Romantic poet Samuel Taylor Coleridge always claimed that he had written hundreds of lines of "Kubla Khan" in his head before that stupid guy from Porlock interrupted. That story didn't really happen. He didn't get it on the page.

In the fourth quarter I start to come around and regain a sense of my surroundings. I'm at a college football game and one of the players I was specifically interested in seeing perform is finally getting into the game. Not Jack Loonam, who as a walk-on will only get in for a single series of plays late in an unimportant game in his senior year, but his high-school teammate from Lexington, South Carolina, Shaq Roland. In a move that makes no sense to me, Old Ball Coach Steve Spurrier (whom I usually refer to as Saint Steve Superior for his arrogant persona) only puts in Shaq at receiver for a single series—but on that 11-play fourth quarter drive, Shaq catches three passes for 48 yards. It's his drive. Was Shaq in Coach's dog-house? I later talk to one of his high-school coaches, Bailey Harris, who thought that maybe Roland lined up wrong early in the game and then got benched until the Gamecocks needed a spark. These big-time head coaches play all kinds of head games with impressionable young athletes. The Old Ball Coach may have felt he needed to make it clear who was boss.

However things turn out for him in this game, Shaq Roland has already lived through an exaggerated version of the SEC's recruiting meat-market. Harris, who was Shaq's basketball coach at Lexington, told me that Roland had a second locker in which he kept all the unopened recruiting letters he received. Nick Saban was Skyping Shaq from Tuscaloosa the day after the tornado struck the city, and Rocky White, one of Shaq's football coaches at Lexington, thought that if the decision were Shaq's to make, the young man would have gone to play at Alabama. But I found out from talking to a number of college coaches in Houston and at Georgia that the student-athlete himself isn't always the decision-maker. Sometimes it's the parent, or the surrogate parent, or the high-school coach. In Shaq's case, the wide receiver was going to South Carolina, according to White, because Mom would be just fifteen minutes away and would be going to all the games.

When Jack Loonam was a high-school senior, college programs were recruiting Shaq Roland as a junior—selling him that recruiting illusion: come to this school and get an education and apprenticeship in professional football, and not really pushing too hard on the complementary truth that he might come to this school and get exploited for the profit of the institution and coaches and other administrators, might get thrown away if his behavior or academics or quality of play didn't meet their standards. This swarm of attacking recruiters gave entrepreneurial Jack access to high-level coaches—he just wanted to get a spot on the team at Georgia, a dream he held since that day in fifth grade when he got to sit in the stands with Coach Mark Richt during spring practice. Jack finally connected with Georgia tight-ends coach John Lilly, whom Bailey Harris calls the most honest coach and recruiter he has ever encountered. Lilly could only assure Jack that he would get favorable consideration for what's called a "preferred walk-on" slot. It probably didn't hurt that coaches in the Georgia program remembered the Loonam name from the 2004 homecoming game when Major Tim Loonam was celebrated for his DawgDoc service in Iraq. Jack had already been thinking about Army ROTC, and so he worked out his deal. The Army would offer him a scholarship and the football team would offer him the opportunity to compete for a walk-on spot as a tight end, in the room with Jay Rome and Artie Lynch and Coach Lilly. Entrepreneurial Jack Loonam could take it from there.

Meanwhile, Shaq Roland got away from Lilly, but the coach told me that as a man of faith he prays for the ones who get away, too, that they end up where God wants them. As we know, God works in mysterious ways, and playing for—*sitting on the bench* for—Steve Superior is certainly ... mysterious.

Shaq finally gets into the game in the fourth quarter, and his series leads to the Gamecock's fourth and goal play—a goal line stand in the twilight between the hedges. Fourth and goal—the crowd doesn't need the scoreboard to tell them this is a play to stand up and cheer. This is football at its most elemental. One team has the ball and can score with a gain of only a couple of yards. They have one chance to get it done, and the other team knows that they can win the game if they can just stop their opponents this one last time. The coaches try to over-think it and the analysts try to over-analyze it and the scoreboard goes wild and the music raves and roars, and none of that is necessary. This is just a simple kid's game.

If I've learned anything in this SEC weekend, it's that I don't really know anything about college football, or know so much that I can't sort it out. I mean, I'm a university man, a life-long football fan, a devout Catholic, and I only recently have learned that even in the meat-market of SEC recruiting, there are prayerful men like John Lilly and Mark Richt who take a stand and at least try to resist the temptations, though that may be like trying to hold back a flood tide (and it may not be so much of a stand, since Richt is considered a little underpaid by some Bulldog fans, but he still makes millions of dollars a year and it isn't like he's curing cancer out there). It's fourth and goal and the game itself has a brutal elegance, and there is sometimes justice, such as when Big Brain Saint Steve Superior tries to outsmart prayerful Coach Mark Richt on fourth and goal and just ends up outsmarting his own dumb self. South Carolina lines up in their spread offense and tries to run the ball out of the shotgun, which might be a big-brain call but also high-risk, with the running back moving parallel to and behind the line of scrimmage, waiting for a hole to open up. That's not going to happen tonight, Georgia's done the better recruiting on defense and two "fast-flow" linebackers penetrate the line and make the tackle for a loss. Transfiguration: Fourth and goal for South Carolina turns into first and ten for Georgia.

Then Jesus said, "Father, forgive them, they know not what they do" (Luke 23:34). Do they really not know what they do? Has twilight really fallen and are they—are we—all that stupid? Have they really judged for themselves what is right? Would anyone judge for themselves and think that this is right, all this excess and illusion, all this commerce and mania over what one coach called, in all candor, a little-bitty kid's game?

I don't know.

I don't know what I'll end up writing about this trip, how I will answer these questions, how I will judge for myself what is right. I try to keep faith that in the moment the Holy Spirit will tell me what to do and say (Luke 12:12).

For now, I've got to wrap up my notes and get out of the stadium eventually and find the stupid car and navigate back to the stupid motel. Each day has troubles enough of its own.

SEC Game Day was so freaking exciting I'm just glad I didn't have a heart attack.

SUNDAY: On the plane back to Houston, flipping through my notes, trying to synthesize this epic trip. It is also the Sabbath, the Lord's day,

Farewell to Football?

so I have my copy of *Magnificat* on the tray table, to review the readings for Mass, which I've already read once in my hotel room.

The woman next to me notices the *Magnificat* and strikes up a conversation about religion. One part of me perks up—I have announced an evangelical mission for this trip, after all, and maybe this is my occasion. Another part, the wounded boy or fatherless son part, shrinks back. This woman is assertive if not aggressive about *her* evangelical faith, and she is crossing that invisible border between our seats and I am a little squeamish about my personal space. She asks me to pray so I recite the "Come Holy Spirit," which she vaguely criticizes as being stiff and formal. Well, yes, it's a formal prayer. I'm not going to sit here on a commercial airliner with a complete stranger and let her in on my personal conversation with God. Matthew 6:6 tells us to do that in our inner room.

I am reminded of the Epilogue to Stephen Greenblatt's *Renaissance Self-Fashioning*, that book of literary criticism which has challenged my intellectual growth for three decades. Greenblatt recounts sitting next to a man on a plane who ends up asking the author to recite certain phrases to help the man prepare for a visit to his ailing son, who has lost the power to speak. Among other things, he wants Greenblatt to say "I want to die." The author balks, and then spends several paragraphs in his inimitable intellectual-anecdotal fashion exploring why. His first option is most obvious—what if this guy is a maniac and as soon as Greenblatt says "I want to die," the guy pulls out a knife and stabs him? (This was written around 1980, when such a possibility on a commercial airliner hadn't become as remote as it seems "post-9/11," as we term everything we hate about Security Theatre and the Terrorism Industrial Complex.)

What if this woman is nuts? Her next routine supports that possibility.

She asks me for the first reading for the day. I provide her with the Old Testament passage, which she locates in her own leather-bound Bible. She speed-reads the passage, and then begins ticking off the last letters in the included lines, listing them on a pocket notebook. She runs some arcane calculus on the row of figures, and then looks up a

passage based upon her solution. She seems to have this process down. She reads the passage and then begins interpreting it to me. (At some point, it all grows so strange that her words take on the timbre of the muted-trombone teacher's voice in the *Peanuts* cartoons. This does not signify for me. Rock On, Tower of Babel!)

I want to die, or at least the fatherless son in me wants to die. What if she's nuts but efficacious and her prophesying brings down the plane? Where's my evangelical mission then, if I haven't even started writing the book? What if she starts in on me, wants to read my tea leaves or count the hairs on my chinny-chin-chin to tell me the day and hour of my death?

I recall that Greenblatt's conclusion, letter-perfect for a Berkeley scholar, was that he couldn't say the man's words because he—Greenblatt—could not give up the myth of his own autonomy by letting someone else script his lines. It's clever, and Greenblatt is an appealing critic and not just a Big Brain, but it's wrong, wrong in the worst kind of way, Hollywood-Humanism elevating-the-self wrong, *concupiscence* wrong. Exercising free choice of the will to serve the self instead of God is how Adam and Eve got in all that trouble in the garden, isn't it?

What do I do—follow Greenblatt down the Left Hand Path of the Autonomous Self? Let it ride with this prophetess of the divine calculus—what if she truly and faithfully acts upon the gifts of the Holy Spirit and has been appointed to evangelize me? Am I going to let what Walker Percy called "the sucking hole of self" stop the operation of the Holy Spirit? Is that even possible?

I recall with panicked elation that she had told me at the beginning of our conversation that she knew she could come on strong sometimes, so I could just tell her to stop if I wanted to (she may very well go through life getting told off by offended non-believers). I wanted to, and begged off, tapping out and claiming truthfully that I was very tired, that my mind was already racing with the work I'd done over this long weekend (and it was true: even this morning, on the way to the airport, I had confessed to the DawgDoc that there had come a point in my life not so long ago when I had realized that I had to start saying no to pornography, a common problem that I only began to take seriously when I had to face the real prospect of confessing my sins), and would she mind terribly if we end this particular conversation?

It's an escape, not a resolution.

The rest of the way home, through the airport, on the drive back to my house, this encounter sticks with me. It couldn't have just been an accident. Something was nutty about it, but who was nuts?

Here I was, flying back from Flannery O'Connor's "territory held largely by the devil," the Deep South of Christ-haunted Hazel Motes and The Misfit ("ain't no real pleasure but meanness"), and what was my gospel going to be? Repent of football?

How nutty, naïve, or just plain stupid is the good news that the solution to all the problems in football, all the excess and illusion and the risk of physical injury and exploitation and disordered passions, that all of those ills can be remedied one conscience at a time, through efficacious examination and the ongoing commitment to judge for ourselves what is right?

How pathetic it seems, and yet, from another perspective, maybe that's what freedom looks like to God: *I've given them everything that they need to achieve their salvation, but they've never shown the slightest inclination to do what is necessary to be saved, even after I gave them my Son. Still, it is enough for my purposes that it be possible for them to do it, however unlikely.*

How nutty is it to think like that?

Here was the prophetess of the Southwest airliner, counting letters and tri-graphing scripture with unbounded zeal. Wasn't that how the Old Testament prophets worked, enraging everyone with their unvarnished truth and calls to repentance? Didn't her very nuttiness speak in her favor?

Is that where I'm headed, a future as a Football Crank, some unpleasant combination of Dr. Tom More sipping Early Times toddies and reading Stedmann's account of Verdun amalgamated with Frederick Exley imaging heart attacks caused by the disordered passions of an alcoholic New York Giants fan obsessed with Frank Gifford? Neither of them could really stand the sight of their fellow man, spouted off endless criticism of the culture around them, and made not the least bit of difference. Is that my future?

How can I judge for myself what is right?

Epilogues again: I recall that in the Epilogue of *Love in the Ruins,* Tom More goes to Confession. The priest groans when More admits it's been eleven years since his last confession, stumbles over the doctor's inability to feel sorry for his sins (I recall a priest once disrupted the routine of my confession slightly by doubling the line back to me: "*are you* sorry for your sins?"), and then scalds him by reminding him that trying to do good in the world, to do good work and good deeds, is far more important than repenting of daydreams about temptations and fantasies of adultery and fornication. Score one for the old priest, a good deed done.

All right, then, be it resolved: I'm going to run this whole matter through the examination of conscience and take it into Confession with me, let the priest do his job, and as the old-timers tend to say, give it up to God.

From there, the story is whatever happens.

CHAPTER 15

• • •

Epilogue: Spartacus Super Bowl (2015)

"If just one man says 'No, I won't,' Rome begins to fear."

SPARTACUS (1960)

"'If only 10 percent of mothers in America begin to conceive of football as a dangerous game,' Maroon said, 'that is the end of football.'"

—JOSEPH C. MAROON, M.D. (IN *LEAGUE OF DENIAL*, P. 206)

• • •

FEBRUARY 1, 2015: New England Patriots 28, Seattle Seahawks 24, University of Phoenix Stadium. Late in the third quarter, the Seattle Seahawks might have really started feeling like Defending Super Bowl Champions. After trading touchdowns with the New England Patriots to finish the first half tied at 14, quarterback Russell Wilson and the Seahawks had scored 10 unanswered points in the third quarter to go ahead 24-14 with 4:54 left in the period. Just over 20 minutes of play left, the last third of the game, and the Seahawks would repeat as NFL Champions. The Seattle defense was the best in the league in 2014 when it came to preventing their opponents from scoring, giving up an average of only 15.9 points per game. Going into the closing act of the Super Bowl drama, the numbers predicted that New England had probably finished their scoring for this last day of the NFL season. The Seahawks were in a good position to repeat as Super Bowl Champions.

Last year, they had crushed the Denver Broncos in the Super Bowl, taking the lead on the first play from scrimmage, when a shotgun snap sailed over Peyton Manning's head and into the end zone for a safety. The Seahawks had never looked back, steadily building their lead, scoring every which way. Steven Hauschka kicked field goals, Marshawn Lynch ran it in for a touchdown, Malcolm Smith ran back an interception of a Manning pass for a touchdown, Percy Harvin ran back a kick for a touchdown, Russell Wilson passed to Jermaine Kearse and Doug Baldwin for touchdowns. It ended up a 43-8 dismantling of a Denver team that had started the 2013 season with such a bang, blowing out defending champions the Baltimore Ravens on opening night, when Manning threw seven touchdown passes. I'd watched that game in the motel room in Athens, Georgia. Late in the season, Clay Buhler and I had been in the stadium in Houston in December when Manning broke the record for most touchdown passes in a season, but by the second day of February, 2014, in MetLife Stadium in East Rutherford, New Jersey, the Manning magic had worn off and the torch was passed to the next generation, embodied by Seahawk quarterback Russell Wilson. At 5'11" and 206 pounds, Wilson was considered undersized for an NFL quarterback, and wasn't drafted until the third round (with pick #75), but he had taken advantage of every opportunity, came out of his first NFL training camp as the starter in 2012, and had led the Seahawks to the playoffs every year since.

And now, on the first day of February, 2015, all Wilson and the Seahawks had to do was hold on to the lead to remain Kings of Super Bowl Mountain. The problem was on the other sideline, where a quarterback from Manning's generation wasn't about to let the opportunity pass for another legendary comeback. Tom Brady, pick #199 in the 2000 NFL draft, had won his first Super Bowl after the 2001 season by leading a drive that started on his own 17-yard-line, with 1:21 left in the fourth quarter, with no time-outs, taking his team down to the 31-yard-line of the St. Louis Rams, and from there Adam Vinatieri kicked the game-winning field goal. (Where Jeff Fisher's Titans had come up a yard short against the Rams two years earlier, Brady had gotten the job done.) Now, playing in his sixth Super Bowl following the 2014 season, he had all the time in the world.

The comeback began for the Patriots on defense. Seattle tried to attack undrafted rookie cornerback Malcolm Butler on two successive pass plays late in the third quarter. Butler had only played sparingly for New England in the first half, but Head Coach Bill Belichick and Defensive Coordinator Matt Patricia started working the rookie into the lineup to take the place of Logan Ryan, who had been beaten badly for a touchdown at the end of the first half. In this third-quarter series, Butler came up in run support to stop Marshawn Lynch for a gain of two, then tackled Jermaine Kearse to hold him to a gain of six on a short pass. Just doing his job, the Patriot Way. The turning-point play came on third down, when Wilson looked to connect with Kearse deep down the left sideline. Butler had been trailing the receiver but made up ground and closed to break up the pass, forcing Seattle to punt. Butler, who had taken the long route to make the team, through a "tryout camp" for un-drafted rookies, had gotten better on every play.

The teams traded three-and-out drives to start the fourth quarter, and then Brady began what would become the Comeback Drive, inaus-piciously taking a sack for a loss of eight yards. A short completion to outside receiver Brandon LaFell brought up a crucial third-and-14 play from the Patriots' own 28-yard-line. The breakthrough play involved slot receiver Julian Edelman working the middle of the field, where he took a tremendous shot from a notorious heavy-hitter, Seattle safety Kam Chancellor. Edelman held on to the ball for a gain of 21 yards. The Patriot receiver was visibly stunned but stayed in the game, and even caught another pass on the drive that eventuated in a touchdown pass from Brady to wide receiver Danny Amendola to bring the Patriots back to within a score, 21-24.

I'd seen this before (millions of TV viewers and NFL fans had seen this before at various times in various places), when quarterback Jay

Cutler was visibly dazed from a hit by Texans linebacker Tim Dobbins in that Veterans Day game in 2012, staying on the field for the series before being evaluated on the sideline and ruled out for the game. (We would see it again in the 2015 season, too, when University of Houston hero Case Keenum, now playing for the St. Louis Rams, was left in a game after suffering an obvious head injury that left him crawling on hands and knees.) Here in Super Bowl XLIX, Seattle defensive end Cliff Avril had suffered an obvious head injury in the third quarter and was taken into the locker room, evaluated, and ruled out for the game. Edelman, on the other hand, while enduring the same kind of shot to the head, and evidencing the same suspicious dazed behavior, stayed in the game, and was reportedly evaluated and cleared on the Patriots sideline after the drive was completed. There is always this sense, or maybe it's suspicion, that the Patriots under Belichick do things differently, pushing rules and guidelines to the edge, or maybe past the edge. The Patriot Way, or cheaters? They've been disciplined by the league before, and would be again, but not for this incident.

The game goes on in its infinitely exciting ever-present succession of irreversible spectacular moments, but what happens to the brain in that moment of concussion and in the moments and days and months and years that follow? We know that, as with my collaborator, The Lucky Man, struck by the inobservant driver rushing through Milan traffic in his Renault Clio, the three pounds of the Jell-O-like brain get smashed up against the walls of the box of bones in which it lives, and like all living tissue it suffers trauma. Since the brain operates like an electrical system, if the trauma is severe enough, the lights can go out like a power grid going down after a violent surge. What happens next is only partially understood, and the NFL has been doing its part to both reveal and conceal those findings for decades.

In 2003, *Neurosurgery*, the official journal of the Congress of Neurological Surgeons, began publishing research articles reporting the findings of members of the NFL's Mild Traumatic Brain Injury

(MTBI) Committee, some of the research for which had begun in the early 1990's. In his introductory note, editor Michael L. J. Apuzzo compared the work of the MTBI Committee to "Galen of Pergamon, the Greek philosopher who studied the wounds of the Roman gladiators" (Fainaru-Wada and Fainaru, p. 142). Apuzzo wrote that "Football's participants dwarf Rome's gladiatorial combatants in number, and, in its most sophisticated form, the game's pageantry matches or exceeds the spectacle of Roman-designed events." His message seemed to be something like *how lucky we are to have such a ready source of brain trauma to study!* The gladiatorial spectacle of our most-favorite ritual violence not only invites us to indulge in the worst of excess and illusions, it also sponsors really great brain research!

Those earlier initiatives were taken under NFL Commissioner Paul Tagliabue, who was skeptical but seemed to sustain a lawyer's commitment to discovery processes. When Roger Goodell succeeded him, the league took a different approach, growing more adversarial with the players. Further developments seemed to increase the urgency to do something, which in Goodell's practice seems to mean trying to cover things up, and if possible, make money doing so. Super Bowl champion and Pittsburgh Steeler Mike Webster died in 2002, after a long public descent into dementia, most likely the sequelae to multiple concussions, bringing the concerns about concussion to a higher level as the story of his terminal ordeals slowly became widely known. (The story of how a Pittsburgh pathologist, Bennet Omalu, worked to bring the medical facts about Webster's brain to the public is dramatized in *Concussion,* a 2015 film starring Will Smith.) NFL retirees came to see the owners and Goodell, who took over as Commissioner in 2006, as their opponents rather than partners in a shared enterprise. Things had really changed in the last fifty years.

Pete Rozelle, the Commissioner who oversaw the fundamental transformation and massive growth of the NFL beginning in the 1960s, had been a football man, early in his career a PR assistant with the Los Angeles Rams when Woody Strode and Kenny Washington were breaking the color barrier in 1946, and later the general manager of the team. Rozelle's successor, Paul Tagliabue, who took over in 1989, was a lawyer; Goodell was a league-office lifer, having worked for no one but the NFL since graduating college. The league's relationship with its players got worse in 2009, when the NFL Players Association voted for DeMaurice Smith, a trial lawyer, to succeed as executive director former Raiders offensive lineman Gene Upshaw, who died in 2008. Goodell and Smith: in football terms, that's not a matchup you like.

In 2011, writes Judge Anita Brody, who oversaw the eventual settlement of the case, "retired NFL Football Players filed the first lawsuit against the NFL Parties alleging, *inter alia*, that the NFL Parties breached their duties to the players by failing to take reasonable actions to protect players from the chronic risks created by concussive and sub-concussive head injuries and that the NFL Parties concealed those risks." In 2011, Dave Duerson killed himself, and in 2012 it was Junior Seau, both shooting themselves in the chest to preserve their brains for study, and they both were shown posthumously to suffer from Chronic Traumatic Encephalopathy (CTE, the degenerative disease Omalu had discovered in Webster's brain). As they say, "it was a bad look" for Goodell and the NFL. The settlement, reached in 2013 in the amount of $765 million and then expanded in Brody's implementation in 2014, would have the concealing effect of stopping discovery into the particulars of the case—it would save the NFL an awful lot of bad publicity. Roger Goodell always seems to have plenty of bad publicity to deal with in earning his $44 million annual compensation.

In the excitement of this third act of the NFL title game in February 2015, it was easy to forget what a miserable year the league had gone through, with Goodell as the galvanizing public figure most of the time. From Ray Rice in September and Goodell's seeming indifference to domestic violence—until it became a matter of bad publicity for the league—to his hypocritically scolding Marshawn Lynch for the running back's reticence to talk to the press in January (while the Commissioner declined numerous media requests for interviews at the same time), Goodell had blown most of his opportunities. In January, the Indianapolis Colts complained to the league about the deflation of some footballs after the Patriots beat them (badly, 45-7) in the conference championship game, resulting in surreal press conferences leading up to the Super Bowl in which Tom Brady repeatedly talked about his balls and Bill Belichick somehow connected the scandal to Mona-Lisa Vito in *My Cousin Vinny*. The Patriot Way? Cheaters? *Mona-Lisa Vito?*

Goodell might have been a little raw when it came to Tom Brady, since it was the quarterback's name first on another big lawsuit, Brady v. NFL in 2011, concerning restraint-of-trade, anti-competitive restrictions, and price-fixing related to the collective bargaining agreement and the owners' decision to lock out the players in the offseason. Drawing upon what I consider to be his consistently wrong-headed instincts, Goodell—a sinner, just like me—chose in 2015 to go the full-formal-investigation routine against Brady and the deflated footballs, appointing attorney Ted Wells to spend millions of NFL dollars on a detailed inquiry. One thing after another. The shadow of "Deflategate" hung over the Super Bowl, just as the shadow of Goodell's hammering of New Orleans for "Bountygate" had hung over the Superdome Super Bowl two years before. Cheaters never win? Watch this!

And so, as NBC cut to commercial after Amendola's touchdown pass from Brady, as the billions of neurons in Julian Edelman's brain set about the work of sorting out their connections following the trauma of that collision with Kam Chancellor, my own brain hummed in reverie. I thought about Woody Strode and Spartacus and the Roman Empire. Woody Strode, one of the First Four African American players in pro football, the year before Jackie Robinson broke into the big leagues. Woody Strode, Spartacus's first opponent in the gladiatorial ring in the film directed by Stanley Kubrick named for the slave who became a gladiator and thereafter a leader of a slave rebellion. Late in the film, explaining why it was worth it to undertake the forlorn-hope mission of rebellion against the Roman Empire, Kirk Douglas as Spartacus declares that "if just one man says 'No, I won't,' Rome begins to fear." Woody Strode and the rest of the First Four refused to take "no" for an answer, instead proclaiming their "yes" to pro football even when it meant a lot of grief and abuse and threats from racist fans who wanted to say "no" to progress, all of that on top of the ritual gladiatorial ordeal of the game itself. One thing after another, and now it was the players, active and retired, standing up to Goodell and the NFL Roman Empire and saying, "No, I won't." *I won't let the league and its owners and its Commissioner take from me what I've earned through the sacrifice of my body in the public spectacle of this game—not without a fight. Not without the lawyers taking a shot at it.* Tom Brady, however underinflated his balls may or may not be, must look like Spartacus to Roger Goodell. Ted Wells and a whole legion of lawyers will be dispatched if need be to put down the rebellion.

I always mute the sound and try to leave the room when the Super Bowl cuts to commercials, because those commercials are always such desperate exhortations to indulge our disordered passions (there is one that advertises something called "Game of War," featuring a big-breasted swimsuit model, that seems to mash-up several of the deadly sins in a fast-cut screaming 30 second spot—war is a game now?). Instead, my neurons flashed signals across memory connections, and I returned to that moment when this particular examination of conscience began, when the lights went out in the Superdome, two Super Bowls ago. One thing after another. I wondered if Julian Edelman's lights went out for a moment, too, or if he experienced a brilliant flash of light as the electrochemical charges in his brain sorted themselves out in the aftermath of Chancellor's wicked blow.

I thought about the Football *Examen* questions I'd been ruminating over for two years. "Why is football such a big deal, such a quintessentially *American* big deal, and how important should the game really be? Why do you not judge for yourselves what is right?" A dozen more. I'd come to a few conclusions for myself, but mostly what I discovered was an ongoing and recurrent concupiscence, in me, a sinner after all, and all around me, a willingness to choose the lesser because at least it wasn't the least, a kind of a Cheater's Way. We are evermore lazy, unwilling to muster the energy to choose what is right, and evermore rationalizing, convincing ourselves that there is virtue in not choosing outright wrong. The spirit of the Pharisee is alive and well in American culture, tribal affiliations coming in under the rubrics of race, gender, sexual orientation, political affiliation ... and always echoing the arrogant Pharisee of Luke's Gospel (18:11) in contrasting ourselves with the despised Other: "at least I am not like the (Buddhists, Muslims, gays, conservatives, Tea Partiers, transsexuals, Catholics, Protestants, Evangelicals)."

Am I like Walker Percy's Bad Catholic, Dr. Thomas More, full of love for humanity and completely unable to name a single individual human being that I can even tolerate? I can't stand Roger Goodell, whom I consider Hypocrite in Chief, but I do seem to like, at this moment and to the extent that I can, some of the players. Russell Wilson seems like a good guy. Tom Brady is the All-American Boy. And this kid, Malcolm Butler, I could get to like him. He's writing himself a whale of a Super Bowl story.

And now the commercials are over and we're back to the only thing that survives the scrutiny: the game as it is played on the field, some of the finest athletes in the world competing in a very demanding sport, and this Super Bowl is as good as it gets. Roger Goodell won't be out there, nor will DeMaurice Smith nor Ted Wells. This won't be decided by the ghosts of Pete Rozelle and Gene Upshaw. This will be decided by the 22 players the coaches put out on the field to try and win the championship.

The Seahawks go three-and-out and punt, with Wilson making a bad throw on third down. Now Brady has the ball, and he carves up the Seattle defense from the inside out. Brady throws eight passes on the drive, compared to only two runs, and most of the passes are either to the running back, Shane Vereen, or to Edelman, the slot receiver, though on one occasion the Patriots befuddle the Seahawks defense by lining up tight end Rob Gronkowski on the outside, where a linebacker follows him and struggles to make the tackle after a gain of 13 (earlier, when the Patriots lined up this way to create the mismatch, it resulted in a touchdown). It all looks fairly easy for Brady. He's done this before, and the go-ahead score comes on a play the Patriots ran unsuccessfully earlier in the second half. This time Edelman eludes the coverage with a funny spin move and Brady finds him for the touchdown pass. With the extra point, New England goes up 28-24, but they've left Wilson and the Seahawks plenty of time for a comeback drive of their own—2:02. Brady only needed 1:21 to come back and beat the Rams in his first Super Bowl.

This is what you get when you boil off the excess and illusion: a really good game.

The Seahawks give the Patriots a dose of their own inside-out medicine on the drive-starter, with Wilson completing a pass to running back Marshawn Lynch that goes for 31 yards. This game is going to come right down to the wire. After the two-minute warning, the Seahawks start attacking the Patriots defensive backs. It's matchup football. First Wilson picks on Butler, going deep for Jermaine Kearse, but the defensive back plays it perfectly to break up the pass. Next they go after a matchup of big men: Seattle's wide receiver Chris Matthews (6'5", 218) against New England's cornerback Brandon Browner (6'4", 221) on a deep pass, but that results in an incompletion. Next Wilson goes short right to Ricardo Lockette for 11 yards. He's covered by Logan Ryan, back in the game because the Seahawks are running four wideouts in their two-minute drill and the Patriots are responding with two safeties and four cornerbacks. Matchup football—Belichick used this same grouping to defend against Jim Kelly's K-Gun offense way back in Super Bowl XXV, and that one came right down to the wire, too. On first and 10 at the New England 38, with Seattle down by four points and needing a touchdown to win, it's Malcolm Butler's turn in the barrel again. Wilson goes deep down the right sideline to Kearse, and Butler seems to make the perfect play, breaking up the catch, but then something funny happens. The ball careens into the air after Butler punches it loose from the receiver's hands, and it ends up dropping back into Kearse's grip as the receiver falls on to his back. It's a magical play, and the Seahawks are still alive.

This too is nothing new for the Patriots. In the Super Bowl after the 2007 season, playing against the New York Giants in this very stadium, on that day the Very Holiest of the Houses of the Holy, the Giants beat the Patriots 17-14, with the key play coming on a freak pass reception. David Tyree—not even a starter—went high into the air for a catch, and despite the perfect hit put on him by New England's safety, Rodney Harrison, Tyree kept the ball plastered to his helmet with one hand, keeping New York's drive alive. Some football conspiracy-theorists claim that that loss was karmic retribution for the Cheating Patriots (who that year were in trouble for having recorded opponents in practice, or their sideline signals, or something), and no doubt more than a few in the foil-hat brigade were now picking up eerie Left Hand Path vibes from this miraculous catch by Kearse in the closing moments of another Super Bowl in the University of Phoenix Stadium. Maybe Goodell, fuming at the Spartacus Brady for deflating those balls, for saying "no" to the Commissioner in any shape or form, for tarnishing the Shield, has called upon dark powers to turn this game against the rebellious quarterback. One thing after another.

Seahawks ball on the New England 5, first and goal. They take a time-out. Goal line stand. No one needs to tell the crowd that this is what football is all about. You could take away the stadium and the TV cameras and the two weeks of hype and all of that and just leave the game on the field, and it would still draw a raving crowd. My eleven against your eleven, the essence of competition. For the coaches, it's the agony of decision-making—free choice of the will with the largest television audience in the world looking on. Would Seattle head coach Pete Carroll mess it up the way Saint Steve Superior did in that South Carolina at Georgia game I'd journeyed to Athens to watch, overthinking the thing and taking the game away from the players with a stupid play-call? Would Belichick have to eat another big slice of karmic humble-pie?

At first it looked like the latter rather than the former, as Seattle ran off-tackle with Lynch for a gain of four. One yard left, three chances to get it. But then Carroll and his staff went Superior, calling a pass play with Kearse and Lockette stacked wide right and counting on the two Patriots defensive backs to screw it up as Lockette cut under Kearse, who was supposed to obstruct both defensive backs.

Superior underestimated the Patriot Way. New England had counted on this play coming, though probably not at this crucial point in the game, and the defensive backs had practiced their roles: Browner would hold his ground while Butler drove on the ball. Butler had come a long way to get to the Super Bowl, just keeping faith in his talent and drive to excel, undrafted out of Division II West Alabama University, making the most of his opportunity by way of a tryout camp that the Patriots run just to make sure they don't miss any talent that might have been overlooked in the draft. That was the hard part, making the team. Now it was easy, just trust in your preparation, trust in your coaches, trust that they have given you a plan to create an advantage, trust what you see—and sure enough, the Seahawks run the play that the defensive backs are expecting, however stupid it seems—*they've got Beast Mode and they're going to pass the ball?* The story is whatever happens. The massive Browner absorbs the block, just like they drew it up, and Butler drives on the ball to make the crucial play, an interception that kills Seattle's drive and puts the game away for New England. Butler just had to live the credo of the Patriot Way: Do Your Job.

There it is, we're back at the beginning, one thing after another, and all about football. I'm on the job, a reader and a writer inquiring into why football is such a big deal, such a quintessentially *American* big deal, and how important the game really should be.

Farewell to football? Do I really need to take it that far?

Just do your job.

How do I do my job?

Farewell to Football?

Trust your game-planning and mission-preparation, trust in your process. Write your book. Examine your conscience. Judge for yourself what is right.

Is that my job? Is that my mission in its entirety?

Or is it my job to seek to do the will of God? Or to follow Christ, the Living Word? The Scripture has led me this far, so perhaps the Scripture describes my job:

> "Do you think that I have come to establish peace on
> earth? No, I tell you, but rather division"
>
> (LUKE 12:51).

Divide the excess and illusion from what really matters? Divide the opinion from the truth, the money-grubbing business of football from the noble enterprise of coaching and effort and achievement?

> "I have come to set the earth on fire, and how I wish it
> were already blazing!"
>
> (LUKE 12:49).

Patience. Trust in the process. Have faith.

The story is whatever happens. Write it.

After all, it began with the Word.

Postscript: Sons

As THEY SAY in those NCAA public-service spots on TV, Jack Loonam went pro in something other than football. He was commissioned as a lieutenant in the Army Transportation Corps and assigned to active duty at Fort Hood, Texas, in 2016.

Jaia Benson said farewell to football, and eventually to baseball too, concentrating on basketball. As a junior he played on the 2015-2016 New York State Class AA semi-finalist Shenendehowa Plainsmen team in Clifton Park, New York, and looks forward to contending again as a senior.

Acknowledgements

THIS BOOK OWES its existence, its spirit and heart and soul, to the Dawg Doc, Tim Loonam, DVM. His love of God, his family, and life has inspired me to take this journey deeper into my faith, with the courage that comes from knowing that a brother Buffalo is there with me. At one point or another, he read just about every word in this book, and when it came, his praise came like grace. I hope I've done this Damn Good Dawg justice.

I would also like to thank the following individuals who read parts or all of the draft manuscript and offered tremendous help to me in getting the prose to work, when it does. When it doesn't, I take all the blame.

Jean Ball Dougherty, Barbe Bishop, Clay Buhler, Alec Campbell, Kevin Carroll, Marjorie Chadwick, Rufus Cormier, Paul Dubetz, Patrick Dunshee, Shirl Hoffman, Heidi Kraft, James Langston, Nick Lopez, Michael Mengis, Milton Morgan, Christian Nagle, Pete Nealley, Patrick Newell, Dan Perry, Teresa Rivas, the late Jackie Stillman Halowack, Deacon Ed Stoessel, David Sylvia, Geoff Winningham, and David Youngerman.

I would also like to thank the following individuals for all the other kinds of help it takes to bring a book project through to completion.

Don Anderson, Leonard Bachman, Claude Felton, Father Ken Heberlein, Michael Hurd, Maureen Maloney Perry, Ross Rich, Richard Scamell, Amy Smith, and Matt Southall.

Sources

THIS BOOK WAS developed through both ethnographic and bibliographic research.

Ethnographic sources: whenever a source is identified in the text with an attributive tag like "said to me" or "told me later," the source contributed an interview, a questionnaire response, or both. I want to thank the following contributors for their invaluable help with this project:

Jeff Ackerman, Jaia Benson, Matt Benson, Perry Bowers, Clay Buhler, Travis Bush, Alec Campbell, Dr. Marjorie Chadwick, Mike Chase, Jamie Christian, Christopher Cola, Rufus Cormier, Ron Courson, Mike Dowling, LTC Kurt Felpel, Bailey Harris, Alex Hilton, COL Hawk Holloway, Case Keenum, Dr. Heidi Kraft, Cody LaRoque, Jared Leising, Jerry LeVias, Tony Levine, John Lilly, Jack Loonam, Dr. Tim Loonam, Betsy Loonam, Arthur Lynch, Carline Lynch, Carlin Lynch, Milton Morgan, Maria Peden, Ann Marie Perry Zeaser, LTC Jason Pike, John Pluta, Mark Richt, Jay Rome, Ketric Sanford, Dr. Julianne Schmidt, Darrell Smith, Adam Spence, Courtney Starr, Craig Starr, Deacon Ed Stoessel (Ph. D.), Sondra Tennessee, Tory Teykel, Dr. Veronique Tran, Joe I. (Rocky) White, and David Youngerman.

Bibliographic sources: I have used what I hope will be the least-intrusive means for attributing bibliographic sources. I try to identify the author, the title, or both, in the text, and then cite specific page numbers as needed parenthetically. Full citations are provided by chapter below.

For canonical and ancient texts, I've used references appropriate to the source, so that the reader can find the passage in various translations and editions other than the one I used: act/scene for Shakespeare plays; book/line for poems; Stephanus edition index numbers for Platonic dialogues; book/section/paragraph for Saint Augustine; chapter numbers for Machiavelli; etc.

All citations to Scripture are to the New American Bible.

The Catechism of the Catholic Church is available for online viewing and search at: http://ccc.usccb.org/flipbooks/catechism/index.html

Chapter 1. Super Bowl XLVII: Farewell to Football?

Howard Cosell, with the editorial assistance of Mickey Herskowitz. *Cosell*. Chicago: Playboy Press, 1973.

Frederick Exley. *A Fan's Notes*. New York: Vintage Contemporaries, 1968.

Franklin Foer and Chris Hughes. "Barack Obama Is Not Pleased: The president on his enemies, the media, and the future of football." *New Republic* (January 27, 2013). http://www.newrepublic.com/article/112190/obama-interview-2013-sit-down-president

Michael MacCambridge. *America's Game: The Epic Story of How Pro Football Captured a Nation*. New York: Anchor Books, 2005.

----. *Lamar Hunt: A Life in Sports*. Kansas City: Andrews McMeel Publishing, 2012.

James Michener. *Sports in America*. New York: Random House, 1976.

Jason Whitlock. "Bryant's problems mirror society's." *ESPN NFL* (November 7, 2013). http://espn.go.com/nfl/story/_/id/9913252/ behind-bryant-tantrums

Chapter 1. a. Examen.
For an excellent survey of the relationship between sports, religion, and popular culture, see: Shirl James Hoffman. *Good Game: Christianity and the Culture of Sports.* Waco, TX: Baylor UP, 2010.

Chapter 2. Houses of the Holy: My First NFL Game.
For a thorough treatment of the connections between occultist Aleister Crowley and Led Zeppelin, especially Jimmy Page, consult: Mick Wall. *When Giants Walked the Earth: A Biography of Led Zeppelin.* New York: St. Martin's, 2008.

Chapter 3: The School of Athens: An Educated Life.
Saint Augustine. *On Free Choice of the Will* (395 AD). Tr. Anna S. Benjamin and L. H. Hackstaff. Indianapolis: Bobbs-Merrill, 1964.

Chapter 4: "Five In a Row Dome Show."
James Gast. *The Astrodome: Building an American Spectacle.* Boston: Aspinwall Press, 2014.

Stephen Greenblatt. *Renaissance Self-Fashioning: From More to Shakespeare.* Chicago: University of Chicago Press, 1980.

"Jefferson County Criminal District judge Layne Walker will not seek a third term." *12 News Now.com* (December 8, 2013, updated December 18, 2013). http://www.12newsnow.com/story/24165166/ jefferson-county-criminal-district-judge-layne-walker-wont-seek-a-third-term

Walker Percy. *Love in the Ruins: The Adventures of a Bad Catholic at a Time Near the End of the World.* New York: Farrar, Straus and Giroux, 1971.

Carl Riley. "Merger a championship move." *The Houston Post* (December 19, 1982): 19C.

W. H. Stickney Jr. "Ball says togetherness helped Bruins overcome." *The Houston Chronicle* (December 19, 1982): 2-19.

-----. "West Brook seizes 5A flag 21-10." *The Houston Chronicle* (December 19, 1982): 2-1.

Geoff Winningham. "Football, Game of Life." *Texas Monthly* (October 1983): 154-160, 236-254.

Chapter 5. Monday Night Football: Everybody Wants to Rule the World.
T. R. Fehrenbach. *This Kind of War: The Classic Korean War History* (1963). Dulles, VA: Potomac Books, 2008.

Chapter 6. Free Fallin'.
Ulysses S. Grant. *Personal Memoirs of U. S. Grant In Two Volumes* (1885). New York: Barnes and Noble, 2003.

David Halberstam. *The Education of a Coach.* New York: Hyperion, 2005.

Mark Perry. *Grant and Twain: The Story of a Friendship That Changed America.* New York: Random House, 2004.

Colin L. Powell with Joseph E. Persico. *My American Journey.* New York: Random House, 1995.

H. Norman Schwarzkopf. *It Doesn't Take a Hero: The Autobiography.* New York: Bantam, 1992.

Lawrence Wright. *Going Clear: Scientology, Hollywood, and the Prison of Belief.* New York: Alfred A. Knopf, 2013.

Chapter 7. Perfect Starts.
Tom Rowe. "Norwich blanks JC to claim Class B crown." *The Evening Sun* (Norwich, NY; November 16, 1993).

Steve Wulf. "My Kind of Town." *Sports Illustrated* 79.26 (December 27, 1993): 102-109.

Chapter 8. The Last Season in the Astrodome.
Data concerning NCAA finances can be viewed and searched at: http://sports.usatoday.com/ncaa/finances

Saint Augustine. *On Christian Doctrine* (427 AD). Tr. D. W. Robertson, Jr. Upper Saddle River, NJ: Prentice Hall/Library of Liberal Arts, 1958.

Kevin Carroll. *Houston Oilers: The Early Years.* Austin, TX: Eakin Press, 2001.

Ed Fowler. *Loser Takes All: Bud Adams, Bad Football, & Big Business.* Atlanta: Longstreet Press, 1997.

Tex Maule. "The Best Football Game Ever Played." *Sports Illustrated* 10.1 (January 5, 1959): 8-11, 60.

Michel Foucault. *The Foucault Reader.* Ed. Paul Rabinow. New York: Pantheon, 1984.

Niccolo Machiavelli. *The Prince* (1513). Ed. Peter Bondanella, Tr. Bondanella and Mark Musa. Oxford: Oxford UP, 1979.

Chapter 10. The Adventures of Cardboard Tim in Territory Held Largely by the Devil.
William Peter Blatty. *The Exorcist.* New York: Harper Collins, 1971.

Mike Dowling with Damien Lewis. *Sergeant Rex: The Unbreakable Bond Between a Marine and His Military Working Dog.* New York: Atria Paperback, 2011.

Dr. Heidi Squier Kraft. *Rule Number Two: Lessons I Learned in a Combat Hospital.* New York: Back Bay Books, 2007.

Flannery O'Connor. "On Her Own Work." *Mystery and Manners: Occasional Prose.* Selected and edited by Sally and Robert Fitzgerald. New York: Farrar, Straus and Giroux, 1969.

Chapter 11. "I" Is for "Ike," Like the Hurricane.
"NFL Game Day." *Houston Chronicle* (September 22, 2008): H-5.

David Plotz. "Off Base (Washington Diarist)." *The New Republic* 431.4 (December 20, 1999): 50.

Chapter 12. Just Getting There, Part II.
Mark Hyman. *The Most Expensive Game in Town: The Rising Cost of Youth Sports and the Toll on Today's Families.* Boston: Beach Press, 2012.

Vince Lombardi with W. C. Heinz. *Run to Daylight!* (1963) New York: Fireside, 1989.

Larry Merchant. ... *And Every Day You Take Another Bite.* Garden City, NY: Doubleday, 1971.

George Plimpton. *One More July: A Football Dialogue with Billy Curry*. New York: Harper & Row, 1977.

Chapter 13. Veterans Day: Winning Ugly.
Norman Doidge, M. D. *The Brain That Changes Itself: Stories of Personal Triumphs from the Frontiers of Brain Science*. New York: Penguin, 2007.

Luigi Giussani. *The Religious Sense*. Tr. John Zucchi. Montreal: McGill-Queen's UP, 1997.

Chapter 14. The School of Athens, continued: The Cost of an Education.
Morris Berman. *The Twilight of American Culture*. New York: Norton, 2000.

Mark Fainaru-Wada and Steve Fainaru. *League of Denial: The NFL, Concussions, and the Battle for Truth*. New York: Crown Archetype, 2013.

Thomas Merton. *The Seven Storey Mountain*. New York: Harcourt, 1948.

Chapter 15. Epilogue: Spartacus Super Bowl.
Judge Anita B. Brody. Denial of Preliminary Approval in re: National Football League Players' Concussion Injury Litigation. Case Number 2:2012md02323, filed January 31, 2012. Pennsylvania Eastern District Court. January 14, 2014.

Index

Farewell to Football?

Steven Liparulo

Author Biography

Dr. Steven Liparulo graduated with a PhD from the University of Houston Creative Writing Program in 2002 and was associate director for writing programs at the University of Houston Writing Center from 2003 to 2016.

He completed undergraduate degrees in English and philosophy from Binghamton University while earning an Army ROTC commission at Cornell University in 1983.

A graduate of US Army Airborne, Ranger, and Special Forces schools, he served as an infantry officer in the Republic of Korea and as a Special Forces A-Team Leader at Fort Devens, Massachusetts.

After Army service, he taught high school in Norwich, New York, and earned master's degrees in teaching and English literature from his undergraduate alma mater.

His work has appeared in *Arizona Quarterly*; *War, Literature, and the Arts*; *Assessing Writing*; *Gulf Coast*; and the Mark Heberle-edited book *Thirty Years After: New Essays on Vietnam War Literature, Film, and Art*.

Made in the USA
Middletown, DE
08 June 2016